GROWTH AND SURVIVAL

Bridging disparate literatures on courts and the legal profession in China, Jonathan J. Kinkel introduces an innovative cross-disciplinary framework to understand the reality of Chinese politics and society. Fusing a variety of perspectives from social ecology, historical institutionalism, and empirical legal studies, Kinkel contextualizes patterns of court reform within China's rapid economic and social transformations. This book's extensive case studies emphasize the dynamic expansion of the legal system in the post-Mao reform period and demonstrate that law firm growth in large cities, especially in the early twenty-first century, pressured courts at the local and national levels to enhance judicial autonomy. Advancing debates on the multiplicity of political–legal regimes, this book offers a comprehensive, empirical account of how reforms in both the public and private arenas can interact and operate alongside one another.

JONATHAN J. KINKEL is a lecturer in the School of Politics and Global Studies at Arizona State University, where his research has focused on the intersection between comparative politics, law and society, and Chinese studies. He is also an Associate in Research with the Fairbank Center for Chinese Studies at Harvard University. He is a past recipient of the Best Graduate Student Paper award from Law & Social Inquiry (LSI), and his research has appeared in journals including *LSI*, *China Quarterly*, and the *Journal of East Asian Studies*. This is his first book.

GROWTH AND SURVIVAL

An Ecological Analysis of Court Reform in Urban China

JONATHAN J. KINKEL
Arizona State University

CAMBRIDGE
UNIVERSITY PRESS

CAMBRIDGE UNIVERSITY PRESS

Shaftesbury Road, Cambridge CB2 8EA, United Kingdom

One Liberty Plaza, 20th Floor, New York, NY 10006, USA

477 Williamstown Road, Port Melbourne, VIC 3207, Australia

314–321, 3rd Floor, Plot 3, Splendor Forum, Jasola District Centre, New Delhi – 110025, India

103 Penang Road, #05–06/07, Visioncrest Commercial, Singapore 238467

Cambridge University Press is part of Cambridge University Press & Assessment, a department of the University of Cambridge.

We share the University's mission to contribute to society through the pursuit of education, learning and research at the highest international levels of excellence.

www.cambridge.org
Information on this title: www.cambridge.org/9781009078184

DOI: 10.1017/9781009086868

First published 2022
First paperback edition 2026

A catalogue record for this publication is available from the British Library

Library of Congress Cataloging-in-Publication data
Names: Kinkel, Jonathan J., author.
Title: Growth and survival : an ecological analysis of court reform in urban China / Jonathan J. Kinkel, Arizona State University.
Description: Cambridge, United Kingdom ; New York, NY : Cambridge University Press, 2022. | Includes bibliographical references and index.
Identifiers: LCCN 2021970022 | ISBN 9781316514368 (hardback) | ISBN 9781009086868 (ebook)
Subjects: LCSH: Courts – China. | Judges – China. | Justice, Administration of – China.
Classification: LCC KNQ1580 .K56 2022 | DDC 347.5101–dc23/eng/20220131
LC record available at https://lccn.loc.gov/2021970022

ISBN 978-1-316-51436-8 Hardback
ISBN 978-1-009-07818-4 Paperback

for Rey

CONTENTS

FIGURES

TABLES

ACKNOWLEDGMENTS

I am more than fortunate to have received the support of many friends and colleagues during the years spent writing this book. First, my advisers and dissertation committee members at the University of Texas deserve much of the credit, and none of the blame, for the following pages. This project would not have been possible without Dan Brinks' constructive, incisive feedback on seemingly countless drafts of chapters and article manuscripts. Bill Hurst has been as important an influence as anyone on this project, intellectually and personally; I thank Bill not only for his mentorship, but also for his collegial and collaborative spirit. Zachary Elkins, Patricia Maclachlan, and H. W. Perry never assumed secondary status in their roles as committee members, providing indispensable advice and timely revisions to draft manuscripts. As scholars whose substantive interests in the discipline overlap in many ways with mine, their non-China perspectives have proven both fresh and valuable.

Many others provided important help revising earlier drafts or offered comments at various conferences and invited talks in the past few years. I particularly thank Mary Gallagher, Nico Howson, Sida Liu, Eva Pils, Ethan Michelson, Rachel Stern, and Yuhua Wang. For all of the guidance from these scholars and from my dissertation committee, any remaining flaws in reasoning are mine alone.

I would not have been able to conduct the fieldwork in China upon which this book relies without the help of Professor Wang Qian at East China University of Political Science and Law (ECUPL) in Shanghai, who hosted my research and helped arrange for me to serve as a visiting professor at ECUPL during 2012–2013. I am grateful for the financial support of the Boren Fellowship, the University of Texas at Austin's Government Department, the University of Texas College of Liberal Arts, the Chinese University of Hong Kong, and Arizona State University, which all provided funding at various points of my research and writing from 2012 to 2021.

Many Mandarin teachers in the United States and China have corrected my tones, comprehension, and basic writing skills over the years, providing me with the indispensable language foundation that I used to conduct this study's interviews and documentary analysis. More Chinese teachers than I can remember deserve my gratitude, but I would like to particularly thank Camille Hsieh and Jeanette Chen for their patience and persistence at a time when my naivete in the language would have been comical if not for my sincerity.

Numerous friends in China who cannot be named here provided indispensable help finding contacts and arranging interviews and stays in several cities throughout China, and I owe them all a debt of gratitude. I also thank Christian Sorace, Eddie Schmitt, Bill McCormick, and many others for their friendships at difficult moments of graduate school and the book drafting process.

At Cambridge University Press, I sincerely thank Finola O'Sullivan and Joe Ng for encouragement and support of the project, as well as three anonymous reviewers who provided constructive and helpful reviews that shaped the manuscript in significant ways.

Most importantly, I would like to thank my family for constantly supporting me before, during, and after this project was launched. My parents no doubt did more in this regard than anyone. Danielle and Ben have always provided encouragement and a warm, happy home-away-from-home on the many trips I have taken to Boston for "a little R&R" (relaxation and research). Of course, my wife Nichole has lived this book as much as I have, and looking back, the much-needed distractions she and our daughters brought me over the past few years will always be the most cherished part of the time spent moving this project along.

ABBREVIATIONS

CASS	Chinese Academy of Social Sciences
CCP	Chinese Communist Party
CQAS	Case Quality Assessment System
ECUPL	East China University of Political Science and Law
FDI	foreign direct investment
IP	intellectual property
KMT	*Kuomintang*
MOJ	Ministry of Justice
OD	Organization Department (of the CCP)
PRC	People's Republic of China
SAIC	State Administration for Industry and Commerce
SEZ	Special Economic Zone
SPC	Supreme People's Court
TMRS	Target Management Responsibility System
TRIPs	Trade-related intellectual property rights
USCBC	US-China Business Council
WTO	World Trade Organization

1

Introduction

Despite the consolidation of Communist power and the encouragement of President Xi Jinping's cult of personality (Economy, 2019; Hernandez, 2018; Hernandez & Carlsen, 2017), the People's Republic of China (PRC) has also moved to expand judicial autonomy during Xi's term in office. As recently as 2016, *The New York Times* claimed that "China Grants Courts Greater Autonomy on Limited Matters" (Johnson, 2016), while *The Wall Street Journal* noted in 2014 that "China Tries to Hold On to Judges by Offering Freer Hand" (Chin, 2014) and *The Economist* opined that "Judges are Often Impotent in China's Courtrooms. That Might Be Changing" (*The Economist*, 2014).

In the years leading up to these headlines (2012–2014), I conducted nearly 15 months of in-China fieldwork, during which I also documented significant variation between urban court systems in China (Shanghai, Shenzhen, and Chengdu) regarding critical elements of personal judicial autonomy and the implementation of judicial selection and promotion mechanisms (Brinks & Blass, 2018; Peerenboom, 2010). Competitive promotion systems for mid-ranking judges in some case study localities featured enhanced transparency, competition, and the routinization of judicial promotion procedures that departed from previous systems of direct nomination and appointment by local Party leaders. Local variation regarding these judicial promotion mechanisms also tracks with other differences regarding these courts' compliance with transparency mandates, judicial opinion writing, and the use of mediation in courts. In an otherwise formally unitary political system, why would court systems in some large urban localities have employed more autonomous judges, while other urban courts have moved more slowly with similar reforms?

The extant literatures on comparative courts and Chinese judicial politics do not explain this local variation in judicial autonomy between similarly developed localities in a single-county authoritarian setting. This is not to say, however, that recent scholarly work has not significantly advanced our understanding of China's court system in the late post-Mao reform era. Ng and He, for instance, provide a rich account of court decision-making in China, examining a wide variety of courts, judicial actors, and possible factors influencing judicial work (Ng & He, 2017). Although the authors find substantial local variation in the ways that courts are embedded in their local contexts, especially between urban and rural courts, their findings do not say much about differences between urban localities, nor do the authors provide a research design aimed at the systematic explanation of specific patterns of local variation. Yuhua Wang's approach, by contrast, analyzes data at varying levels (a multilevel time-series and cross-sectional research design) to draw more verifiable conclusions regarding the political subtleties of court reform in China at the local level. Wang's "demand-side" theory argues that in localities where foreign-invested enterprises from outside the "China Circle" of Taiwan, Hong Kong, and Macao are significant players in the local economy, "local governments must tie their hands and build a strong court system" (Y. Wang, 2015, p. 43), thereby establishing a partial rule of law limited to economic and commercial affairs (i.e., allowing for instrumental use of law and courts in criminal and politically sensitive cases).

Although Wang's book provides many insights, including the suggestion that national leaders have an interest in using partial rule of law as economic infrastructure and that the nature of foreign investment can influence judicial outcomes, Wang's finding that foreign investors have tended to credibly lobby local governments of PRC for changes and increases in autonomy to the local courts might not necessarily apply throughout China. Companies tend to avoid court if possible, and concern regarding unfair courts and judges, for instance, is not mentioned by US company officials surveyed regarding the in-China business environment by the US-China Business Council between 2013 and 2019.[1] This is not to suggest that foreign companies face no business obstacles in Chinese courts, but these survey results seem to be inconsistent with a theory that judicial impartiality is a problem of such magnitude that foreign businesses would devote the substantial resources needed to move the needle on this topic at the local level in China.

State-centered, "top-down" approaches of court reform in China also present potential alternative theoretical explanations, especially considering the extent of state and Chinese Communist Party's (CCP) involvement in

[1] US-China Business Council Member Surveys regarding the business environment in China can be found for 2019 and several previous years at the following website: www.uschina.org/reports/uscbc-2019-member-survey. Relevant PDF copies of surveys are on file with the author.

court politics in China, as well as the importance of reforms at the national level occurring in 2014–2016. Zhu Suli finds, for instance, that the CCP is "the major force mobilizing, promoting, and implementing reform within the judiciary" in contemporary China, an approach similar to that of Li (Ling Li, 2012; Zhu, 2010, pp. 52–53). However, state-centric perspectives can also neglect changes in the degree of state intervention in the law and the legal system's own response to the state. In the context of headlines that opened this chapter, it also appears that central state- or party-centric explanations of judicial reform do not sufficiently account for the possibility that local dynamics can create pressure for national-level reform. Why would the PRC Party-State have partially augmented judicial autonomy in the reforms of 2014–2016 during an era of broader authoritarian consolidation?

To take the Party's official rationale – that it was seeking to root out corruption and limit local protectionism in the judiciary – at face value would obscure the full picture of court reform dynamics, especially those in urban China, which unfolded over the course of several years. Rather than a sudden epiphany, national judicial reforms beginning in 2014 were a partial acknowledgment that underlying factors, many of which can only be understood when examining local-level detail in China, have motivated the Party leadership's outlook on the court system. As explained in more detail throughout this book, the economic reforms implemented under Deng Xiaoping (after 1978) ushered in an era of unprecedented construction, deregulation, and re-regulation of the private legal profession (including vastly expanding the number of lawyers who were employed to consult and represent inbound foreign investors and their joint venture partners), which have placed intense pressure on local courts and governments to staff the legal institutions so critical to China's economic development over the past four decades (Alford, 1995; Blecher, 2003; S. Liu & Wu, 2016; Peerenboom, 2002; Stern & Li, 2016). In particular, the high-end legal service markets that have proliferated in urban China since 1992 offer judges potentially lucrative alternative careers (S. Liu & Wu, 2016), threatening court leaders' abilities to retain well-qualified judges to staff their courts. When young, talented judges can easily quit their jobs and find high-paying local employment as lawyers, court leaders have sought to retain these judges by resorting to one of the only methods at their disposal for stemming judicial attrition: strategically reforming promotion mechanisms and increasing overall court transparency. More competitive and transparent promotion clarifies the path to career success for ordinary, mid-ranking judges, providing ordinary judges with greater assurance of upward career mobility.

Table 1.1. *Periodization of political–legal reform in post-Mao China, with focus on 1992–2016*

Years	General characteristics of political–legal reforms during the period
1966–1976	Cultural Revolution Decade; courts highly politicized, especially during early years of Cultural Revolution, but continue functioning; law schools largely shuttered and lawyers still almost entirely marginalized in the wake of the Anti-Rightist Campaign
1976–1992	Post-Mao leadership succession struggle; Deng Xiaoping develops a legal system for a variety of purposes, including support for economic liberalization and political control; pre-1989 gains in construction of the legal profession give way to foreign investment flight and domestic reform uncertainty; the state still possesses ownership over 98% of law firms in 1991
1992–2001	**Resumption and acceleration of liberalizing economic reforms and plans for WTO accession; foreign law firms' presence in China legalized in 1992; only 22% of law firms are state-owned in 2002**
2001–2014	**Privatization and internationalization of legal profession continue in the aftermath of WTO accession; development of legal profession varies by locality (discussed in detail in Chapter 4); courts begin to implement reforms to judicial selection and promotion (discussed further in Chapter 5)**
2014–2016	**National judicial reforms separate civil service and court bureaucracies, allowing for increases in judicial remuneration, professionalism, and status across the country**
2016 and beyond	Broad judicial and legal retrenchment in the context of law-related political and economic paradigm shifts, both domestic and international (examined in more detail in Chapter 7)

Ultimately, court leaders' decisions to reform promotion mechanisms produced the variation in judicial autonomy that I observed in my fieldwork (Kinkel, 2015).

Reflecting a broadly historical institutionalist perspective, Table 1.1 provides a basic periodization of these developments, with the 1992–2016 period in bold to highlight its significance to the main argument of this book.

Aside from highlighting that the period between 1992 and 2016 has been especially important in the development of the court and legal system in China, Table 1.1 indicates that a period of legal retrenchment has also occurred in the wake of 2016 reforms, a topic taken up in more detail in Chapter 7 of this book. Taken together, these developments have led over time to gradual, intertwined spatial differentiation of local legal service markets and expansions of personal judicial autonomy in urban China, demonstrating the value of closely studying legal reforms during the 1992–2016 period.

A New Theoretical Approach to Court Reform in China

In making this argument, this book draws upon historical institutionalist and social ecology approaches to explain change in China's urban legal system. The temporal parameters placed on this study illuminate changes in China's court system over time that involve historical institutional layering, or "incremental amendments to existing rules or the enactment of new rules without voiding others" (Tsai, 2016). To understand how layered institutions can produce local level variation, I also employ human ecology–based approaches to organizational change, which find that social forms of law can change through interaction and cooperative competition between interrelated actors (who cooperate under certain conditions despite individuals' self-interested pursuit of their own survival) (Hannan & Freeman, 1977; S. Liu & Emirbayer, 2016; S. Liu & Wu, 2016; Ng & He, 2017; Park & Burgess, 1969). In urban China, and likely throughout the country, court leaders' professional growth and survival has been intertwined with their courts' collectively assessed performance on quantitative indicators, which itself is tied to the retention of the mid-career judges who can decide cases quickly and accurately. The globally unprecedented growth of the Chinese legal profession in the past two decades has made it difficult to stem the attrition of mid-career, case-deciding judges (S. Liu & Wu, 2016; X. Liu, 2014), and urban court leaders' decisions to strategically reform judicial selection and promotion mechanisms can be seen as an interactive response aimed at preserving court leaders' hierarchical privilege and the basic organizational structure of their courts – all in an environment of competitive cooperation.

The development of local pockets of judicial autonomy in China, as documented in this book, shows that the impetus for greater legal and judicial autonomy, in a rapidly developing authoritarian context, can stem not from the leadership's conscious realization that autonomous law is needed for development, nor from the social mobilization of professionals or other legal reformers, but rather from the more immediate concerns of legal actors who find themselves in a rapidly changing services market – a professional *ecology* that includes judges as well as lawyers. In this way, even an authoritarian regime has an interest (especially in a context of rapid economic globalization) in reforming its court system to attract foreign investment and, at a more basic level, to serve a dispute resolution function that grows increasingly more complex and labor intensive with each economic expansion.

This book challenges preexisting explanations presented in the comparative law and courts literature regarding the association between economic development and several aspects of legal reform, including constitutional authority, the degree of official corruption, and judicial autonomy (see, e.g., Moustafa, 2007; Trubek & Galanter, 1974). First, the argument of this book challenges a long-standing assumption that democracy is a prerequisite for the political empowerment of judges (Landes & Posner, 1975; Tate & Vallinder, 1995) and examines the various functional roles played by courts in authoritarian regimes, regarding which the role of facilitating trade and investment is particularly relevant here (Ginsburg & Moustafa, 2008; Moustafa, 2007). Moustafa's study of the Egyptian Constitutional Court addresses a common political-economic goal shared by many authoritarian and democratic regimes: facilitating trade and investment and infusing the state with new sources of capital. In Moustafa's analysis, the regime's pursuit of this goal in Egypt surprisingly led to the creation of an autonomous Supreme Constitutional Court with powers of judicial review that "was designed to assuage investor concerns and guarantee institutional constraints on executive actions…" (Moustafa, 2007, p. 5).

To address the shortcomings of existing theories of court reform in China and apply lessons learned from other cases of authoritarian judicial change, I emphasize qualitative methods such as conducting fine-grained, semi-structured interviews and analyzing written source materials to highlight the factors mediating the relationship between economic development and judicial autonomy in China's urban courts. Even the most systematic research on the emergence of judicial autonomy in China often relies on second-hand perceptions of judicial practice to measure the actual outcomes related to judges and courts (Michelson & Read, 2011; Y. Wang, 2015, p. 60). In this book, conversely, I use information taken directly from courts and judges themselves not only to identify the factors responsible for local variation in Chinese judicial autonomy, but also to cast light on the broader dynamics of judicial autonomy in China and to contribute empirically and theoretically to emerging literature in comparative politics, China studies, and socio-legal research. These sources support the theory, based in the literature on social ecology (S. Liu, 2015), that the variation in outcomes between these three case studies is tied to revenues, remuneration, and labor markets for legal professionals in rapidly developing urban areas, i.e., factors of economic development that are most salient to the professional survival and growth of the judicial leadership tasked with reforming courts at the local level in China.

Similar Cases, Different Outcomes

This study leverages subtle, significant local differences within China, a country of vast size and fragmentation (Lieberthal & Oksenberg, 1988; S. Liu, 2011b; Mertha, 2009), to generate new theories regarding the relationship between economic development and court reform in China. As such, this book adopts an inductive approach to hypothesis generation that explains fine-grained variation between three urban localities in China: Shanghai, Shenzhen, and Chengdu. Such an approach seeks to identify city-level variations in judicial selection mechanisms between these relatively similar, large, important urban centers in China, which then allows for the generation of theories to highlight the precise features of each case that contribute to the variation in outcomes observed in the courts. I narrowed the selection of cases to the specific urban court systems of Shanghai, Shenzhen, and Chengdu to focus directly on differences in judicial autonomy associated with levels of economic development suggested in previous research; accordingly, I selected cases based on variation in local models of reform-era economic development, which helps narrow the range of variation regarding social, economic, and cultural factors that could also serve as explanatory variables for the emergence of differing levels of judicial autonomy (see Tsai, 2007, pp. 152–166). For example, during the primary research period (2012–2014), all three case study cities featured resident populations (*changzhu renkou*) over 10,000,000, well-developed secondary and tertiary sectors, and comparable levels of state sector involvement in the local economy (Shanghai Bureau of Statistics, 2011; Shenzhen Bureau of Statistics, 2011; Chengdu Bureau of Statistics, 2011).

In recognition, however, that "Local idiosyncrasies … and situated knowledge of the ever-changing political context are all part of the decision-making processes in legal and regulatory governance" (Valverde, 2009, p. 142), these three large urban centers also differ on several factors related to economic development and judicial politics, including the development of private markets for legal services. Geographically speaking, Shanghai, Shenzhen, and Chengdu span coastal and interior geographies of mainland China, which contributes as well to the variation in the local legal profession observed in each case study locality. Especially after 2001, Shanghai and Shenzhen have resembled "high-end" legal services markets, whereas Chengdu has been more characteristic of a "battleground" market (S. Liu, 2011a, 2011b); this important typological distinction appears to be associated with more pronounced pressure for judicial reforms in Shanghai and Shenzhen relative to Chengdu, a point that is the focus of Chapters 4 and 5 of this book.

As noted above, this book aims to fuse temporal analysis with the examination of spatial difference in the forms of law and to avoid prioritizing legal geography at the expense of legal history (see Valverde, 2015). As such, the temporal periodization in Table 1.1 highlights the period between 1992 and 2016 because of its importance to the development of the court and legal system in China. After 1992, in the wake of China's post-Tiananmen recommitment to liberalizing reforms and the subsequent return of substantial foreign investment, internationalization and privatization of legal professionals were rebooted in a wave of economic readjustments that raised the standards, salaries, and status of the legal profession as the speed and magnitude of law firm growth in China in the early twenty-first century reached levels previously unseen in the global history of the legal profession (S. Liu & Wu, 2016, p. 800). The dramatic increase in foreign direct investment (FDI) and law firms is summarized in Figure 1.1.

This book argues that economic development, buoyed by substantial foreign investment inflows during the post-Mao period and the large-scale expansion of the legal profession, has led to court change in urban China[2]: for instance, the legal profession was largely privatized by 2002 (Michelson, 2003, p. 66), and the expansion of China's legal services market continued through sweeping nationwide judicial reforms in 2014–2016

[2] In this book, the main argument is largely agnostic on the causal mechanisms affecting economic development, FDI, and law firm growth; however, Chapter 7 details a likely causal pathway for FDI to impact law firm growth (which this book then claims influences judicial autonomy), as well as possible strategies for testing this pathway in future research.

Figure 1.1 FDI and law firm growth. *Sources:* Cai and Yang (2005), Michelson (2003, p. 472), China Law Yearbook (various years), China Yearbook of Lawyers (various years), Stern (2010), Xinhua News Agency (2017).

that unhooked judges from the broader civil service hierarchy. Viewed from a broader perspective, these developments have contributed, at historically significant moments, to intertwined spatial differentiation of local legal service markets and expansion of personal judicial autonomy in urban China, demonstrating the importance of incorporating a temporal approach to the examination of these changes.

Chapter Summaries

This introductory chapter has summarized both the general contours of local variation in judicial autonomy (the primary focus of the book), and it also poses important questions regarding the timing and scope of judicial personnel reforms at the national level, especially those occurring in 2014–2016 that separated the judiciary from the general PRC civil service bureaucracy. Chapter 2 presents the explanatory theory in fuller detail, demonstrating how a historical-institutionalist framework based on and informed by the insights of social ecology can illuminate the ramifications, for local courts and judicial selection mechanisms, of China's largely post-1978 efforts to construct a legal profession. Chapter 3 lays out the relevant background context of China's judicial system, including specific details on the Case Quality Assessment System (CQAS, an employee performance evaluation system), and how formal and informal rules under the CQAS have interacted within the structure provided by a Guiding Opinion of the Supreme People's Court (SPC) to incentivize the actions of judges in the PRC.

Chapter 4 is a crucial cog of the book's main argument, documenting spatial and temporal variation in local markets for legal services that aligns with local reforms to judicial promotion mechanisms, the timing of which since the turn of the twenty-first century is consistent with an attempt by court leaders to prevent talented judges from leaving for careers in local law firms. This chapter adopts a macro-level perspective on service sector characteristics that interact with the incentives produced by the judicial evaluation system described in Chapter 3, which provide substantial pressure for the emergence of court institutions that provide judges with more professional careers. To document more precisely how institutional outcomes vary across my court system case studies, Chapter 5 focuses on variations in my outcome variable: personal judicial autonomy. My findings show that the particular patterns of local variation in judicial appointment and promotion in urban China have varied distinctly by case study locality, with promotion mechanisms in Shanghai much more open, competitive, and transparent than, for instance, those in Chengdu. Chapter 6 then examines and critiques a competing, top-down theory based on centralized CCP personnel reforms, showing that even though the Party and the central state have selectively emphasized the bureaucratic specialization and professionalization of China's urban court system, these efforts explain neither the case study variation that I observed during in-country fieldwork nor the timing and scope of the 2014–2016 nationwide judicial personnel reforms.

Chapter 7 devotes more sustained attention to the possibility that the local-level court changes documented in this book account for the much broader, highly publicized national-level judicial reforms launched in 2014. The conclusion also places these changes in a global context that includes international, law-related flare-ups since 2016 related to heightened trade tensions with several nations (including China's largest trading partner, the United States) and ongoing societal and political tensions in Hong Kong. Chapter 7 also considers whether the main findings of the book might apply to debates regarding the autonomy and decision-making of judges in political settings outside of China – authoritarian or otherwise.

Conclusion

This book aims to specify the intervening variables and the underlying causal mechanisms supporting an empirical association between development and "economic rule of law" in China, filling theoretical gaps in research on authoritarian and Chinese legal politics. Using a subnational comparison of three largely similar urban court systems in China, I find that local demand for private legal services has been the primary factor influencing the political calculus related to judicial autonomy. To gauge the degree of judicial autonomy in a local court system, I examine judicial promotion mechanisms, compliance with judicial transparency mandates, the extent to which judges justify their case decisions with written reasons, levels of mediation, and degree of bureaucratic specialization; ultimately, I find that Shanghai's local courts displayed the highest degree of judicial autonomy, followed by Shenzhen and Chengdu.

Borrowing primarily from concepts rooted in the literatures on institutional change and social ecology, this book finds that when a market for private legal services can provide highly trained legal professionals a viable alternative to careers in courts, court leaders have tended to face greater pressure to reform judicial designs. Because court leaders' own promotion chances have turned on the efficiency, fairness, and social impact of cases resolved by their subordinates, court leaders have been incentivized to craft court institutions that provide more professional career opportunities when facing the prospect of substantial judicial attrition. By contrast, court officials were less likely to professionalize career trajectories for their subordinate judges when mid-ranking judges had limited career alternatives to working as a civil servant, judge, or other law-related workers in the Party or government bureaucracy. The dynamic interaction of economic development, the legal profession, and the court system not only appears to explain variation in judicial autonomy across China, but also suggests a compelling explanation for national-level changes to the judiciary in 2014–2016 discussed at the beginning of this chapter.

2

An Ecological Theory of Court Reform in Urban China

At the outset of the post-Mao reform era in 1978, the accounts of several researchers suggest that there were few, if any, lawyers or law schools in China (cf. Alford, 1995; Cohen, 1979, p. 359; Stern, 2013, p. 21). The Anti-Rightist Campaign of 1957 was particularly brutal for lawyers, and so was the Cultural Revolution Decade (1966–1976), during which "all but a handful" of law schools were shut down (Cohen, 2016; Peerenboom, 2002, pp. 345–347; cf. Stern, 2013, p. 21). Courts, by contrast, had seen their institutional groundwork laid in the 1954 constitution, and Chinese courts employed as many as 60,439 judges just a few years after Mao's death (cf. Clarke, 2003, p. 174; Stern, 2013, p. 21); the depoliticization of legal institutions during the later stages of the Cultural Revolution also suggests that courts in many regions of mainland China did not need to be rebuilt from scratch after 1978 (Hurst, 2011).

In other words, courts were an established PRC legal institution at the outset of post-Mao reforms, whereas Chinese lawyers comprised a nascent professional class exhibiting negligible formal organization and exerting little to no political or policy impact on China's legal system. The globally unprecedented growth of the legal profession in the subsequent decades, however, has led to significant changes in China's courts and its broader legal system, and a primary task of this book is to tell the story of how these changes occurred. State-led efforts to construct a professional class of lawyers largely began in the early 1980s – efforts that featured some limited privatization of the legal profession alongside the opening of China's command economy to substantial foreign investment and interaction. Reforms to the legal profession were essentially brought to a halt by violent state repression in Beijing and throughout the country in 1989; construction of China's formal legal profession was not resumed until after 1992, in the wake of China's recommitment to liberalizing reforms and the subsequent return of substantial foreign investment. Public messaging including Deng Xiaoping's 1992 Southern Tour and former Vice-Premier Zhu Rongji's statements in September of that year underlined "… the determination of the party to continue the basic policies," such as legal reform and institution building (Y. Wang, 2015, p. 46). After 1992, internationalization and privatization of legal professionals were rebooted in a wave of economic reforms and adjustments, raising the standards, salaries, and status of the legal profession, leading to law firm growth in the early twenty-first century in China whose speed and magnitude are unmatched "in the global history of the legal profession" (S. Liu & Wu, 2016, p. 800). As argued throughout this book, the growth of the legal profession around this time began pressuring courts to recalibrate various institutional practices related to judicial autonomy, particularly in urban areas, in order to stem the attrition of judges leaving courts for law firm employment opportunities.

Many national- and local-level arguments of this book are based on interrelated timing and sequencing of system-wide events, reforms, and practices throughout the post-Mao Chinese legal system. The phase after 1992 is a critical period for the judiciary and the broader growth of the legal profession in China, which witnessed a return of foreign investment that coincided with the Chinese government's release of the first regulations governing foreign law firms, legalizing the firms' presence in China (Stern & Li, 2016, p. 190). It was also not until after 1992 that the corporate legal market came into existence in China (S. Liu & Wu, 2016, p. 800). Although hiring licensed Chinese lawyers and providing official representation for Chinese legal matters remained off limits, many foreign firms worked around these restrictions by guiding inbound investment (Stern & Li, 2016, p. 190), a trend that continued through China's accession to the World Trade Organization (WTO) in 2001.

Developments in the post-1992 period also largely coincided with the resumed privatization of the Chinese legal profession (a topic discussed in greater detail in Chapter 4); although by 1986, the majority of law firms had detached themselves from the state (Michelson, 2003), the post-1992 era would see the State Council and the Ministry of Justice (MOJ) "unhook" (*tuogou gaizhi*) and otherwise privatize China's legal profession, converting all remaining state-owned law firms to partnerships (Michelson, 2003, pp. 59, 66). This campaign to privatize the legal service industry was largely successful: in 1991, the state possessed ownership over 98 percent of law firms, only 22 percent of firms were state-owned by 2002 (Michelson, 2003, p. 66). These shifts created a pool of Chinese lawyers free to collaborate with foreign firms in a gray zone of lucrative legal practice at the blurred boundary of PRC regulations (S. Liu, 2008; Stern & Li, 2016), which has led to intertwined spatial differentiation of local legal service markets and reforms to judicial selection procedures in China's courts (documented in more detail in Chapters 4 and 5).

Certainly, by 2016, China's legal landscape had been dramatically altered, with the legal profession built into a corps of over 250,000 lawyers, outstripping a judicial headcount of approximately 200,000 (J. Cohen, 2016).[1] As discussed later in this chapter, this dramatic expansion of the legal profession relative to the courts has substantially impacted legal system reform in China, especially mechanisms of judicial selection and promotion and other elements of judicial decision-making in urban China.

The Central Puzzle and Extant Theoretical Explanations

In Chapter 1, I describe significant variation between three urban court systems in China (Shanghai, Shenzhen, and Chengdu) regarding the implementation of judicial selection and promotion mechanisms, which are critical elements of personal judicial autonomy (Brinks & Blass, 2018; Peerenboom, 2010). I find that this variation also tracks other differences regarding these courts' compliance with transparency mandates, judicial opinion writing, and the use of mediation in courts. In an otherwise unitary political system, why would this local variation appear?

Various types of democratic decentralization have traditionally been seen as the necessary conditions for supplying the fragmentation necessary to convince rulers that delegating more authority to the judicial sphere of government is in their self-interest (Chavez, 2004, pp. 466–467; Ginsburg, 2003, p. 18). Comparative law and politics research exploring factors leading to greater judicial power emphasize a link between democratic accountability and robust checks on authority, finding that "competitive elections in democratic regimes keep politicians accountable to voters and prevent them from engaging in predatory behavior" (North, 1990; see Wang, 2015, p. 16). Of course, democracy-based explanations do not provide much insight into court developments in authoritarian

[1] It is very difficult to assign a precise number of judges in China who actually decide cases; although officially there are approximately 195,000 judges in China (Johnson, 2016; Ng & He, 2017, p. 3), Ng and He characterize official statistics on this metric as "sketchy"; only some seven out of ten "judges" are engaged in "judicial work" (Ng & He, 2017, p. 4, note 2, p. 209). The SPC Five-Year Plan covering 2014–2018 in Article 49 even formally recognized that China needs to "Establish a system specifying the number of judges." Stern's data suggest that the number of lawyers had outstripped the number of judges already by at least 2010 (Stern, 2013, p. 21).

China, and even in liberal democracies, national high courts also tend to march in step with the dominant political regime (Dahl, 1957). In addition, the importance of law and legal institutions to the political stability of authoritarian and democratic rulers alike (Lijphart, 1977; North & Weingast, 1989; Toharia, 1975; Ulc, 1972) undermines a universal claim that democracy is a prerequisite for the expansion of judicial autonomy and authority.

A growing scholarly literature on institutional change in nondemocratic political systems has emerged in recent years to provide greater insight into courts in China and other authoritarian regimes (see, e.g., Ginsburg & Moustafa, 2008; Hilbink & Woods, 2009; Kapiszewski, 2012; Moustafa, 2007; Ng & He, 2017; Wang, 2015). Much of this literature shares a common assumption that authoritarian leaders face a dilemma; empowering judges, granting legal rights to some individuals, and introducing laws that could potentially restrict sovereign authority can also help produce the predictability needed to provide credible commitments to foreign investors that many see as necessary for attracting new sources of capital and consolidating sovereign authority (see Moustafa, 2007, p. 5). The enhanced formality and institutionalization often associated with courts can also play various functional roles, such as establishing social control and bolstering regime legitimacy (Ginsburg & Moustafa, 2008; Moustafa, 2007). What I call an "authoritarian judicial dilemma" results from the ruler's dueling interests, on the one hand, in using law to enhance power and, on the other hand, in preventing empowered judges from invalidating bedrock regime policies and activist lawyers from mobilizing societal actors to demand changes that could weaken or threaten authoritarian rule.

Some scholars of China and other authoritarian court systems seemingly suggest that the central state might simply be navigating these tensions in a strategic fashion, implementing decisions in a top-down manner to expand judicial autonomy and authority throughout the country. Zhu's (2010, pp. 52–53) analysis of change in China's court system, for instance, is based on the premise that the CCP is "the major force mobilizing, promoting, and implementing reform within the judiciary" in contemporary China. In similar Party–State-centric fashion, Li finds that judicial behavior is brought about by "the particular decision-making mechanism guided by the Chinese Communist Party's instrumental rule-by-law ideal" (Ling Li, 2012). Greater "independence, competence, and fairness" in China's court system have been linked largely to state efforts to improve the quality of legal education in China, which, in theory at least, has led to a greater supply of qualified and competent judicial personnel (Fu, 2003). However, state-centric theories do not account for the decidedly local variation in judicial autonomy across China, and they also neglect changes in the depth and extent of state intervention in the law, the dynamic development of the legal system, and the legal system's own response to the state (X. Li & Cheng, 2013, p. 59; C. F. Minzner, 2009, p. 110).

The premise that authoritarian judicial institutions often serve as economic infrastructure, which might motivate state leaders to establish judicial institutions with varying degrees of autonomy for the purposes of facilitating trade and investment, might serve as an alternative foundational premise to the assumptions of top-down frameworks (see Ginsburg & Moustafa, 2008, p. 4; Moustafa, 2007). Cross-national quantitative analysis suggests that rule of law and economic development are closely related and tend to be mutually reinforcing (Peerenboom, 2009; Rigobon & Rodrik, 2005), and within China, Michelson and Read find that positive public attitudes toward local courts are associated with higher levels of economic development (Michelson & Read, 2011). Similarly, scholars have claimed that fairer judges are found in localities exhibiting higher per capita GDP, and others have found that legal reforms in China are much more likely to be consolidated in the economically advanced coastal regions than those in the nation's hinterlands (Michelson & Read, 2011, p. 195; Y. Wang, 2015, p. 4; Y. Wang & Shen, 2009). The finding that economic development *writ large* influences judicial autonomy does not tell us much, however, as development, rapidly emerging markets, and globalization have occurred in many localities, including many parts of China, but not all have seen expansions in judicial autonomy.

Wang's "demand-side theory" addresses this problem, presenting an elegant argument explaining how and why particular aspects of economic development might impact the court system to claim that "authoritarian rulers will respect the rule of law when they need the cooperation of organized interest groups that control valuable and mobile assets but are not politically connected" (Y. Wang, 2015). In Wang's account, these interest groups are foreign-owned enterprises that, among other characteristics, do not have many political connections in China and can influence judicial politics either by lobbying the government (voice) or moving, hiding, or destroying their assets (exit) (Y. Wang, 2015, pp. 7, 40).

Although Wang's research is a major contribution to the field, especially the insight that the particular nature of foreign investment can have a substantial impact on institutional change in a given locality, it leaves some questions unanswered. For instance, Wang ascribes foreign enterprises with substantial leverage to compel local officials in China to expand judicial autonomy, even though he also suggests that these foreign enterprises have limited political clout in China. Other potentially open questions include whether foreign investors in China prioritize judicial reform as part of their business strategies – for instance, concern regarding unfair courts and judges is not mentioned by US company officials (to give but one example of a prominent FDI source country) surveyed regarding the in-China business environment by the US-China Business Council between 2013 and 2019. In these surveys, respondents list law-related business obstacles such as "administrative licensing," direct subsidies for domestic companies, and foreign investment barriers ahead of any problems with adjudication in Chinese courts; court-related complaints are even less prevalent than appraisals finding no signs of local protectionism in China.[2]

Wang's argument also does not focus on changes within the court system itself, instead analyzing courts largely using external measures such as local governments' funding allocations for courts and the perceptions of local citizens who have never used the court system (Y. Wang, 2015, p. 121). The likely ambivalence of many political leaders regarding legal system reform (discussed more extensively later in this chapter) seems to suggest limitations to their unilateral involvement in local court reform, however. More specifically, a focus on courts themselves – including court leaders' actions and their impact on ordinary judges – appears necessary to advancing our understanding of judicial reform in China. Ng and He's recent book moves in this direction, adopting a socio-legal perspective that provides a fresh look and a seemingly comprehensive assessment of court operations in China (Ng & He, 2017), examining a wide variety of courts, judicial actors, and possible factors influencing judicial work throughout China. Their concept of embeddedness draws on the sociological approach of organizational ecology, finding that courts seek to enhance their survival, which leads to variation between "work unit" (*danwei*) and "law firm" types of courts; variation between these typologies is brought about by a complex interaction of factors that represent different social, political, economic, and cultural facets of embeddedness (Ng & He, 2017, p. 14). Although Ng and

[2] Again, US-China Business Council Member Surveys on the business environment in China can be found for 2019 and several previous years at the following website: www.uschina.org/reports/uscbc-2019-member-survey

He's socio-legal approach provides vivid accounts of court operations in the larger context of China's political system, including detailed descriptions of urban- and rural-level court variation, it only hints at factors or variables that might explain change in China's court and legal system.

To contribute to this growing field, I borrow from the broad scholarly landscape just discussed, but also seek to move forward by using an historical and comparative research design with the analytical leverage necessary for identifying more precisely the institutional features that lead to specific types of autonomy, transparency, and judging in a more focused subset of urban courts. The result is a synthesized ecological framework that, though it frequently draws from the research of other scholars, presents an original, modestly positivist application of a theory of social forms to the incremental changes to personal judicial autonomy in China since 1992 (see, e.g., Hannan & Freeman, 1977, 1989; S. Liu, 2015; S. Liu & Emirbayer, 2016; Ng & He, 2017; Wang, 2015; Tsai, 2016). In so doing, this book acknowledges that the spatial and temporal dimensions of law are often intertwined (Valverde, 2015, p. 33), i.e., variations in judicial autonomy have appeared even in similar urban localities in China, and these dramatic changes to the legal profession and courts have occurred primarily in the important period after liberalizing trajectories were resumed in 1992 and sweeping judicial reforms separated judges from the civil service bureaucracy in 2016.

Court Change in Urban China through the Lens of Ecology

In a departure from the research discussed above, I contend that the key mechanism impacting court reform during 1992–2016 is the growth, internationalization, and resulting influence of the local legal profession, catalyzed by the professional and social interaction between lawyers, judges, and courts in urban China. During my in-country fieldwork (2012–2014), I learned during interviews that court leaders in urban China were promoted based on their ability to efficiently manage courts, as measured by their courts' scores on quantitative performance indices; high scores on these performance indices were dependent on retaining and motivating a staff of qualified, productive, and diligent judges, who bore responsibility for deciding cases. In some urban localities, however, extensively developed, "high-end" legal services markets provided mid-ranking judges with lucrative alternative career opportunities as lawyers, threatening court leaders' ability to retain experienced, qualified judges to staff courts.[3] In these high-end localities, court leaders have layered new institutions of judicial selection and promotion alongside older practices in hopes of avoiding attrition among mid-career judicial cohorts (see Tsai, 2016). By strategically reforming promotion mechanisms, which could provide judges with greater assurance of upward career mobility, court leaders have resorted to one of the only methods at their disposal for curbing judicial attrition and thereby improving court leaders' own chances for promotion. Ultimately, I find that court leaders' decisions to reform promotion mechanisms produced the variation in judicial autonomy that I observed in my fieldwork (see also Kinkel, 2015; Kinkel & Hurst, 2015).

Survival and Growth: Judicial Motivations, Incentives, and Aspirations

Regarding judicial motivations and incentives, human ecology–based approaches find that individuals operate in their own self-interest to enhance their survival (S. Liu & Wu, 2016; Park & Burgess, 1969). In seeking their own professional survival and career growth, however, the actions of judges and other legal professionals in urban China are not conditioned by zero-sum, winner-take-all competition with colleagues, attorney acquaintances, and court supervisors. Instead, legal actors such as lawyers and judges contribute "… through the mutual exchange of services so established to the common welfare" in a process of "competitive co-operation" (see Hannan & Freeman, 1977; Ng & He, 2017; S. Liu & Emirbayer, 2016; Park & Burgess, 1969, p. 507). In emphasizing both *competition and cooperation*, the ecological approach to the social forms of law taken here is distinct from other theoretical approaches, including those based on the concept of social "fields," which emphasize power struggles, dominance, and subordination between actors as the primary forms of interaction, with professions as spaces of power and domination (Bourdieu, 1987; Kisilowski, 2014; S. Liu, 2015). In a broad sense, a social ecology approach to organizations is a metaphor to biological growth – as Park and Burgess write:

[3] The difference between "high-end" versus other types of local legal markets is discussed in more detail in Chapter 4. I also acknowledge that both the English- and Chinese-language literature on PRC courts have discussed the possibility that both "pull" factors (like increasing attorney salaries) and "push" factors (such as crushing caseloads and other workload burdens under the CQAS detailed in Chapter 3) could create pressure for judicial promotion reforms (see, e.g., Hu, 2015). Research strategies for assessing open empirical questions such as the merits of push vs. pull alternative theories are presented in Chapter 7 of this book.

> The plant community is the best illustration of the type of social organization that is created by competitive co-operation because in the plant community competition is unrestricted.... The economic organization of society, so far as it is an effect of free competition, is an ecological organization. There is a human as well as a plant and an animal ecology. (Park & Burgess, 1969, pp. 506–508)

Consistent with the concept of interaction that can be both competitive and cooperative, it appears that the analogy to plant life is apt indeed – plants can simultaneously compete fiercely for sunlight while also cooperating by sharing nutrients in times of physical stress (Simard, 2021). In the midst of privatization, professional jurisdictions might likewise feature actors who compete against colleagues for promotion or for a high-salaried law firm position in one scenario, while partnering together on a collaborative venture in the next.

At the same time, assumptions regarding competition among individual actors might also seem similar to those that underlie the purely instrumental preferences of many rationalist frameworks. Many of my judicial interviewees suggested, however, that instead of acting on purely materialist incentives, they seemingly aspired to a reciprocity- and exchange-based Weberian conception of "modern officialdom," i.e., the "acceptance of a specific obligation of faithful management in return for a secure existence" (Weber, 1946, p. 199). Importantly, this distinction helps explain why some judges in China might choose to leave their judicial positions, whereas others might be dissuaded from leaving if promotion opportunities and career trajectories were opened and clarified, thereby offering a chance at a "secure existence" in urban China. In short, an ecology approach contemplates the possibility that institutional change can occur through interaction within and among social forms of law; although the basic form of interaction in human ecology is competition, this book challenges traditional approaches by acknowledging that – especially in a rapidly changing and uncertain environment – preferences can be fluid and that processes of negotiation, exchange, reciprocity, and settlement can be part of a broadly strategic approach to navigating a professional environment that also depends on cooperation. In this way, depending on local conditions, some judges might decide to resign their judicial positions for new career opportunities in a burgeoning legal services sector, whereas others might opt to move forward professionally in response to court leaders' decisions to strategically reform judicial selection and promotion mechanisms (which is itself an interactive response on the part of court leaders to preserve their own hierarchical privilege and the basic organizational structure of their courts – all in an environment of competitive cooperation). The fact that many Chinese judges have chosen to significantly reorient their professional lives by resigning their judicial positions also speaks to the fundamentally disruptive influence of the rapidly expanding legal service market in early-twenty-first-century urban China.

Although some neoclassical economic and rational choice frameworks have, in some ways, accepted the premise that institutions can influence individual behavior, much of the rational choice institutionalist approach imputes largely instrumental (materialist or otherwise) individual preferences, even to actors embedded in institutional settings (Katznelson & Weingast, 2005, p. 8). Like Ng and He and others who have applied organizational ecology approaches to court reform in China, the approach of this book differs from those of institutional economists who emphasize efficiency as a mechanism of change; although efficiency considerations are important, and have "powerful consequences for many kinds of organizations ... they do not obviously override institutional and political considerations" (Hannan & Freeman, 1989, p. 339; Ng & He, 2017).

As discussed in more detail in the following three chapters, considerations of survival, and even growth, for court leaders, ordinary judges, and lawyers in urban China have been tightly interconnected since the unprecedented proliferation in Chinese law firms after 1992, and these motivations differ from the material self-interests imputed to actors in most rational-institutionalist frameworks. In this way, law and society research undergirds this book's theoretical structure, in recognition of the unique aspects of courts and legal institutions; at the same time, this book also engages with the "new institutionalism" debates, spanning at least the fields of economics, political science, and sociology over the past several decades (Hall & Taylor, 1996; Kinkel & Hurst, 2011; S. Liu, 2015; Ng & He, 2017; Thelen, 1999; Valverde, 2015; Fioretos et al., 2016). In finding that institutions can influence the decisional calculus of a variety of actors, scholars in this field have also long acknowledged and prioritized the temporal aspects of systemic legal change, a feature that bears strong resemblance to historical institutionalism's focus on legacies of concrete historical processes and their capacity to bring "questions of timing and temporality in politics ... to the center of the analysis of how institutions matter" (Thelen, 1999). In the spirit of this scholarship, I find that the best way to advance the study of China's courts is through "important borrowing and cross-fertilization" that draws upon a number of quite "heterogenous analytical tools that do not have a single provenance ... but instead work well in combination" (Thelen, 1999; Valverde, 2015). Ultimately, a diverse, cross-disciplinary approach is necessary to address and, in many ways, incorporate the insights of the wide-ranging scholarship on China's law and courts that includes at least comparative political science (Wang, 2015; Tsai, 2016), socio-legal studies (Ng & He, 2017; Liu, 2015), and law (T. Zhang, 2012).

Positions in Social Space: Local Court Leaders versus Ordinary Judges

Viewing change in China's courts through the lens of ecology contemplates judges and lawyers assuming particular positions that condition their interests in an ecosystem of legal practice at the local level in China. Some concepts related to "social geometry" from the literature on behavioral theories of law are also helpful here to better understand how, depending on location and direction within a social space, legal actors' decisions can vary in at least vertical and horizontal dimensions (Black, n.d., pp. 40–48; S. Liu, 2014). First, Black's notion of vertical positioning might be fruitfully applied to the divide between the actions of court leaders and ordinary judges in China; although Chinese judges are interested in both survival and professional growth, their hierarchical positions within the judiciary can influence the particular actions taken to pursue these interests. Second, the "horizontal" positioning that Black describes could frame relations between lawyers and judges within a local legal market, helping us understand how the different positioning of these law-related actors in the broader local services market might produce dissimilar responses to promotion and evaluation systems in courts. The horizontal configurations of actors illuminate the ongoing turf battles between different types of lawyers, judges, and other legal professionals in highly volatile professional environments in urban China; as Abbott (1988) finds, various professions can claim jurisdictions in the social space of work – a process that continues to be highly unsettled in urban China. Along with finding niches (Hannan & Freeman, 1977), actors settle into jurisdictions (Abbott, 1988), and the positions of these actors in the larger social space of law are continuously "being constructed and reconstructed by the mobility and interaction of actors as well as broader environmental forces" (S. Liu, 2015).

In urban China, the vertical promotion to a court leadership position largely settles a given judicial actor into a symbiotic relationship with the respective court unit, committing a judge more deeply to a career in the judiciary and opening distance in the judge's horizontal relationship between the court and legal services market in a given locality. As discussed in more detail in Chapter 3, court leaders' professional survival is tethered to their courts' collectively assessed performance on quantitative indicators, which itself is tied to the retention of the mid-career judges who can decide cases quickly and accurately. Based on these same institutions, mid-career judges responsible for deciding cases appeared to have greater horizontal connections to local legal services markets in urban China at least before 2016, with the globally unprecedented growth of the Chinese legal profession in the early twenty-first century making it difficult to stem the attrition of mid-career judges and avoid the court instability that judicial "brain drain" (*liushi renyuan*) can create (X. Liu, 2014).

Court Leaders and the Tolerance Interval for Judicial Reform

Importantly, court leaders possess leeway to reform judicial institutions likely due to the political ambivalence of local political officials (such as Party leaders, provincial governors, mayors, and others at the central and local levels) toward court reform sparked by the authoritarian judicial dilemma mentioned earlier in this chapter. In a similar context, Stern defines ambivalence on the part of political officials as the simultaneous, conflicting impulses to promote law but control courts, which "… generate a medley of conflicting statements, cases, and regulations. In contemporary China, this often translates to ground-level uncertainty. When information is conflicting, and also often incomplete or unreliable, it is difficult to gauge the government's 'tolerance interval,' let alone figure out how to act accordingly" (Epstein et al., 2001; cited in Stern, 2013).

Although Stern's study on environmental litigation most directly examines ambivalence with respect to citizen action, it also observes that political officials tasked with addressing the authoritarian judicial dilemma might have an interest in expanding judicial autonomy (e.g., to use courts as "economic infrastructure"); they would likely do so by providing mixed or ambiguous signals of official preferences – a phenomenon applicable to court reform in urban China. For instance, local courts have been authorized since 1998 to implement "competitive promotion" systems for judicial selection opportunities in both "leading" and "nonleading" positions, which would limit the authority of local CCP units to interfere in promotion decisions; however, competitive promotion is not required, nor are there predictable consequences for lax implementation.[4] Adding complexity to this ambiguity, courts are not provided guidance as to when or how to carry out judicial promotion competitions; yet, they have been allowed to host transparent promotion competitions open to candidates within a system, department, or the general public, according to regulations that were largely ratified by the Law on Civil Servants in 2006.[5] Similarly, regarding transparency, the SPC has previously authorized local courts throughout China to publicly release a variety of information online, including judicial opinions; yet, it is within courts' discretion whether and to what extent to comply (CASS, 2012, p. 33).

These circumstances effectively allow this book to report retrospectively on the degree to which courts have implemented promotion and transparency regulations, which can serve as a useful gauge of personal judicial autonomy.[6] The concept of "policy entrepreneurship," from the literature on policy change and civil society in China, also becomes more relevant in this context. In the early to mid-2000s, the authoritarian policymaking process in China was "increasingly pluralized," and barriers to entry in the policymaking process were lowered, at least for certain actors that include "peripheral officials" (a category within which I would include local court leaders) (see Mertha, 2009). In an increasingly pluralized policy environment, peripheral officials can become "policy entrepreneurs" who advocate not only for proposals or ideas but are also willing "… to invest their resources – time, energy, reputation, and sometimes money – in the hope of a future return … [including] in the form of policies of which they approve" (Mertha, 2009, p. 996). In a fragmented political system like China's, court leaders often act as policy entrepreneurs to reform judicial promotion and compete in political spaces that allow them "… to operate without being snuffed out by the coercive apparatus of the state. Territorial, jurisdictional and other political cleavages provide comparatively fertile ground for various contending interested parties to push their agendas and to arrive at compromises

[4] CCP Organization Department and the CCP Personnel Department Notice on Issuing the Opinion Regarding Party State Organs Implementing Competitive Promotion (*Zhongzubu, Renshibu guanyu yinfa "guanyu dangzheng jiguan tuixing jingzheng shanggang de yijian" de tongzhi*) of July 23, 1998, Central Organization Document Number 33 (1998) (copy on file with author).

[5] Notice on Issuing the Opinion Regarding Party State Organs Implementing Competitive Promotion, Central Organization Document Number 33 (1998).

[6] The section "Conceptualizing and Measuring the Outcome Variable: Personal Judicial Autonomy" directly defines the concept of personal judicial autonomy and explains how it is measured.

that better reflect their own parochial or institutional goals" (Mertha, 2009, p. 997).

Similar to Stern's concept of political ambivalence, Mertha's description of policymaking "space" echoes the finding that there is a tolerance interval within which peripheral officials have leeway to move politically without exposure to an outsize risk of political repression. Accordingly, this book argues that in some localities, court presidents and even vice presidents have navigated a loosely defined tolerance interval to limit the court-packing efforts of local CCP actors, as long as judges do not challenge core interests of the regime. As such, this book largely eschews a Bourdieusian approach to professional "fields" and develops a spatial theory of law that, for the purposes of the present analysis, largely sets aside power struggles, dominance, action-oriented collective mobilization of legal professionals, and other actions that likely fall outside of the state's "tolerance interval" (P. Bourdieu & Wacquant, 1992; Epstein et al., 2001; Karpik & Halliday, 2011, p. 221; Stern, 2013) to better illuminate social spaces with actors, locations, and the relations that associate them (Abbott, 2005). The result is an ecological theory of social forms that has much in common with field theory in its approach to social space but remains distinct in terms of power (Liu, 2015, p. 11).

Assumptions regarding the ambivalence of political leaders with respect to court reform resemble those at play in other work on the SPC's ability to craft policy under certain conditions (see T. Zhang, 2012), but the argument of this book (especially that of Chapter 7) instead begins at the local level, where courts appear to have influenced the national direction of court personnel reforms in 2014–2016 as much as the SPC. Operating within this limited, but tangible, political space, court leaders in urban China would have faced greater pressure to introduce judicial selection and promotion reforms when law firms in high-end legal services localities could threaten to lure their top judges into careers as lawyers. During 2009–2014, for instance, an average of 67 judges resigned *every year* from Shanghai courts, with 74 resignations in 2013, placing substantial pressure on local court leaders to curb judicial attrition (Chin, 2014).[7] At the

[7] As noted previously, calculating the precise number of judges in China is very difficult, and even more so at the local level. However, in a *China Daily* article from 2017, Shanghai High Court President Cui Yadong provided the number 1,000 as the approximate number of Shanghai judges (China Daily Staff, 2017). If this estimate were loosely applied to the previous decade, approximately 6–7 percent of judges in Shanghai, or more, were resigning every year during the mid-2010s.

fourth meeting of the Shanghai delegation to the 2014 National People's Conference, Judge Cui Yadong summed up the burden placed on courts by the loss of highly productive case-deciding judges, first acknowledging the degree of judicial attrition and proclaiming that judicial labor turnover must be confronted and resolved in any systemic judicial reform:

> The judges who leave constitute our backbone (*gugan*), and they are familiar with their professional duties—usually around 40 or 50 years old. This situation, in which the professional backbone of the legal system resigns in high numbers, severely undermines our personnel stability and creates a self-perpetuating cycle where "brain drain" (*liushi renyuan*) gradually becomes larger problem every year. (X. Liu, 2014)

The result of the interaction between court leaders' professional incentives and local demand for legal professionals is variation in the competitiveness, transparency, and routinized use of competitive judicial promotion mechanisms. Interviews with mid-ranking judges support a finding that, despite the attrition of some judges, reforming judicial designs to professionalize career trajectories is nonetheless a viable strategy for retaining many other productive judges who desire greater clarity and more reliable information regarding their chances of professional survival as judges and feel heavy pressure from constant, within-court quantitative rankings and high caseloads.[8] According to several interviews with case-deciding judges, a realistic chance at a merit-based promotion (and the administrative salary raise that such promotions provide) is a plausible strategy for stemming the tide of judges resigning from courts to pursue higher paying jobs in local law firms.[9]

To clarify, though, court leaders in contemporary China focus on retaining judges who have already earned promotions and the authority to decide cases, rather than attracting entry-level candidates for court openings. As of 2014, a recent Chinese law school graduate could have obtained an entry-level court position as an assistant judge (*zhuli shenpanyuan*) or even a position as a clerk (*faguan zhuli*) (see Z. Liu, 2014, p. 148). Only after obtaining at least five years of experience, and sometimes much longer, could a judge have obtained authority to sit on a

[8] *PC2013-65, judge, Foshan, July 2013; PC2013-56, judge, Shanghai, June 2013.* Throughout this book, interviews are cited by a code, preceded by the term "PC" to represent "personal communication" and then the year of the interview. Interview citations are also italicized, and information regarding the interviewee's professional status, the date of the interview, and the location of the interviewee are provided.

[9] *PC2014-2, judge, Shenzhen, June 2014; PC2014-3, judge, Shanghai, June 2014.*

collegial panel (*heyiting*) of up to three judges and decide cases.[10] One interviewee noted that courts are often flooded with applications for entry-level positions, but these high applicant volumes do not necessarily help court leaders because it takes several years to develop the experience needed to decide cases, by which time, judges in training could leave the court and start the recruitment all over again.[11] Ultimately, courts have a much more difficult time stemming the attrition of experienced judges and a much easier time finding entry-level job applicants, leaving court leaders with an institutional interest in retaining adept, case-deciding judges.

Mechanisms of Change: Bridges, Conditions of Interaction, and the Forms and Substance of Law

In explaining local changes to judicial autonomy in China and offering a plausible theory of nationwide judicial reforms in 2014–2016, I broadly emphasize the "social forms of law," i.e., the Weberian notion of "social structures and social processes that constitute the spatial outlook and temporality of the legal system" (S. Liu, 2015, p. 7; see also Weber, 1978, pp. 654–658). The networks of legal agents operating in relation to local court systems in urban China can be seen, broadly speaking, as social forms of law. Instead of focusing on power struggles within professional fields or documenting lawyer mobilization, an ecology-based socio-legal theory can contemplate "the social processes that have the capacity of bridging micro interactions of legal and nonlegal actors and macro social structures of the legal system" (Liu, 2015, p. 15). The Case Quality Assessment System (CQAS, *anjian zhiliang pinggu tixi*), detailed in Chapter 3, does much of this work by supplying judges with their foundational institutional incentives; Chapter 4 then ties these incentives to the historical context and layers of the social process of law by which the legal system in China transformed after 1992. Although this book emphasizes the social forms of law, I also provide evidence suggesting (in Chapter 5, in particular) that these dynamics can also influence the substance of law. The decisions of court leaders in urban China to increase the transparency of their courts and enhance the statutory basis of their judicial decisions also appear to be shifts that are substantive in the sense that they are tied to individual actions of legal agents (Liu, 2015, p. 7).

10 *PC2014-2, judge, Shenzhen, June 2014.*
11 *PC2014-3, judge, Shanghai, June 2014.*

Much of this argument is held together by an understanding of the different motives operating at least before the 2014–2016 national-level judicial reforms between ordinary, mid-career, case-deciding judges and court leaders (i.e., court presidents and vice presidents) under rigid, quantified performance evaluation systems, which have bridged the interaction between micro- and macro-level court structures. Chapter 3 details that the foundational institutional incentives of the CQAS pressure ordinary, case-deciding judges to resolve large numbers of cases very efficiently; on the other hand, the institutional incentives of court leaders, and how these incentives are related to attracting and retaining qualified, mid-ranking judges who decide cases, help demonstrate that local demand for private legal services pressured court leaders to reform judicial designs. Before 2014, and perhaps thereafter, the CQAS evaluated court leaders (e.g., court presidents and vice presidents) based on the quantitative scores of their courts as collectives. High scores – and court leaders' chances for promotion – thus depended on retaining highly productive, qualified subordinate judges who decide cases. During interviews, judges consistently told me that the institutional pressures exerted within the court hierarchy via judicial performance evaluations most affected their daily work lives and also provided their primary motivation for their work habits in deciding cases.[12]

Court leaders' incentives are institutionally structured by the CQAS, which grew increasingly complex in the early twenty-first century and was unified nationally by the SPC in 2011. The complex features of the CQAS were authorized by the straightforward and simple description of judicial performance evaluation in the Judges Law of China, which states, "Appraisal of judges shall be conducted by the Peoples' Courts the judges belong to.... The result of appraisal shall be taken as the basis for award, punishment, training, dismissal of a judge, and for readjustment of his or her grade and salary."[13] Putting this legislation into practice, a wide range of statistics, formulas, and measurements structure judicial performance appraisals: the 2011 SPC Guiding Opinion Regarding Launching Case Quality Assessment Work (hereinafter, "Guiding Opinion") instructs local courts to use at least 31 indices to quantitatively assess judges' and

[12] *PC2013-43, judge, Shenzhen, April 2013; PC2013-56, judge, Shanghai, June 2013; PC2013-49, judge, Shanghai, May 2013; PC2013-51, judge, Chengdu, May 2013.*

[13] Judges Law of the PRC, Articles 19 and 22. References in this book are to the original Judges Law passed in 1995 (which was effective during 1992–2016), unless otherwise noted.

courts' performance in three separate categories: "fairness" (*gongzheng*), "efficiency" (*xiaolü*), and "social impact" (*xiaoguo*).[14]

According to Article 1 of the Guiding Opinion on the CQAS, court leaders are evaluated by aggregated (*zonghe*) indices regarding the performance of their courts and the subordinate judges and units within each court's jurisdiction.[15] Aggregating the performance scores of individual judges under the CQAS allows political elites to assess the performances of individual court divisions and courts as collectives by viewing aggregated CQAS results in comparison with similar units in other jurisdictions and locations throughout the country.[16] These composite court rankings allow comparison and classification of court presidents and vice presidents' court management performance, as explicitly mandated by the Guiding Opinion: "For every half-year and year-long period, the SPC will engage in analysis of assessment statistics and indices, and publish an 'All-Country Case Quality Analysis Report'; summarize the case quality situations of Higher-Level Courts, Intermediate-Level Courts, and Basic-Level [i.e., first-instance] People's Courts, and at regular intervals provide feedback (*fankui*) regarding every level court's case quality assessment situation."[17] Using software and spreadsheets mandated for use under the Guiding Opinion, the SPC and High Courts throughout China distribute cumulative court and divisional index results, upon which lower levels of the court system should rely in an attempt to guarantee the objectivity of the assessments (J. Zhang, 2011).[18] In response to cross-provincial analysis and "feedback" provided in the SPC reports on CQAS performance, municipal courts discuss their cumulative CQAS scores in comparison with other court systems throughout the country.[19]

Hence, the performance of court leaders is assessed based on the collective performance of their entire courts – during the period under study, these leading "judges" did not decide cases on a regular basis;

[14] 2011 SPC Guiding Opinion Regarding Launching Case Quality Assessment Work (*Zuigao renmin fayuan guanyu kaizhan anjian zhiliang pinggu gongzuo de zhidao yijian*), Articles 8–10 ("2011 Guiding Opinion").

[15] 2011 Guiding Opinion, Article 1.

[16] Examples of similar, comparable courts would be all first-instance District Courts in a municipality or all Intermediate Courts in a given province or region.

[17] 2011 Guiding Opinion, Article 24.

[18] 2011 Guiding Opinion, Articles 17 and 27.

[19] *PC2014-3, judge, Shanghai, July 2014; PC2012-23, judge, Shenzhen, September 2012; PC2012-30, judge, Wenzhou, October 2012.*

Table 2.1. *Overview of judicial rankings at an intermediate-level court in urban China (as of 2014)*

Position	Function	Cadre status	Promotion style
Assistant Judge (*zhuli shenpanyuan*)	Provides research and logistical assistance to Associate Judge	Cadre	Watered-down competitive promotion
Associate Judge (*shenpanyuan*)	Adjudicates cases; possesses soft veto power on case decisions as a member of a three-judge panel	Cadre	Watered-down competitive promotion
Chief of Judicial Panel (*heyiting shenpanzhang*)	Final, tie-breaking decision-maker in case disputes handled by three-judge panels	Cadre	
Division Vice Chief (*futingzhang*)	Management and assignment of case disputes; serves on three-judge panels	Mid-level cadre	Competitive promotion
Division Chief (*tingzhang*)	Management of cases and assignment of Judicial Panel Chief	Mid-level cadre	Competitive promotion
Vice President (*fuyuanzhang*)	Management of whole court operations	Leading cadre	Direct selection (Z. Liu, 2012)
President (*yuanzhang*)	Management of whole court operations	Leading cadre	Direct selection (Z. Liu, 2012)

Sources: PC2013-4, judge, Shenzhen, January 2013; PC2013-3, Shenzhen, January 2013 (Z. Liu, 2012, 2014).

instead, they were responsible for "managing" the court in the way that a CEO might run a company (for an overview of the status and functions of different court personnel, see Table 2.1). On the other hand, ordinary judges are assessed for promotion individually, based on how quickly and accurately they decide cases. Interacting with these institutional incentives, the relative local demand for legal services increases the value of mid-career judges, thereby pressuring court leaders to retain efficient, qualified judges and raising the opportunity costs for young legal professionals who decline to pursue potentially lucrative careers as lawyers.

Although these judicial performance mechanisms incentivize court leaders to retain the most efficient and productive judicial workers (as measured by several indices, including cases cleared per year or per month), court leaders have possessed limited means to achieve this objective. Because salaries have been controlled by the State Council at the national level, I observed that local court leaders could not offer their subordinates meaningful income raises to account for the rapidly rising cost of living in urban China. One of the few means at their disposal for retaining highly qualified judges is rendering judicial promotion mechanisms more transparent to clarify subordinate judges' potential for professional survival and possibilities of career growth.[20] From the perspective of ordinary judges, a merit-based promotion system creates a sense of honor and accomplishment that one judge characterized as a motivational substitute for high salaries.[21] From the perspective of court leaders, Shanghai Court President Cui Yadong stated that to prevent large numbers of experienced judges from resigning their posts, courts must "advance judicial personnel construction regularization, specialization, and professionalization, and at the same time, establish a judicial personnel system that adapts to the special features of professionalism" (X. Liu, 2014).

With respect to forms, however, the ecological approach also calls for an explanation of the temporality of socio-legal processes and their structural effects (S. Liu, 2015, p. 19). In this book, the variations between judicial promotion mechanisms (judicial administrative hierarchies) are initially explained by variation in local legal services markets – more specifically, the difference between high-end and battleground markets that has only become influential (and perhaps only truly appeared) after 1992. As noted at the beginning of this chapter, my explanation for local and

[20] *PC2013-57, judge, Shanghai, June 2013; PC2013-53, judge, Shanghai, May 2013; PC2012-2, judge, Shenzhen, June 2012; PC2012-6, judge, Shenzhen, June 2012; PC2013-51, judge, Chengdu, May 2013.*

[21] *PC2013-51, judge, Chengdu, May 2013.*

national-level court reforms is bolstered by the interrelated timing and sequencing of the privatization and growth of the legal profession, especially after 1992, which accelerated as part of China's 2001 WTO accession; not long after, significant reforms were introduced to the selection and promotion of local courts in China.

Although this book adopts an ecological approach to explaining change in China's legal system, it also goes beyond previous applications of organizational ecology by advancing modest causal relationships between macro- and micro-level institutional layers, actors, and events. While Liu is correct to suggest that changes to the forms and substance of law might be socially contingent, and are likely not statistically predictable, the argument of this book takes a more positivist approach, suggesting that modest causal claims might also be supported by an ecological framework (S. Liu, 2015). In some ways, this approach resembles Ng and He's (2017) "embedded courts" approach, mentioned above, that also draws on a socio-legal application of organizational ecology to illuminate courts' efforts to enhance their survival, which leads to variation between archetypical "*danwei*" and "law firm" courts in China; however, I have designed this book to examine more specific, intra-urban variations with the goal of elucidating more precisely the plausibility of distinctive causal pathways (see Ng & He, 2017, p. 14).

The methods that I use to further refine the research on institutional change in China's courts include fine-grained, qualitative interviews and examination of written source materials that more clearly specify the factors mediating the relationship between economic development and judicial autonomy in China's urban courts. As judges explained to me, their livelihoods in urban localities with rapidly rising costs of living were increasingly insecure; judges and other public officials did not enjoy the social esteem commensurate with the Weberian sense of modern officialdom mentioned above, perceiving a diminished social status for judges relative to the lightly regulated lawyer profession and employees in growing private companies. Judges mentioned that meaningful upward career mobility would represent at least one factor that could bring them closer to the pure type of modern officialdom to which they seemingly aspired. At the same time, the ability of court leaders to alter these promotion mechanisms ultimately serves as possible means to motivate judges to remain in their careers in the court system. Eventually, as Chinese judges who rule on disputes have opportunities for more merit-based promotion and work in courts that increasingly value transparency, they should be more autonomous from the myriad social and political pressures influencing their decisions in the disputes before them.

Conceptualizing and Measuring the Outcome Variable: Personal Judicial Autonomy

The Concept of Personal Judicial Autonomy

In this book, the outcome variable is "personal judicial autonomy," which is found when judicial terms of office are "reasonably secure" and when judicial appointments and promotions are relatively depoliticized, fair, and carried out according to pre-established rules (Peerenboom, 2010, p. 71). Although this conceptualization draws heavily from Peerenboom's concept of personal judicial "independence," I use the term "autonomy" in recognition of an important distinction in terminology: "[T]he traditional variable to describe judiciaries, independence, has considerable affinity with … autonomy," but the concept of autonomy "does not unrealistically require courts to be completely unmoored from their political and social surroundings"; at the same time, autonomy still speaks to "the normative ideal that courts exist to serve as neutral impartial third parties to resolve disputes" (Brinks & Blass, 2018, pp. 23–28). Moreover, Peerenboom's conception of independence is explicitly geared toward actively promoting judicial independence in China, whereas the primary scope of this book is explanatory. Ultimately, the outcome variable "personal judicial autonomy" strikes a proper balance between the measurable aspects of Peerenboom's concept of "personal independence" and the conceptually precise elements of Brinks and Blass' "autonomy."

Personnel decisions regarding judges, including appointment, promotion, removal, and "court packing," are crucial to understanding whether courts possess the *a priori* autonomy necessary to render fair decisions in the legal disputes before them (Chavez, 2004; Dahl, 1957; Peerenboom, 2010). As part of the social forms of law operating at the local level in China, the structural governmental arrangements relevant to judicial selection can capture much of what is meant by judicial autonomy: Merit-based promotion cultivates the conditions necessary for impartial decisions by minimizing judges' worries that in politically sensitive cases, their professional livelihoods might hang in the balance (Hilbink & Woods, 2009; Solomon, 2007b; Weber, 1978). For example, in Chavez's study of authoritarian judicial politics in Argentina, most dimensions of judicial autonomy are measured using personnel-related factors such as whether the executive used opaque processes to appoint pliant judges, pack the courts, or violate judicial tenure (Chavez, 2004, p. 465). Even models of U.S. Supreme Court Justices' case decisions are firmly rooted in an assumption that the justices possess a freedom from politicized retribution that flows from their life tenure (Landes & Posner, 1975; Segal & Spaeth, 2002, pp. 92–93).

Peerenboom also finds that "personal" judicial autonomy is a prerequisite for "decisional" autonomy, which "refers to the ability of judges to decide cases independently in accordance with law and without (undue inappropriate, or illegal) interference from other parties or entities" (Peerenboom, 2010, p. 71); the interrelated nature of personal and decisional judicial autonomy also mirrors the conceptual overlap that can occur between the social forms and substance of law (Weber, 1978). Acknowledging the connection between personal and decisional autonomy, I further examine the measures of decisional autonomy in judicial opinions, mediation frequency, and transparency scores to determine whether they correspond in substantive ways with fluctuations in judges' job-related personal autonomy. If this is the case, it is more likely that the conclusions regarding personal judicial autonomy are reliable.

Addressing "judicial autonomy" in China does not suggest that judges, especially in criminal cases, are free to rule on cases – especially those of a politically and/or socially sensitive nature – as they please. Instead, this form of autonomy is a relative and disaggregated concept meant to assess the changes to workplace practice in Chinese courts that have substantial consequences for judicial decision-making. Contemplating networks of legal systems in which multiple informal and formal networks of law operate together (Santos, 1987), a disaggregated outcome variable relates well to similarly unpacked concepts employed in studies on authoritarian legal systems in China and elsewhere, including Peerenboom's "thick" and "thin" rule of law, Wang's "partial" rule of law, and Moustafa's circumscribed notion of "constitutional power" (Moustafa, 2007; Peerenboom, 2002; Y. Wang, 2015). Focusing on a partial conception of autonomy is also designed to fit the unique demands of conducting an empirical examination of court systems in authoritarian regimes. Broader concepts are difficult to employ in empirical studies due to their ambiguity and fuzziness (Wang, 2015), as indeed, depending on the context, "rule of law" can refer to libertarian or socialist principles (Peerenboom, 2003). Likewise, the concept of "judicial independence" is difficult to apply to a regime as authoritarian as the PRC, given that even the ostensibly "independent" courts of the British common law system were hardly *politically* independent: "The theory of the British constitution has always been one of complete, absolute, and unified sovereignty" (Shapiro, 1981, pp. 66–67). The institutional roots of PRC courts, steeped in Leninist politics, render a broad application of the concept of judicial independence or rule of law even less applicable to the Chinese case (see also Hurst, 2018).

Empirically speaking, focusing on these more specific dynamics of judicial design will illuminate under-explored mechanisms that are crucial to producing judicial autonomy, as "the criteria for becoming a judge and for being promoted are not publicly available, nor is the selection and promotion process transparent or subject to public monitoring" (Peerenboom, 2010, p. 77). Using judicial autonomy as an outcome variable also complements the survey methods that underpin much of the extant systematic research on judicial autonomy in China and rely on external measures to measure judicial autonomy – such as the perceptions of citizens who have not had contact with courts (Michelson & Read, 2011; Y. Wang, 2015). Given the limits to obtaining reliable data on China's judicial institutions, measures like these are best used in tandem with each other to sketch modest conclusions regarding the dynamics of court politics in China.

Measuring Personal Judicial Autonomy

To measure the concept of personal judicial autonomy, I first assess the degrees of competition, routinization, and transparency in courts to gain an understanding of the extent to which judicial terms of office are "reasonably secure" and when judicial appointments and promotions are relatively depoliticized, fair, and carried out according to pre-established rules (Peerenboom, 2010, p. 71; Weber, 1946). Importantly, measuring autonomy in this way illuminates whether courts' implementation of competitive judicial promotion mechanisms can credibly disrupt the authority of CCP units and other political leaders from directly and unilaterally selecting preferred judicial candidates – which was the standard practice throughout at least the 1990s under the "nominated appointment" system for selecting mid-level judicial cadres (Wei, 2010).[22] When Shanghai Courts host "all-city" competitions, for instance, local CCP authorities' ability to directly influence promotion outcomes is fragmented and diminished by the results of exams, interviews, and performance evaluations used to select promotion candidates.

To assess courts' compliance with transparency guidelines, I examine transparency index scores from the Chinese Academy of Social Sciences

[22] *PC2013-1, judge, Shenzhen, January 2013.*

(CASS), which assesses courts for the extent to which they provide timely information to the public via online websites – as ordered by the SPC (CASS: Chinese Academy of Social Sciences Legal Studies Department Rule of Law National Status Research Group, 2012). The SPC requires local courts throughout China to establish official websites and publish online information related to court work and the litigation process, including written judgments of current judicial cases (CASS, 2012). According to SPC rules effective at that time, courts should, "according to regulations, put judicial opinions of all types online" (CASS, 2012, p. 33).[23] The ambiguity of these court mandates is instructive because it helps identify which specific courts not only comply with but also exceed the suggestions of nonbinding regulations aimed at educating the public, thereby enhancing transparency and access to an official rationale for judicial decisions.[24] The Transparency Index includes five issue areas: online transparency regarding courts' general information (20 points), guidance regarding court procedure for litigants (15), judgment information (25), enforcement information (15), and judicial/court (*sifa*) statistics (25) – measures that cumulatively yield a 100-point, composite transparency scale (Lin Li & Tian, 2013, p. 216). Although CASS data and mediation rates should not be taken at face value or viewed in isolation, these data can nonetheless help corroborate the accounts provided by judges and lawyers during interviews. Given that this book is not intended to test hypotheses, but to create new theories using a controlled comparison case study (see Van Evera, 1997), I take an approach similar to that of Hilbink (2007), who triangulated and contextualized the statements of individual interviewees using several techniques, including interviewing a variety of actors and cross-checking against documentary materials (pp. 10–11).

In addition to focusing on courts' judicial promotion institutions, I have obtained data related to judges "decisional" autonomy, which includes a complete set of written court opinions related to intellectual

[23] On this point, the CASS report cites Several Opinions of the SPC Regarding the Work of Strengthening Adjudicatory Transparency (*Zuigao renmin fayuan guanyu jiaqiang renmin fayuan shenpan gongkai gongzuo ruogan yijian*) and Decision of the SPC Regarding Confirming the Scope of Court Transparency (*Guanyu queding sifa gongkai shifan fayuan de jue'ding*).

[24] Susan Finder provides highly detailed explanation of the hierarchy, function, and utility of the various types of documents issued by the SPC, see, e.g., the article available at the following link: http://supremepeoplescourtmonitor.com/2013/06/04/the-supreme-peoples-court-interpretations-of-law-as-a-form-of-official-document (copy of blog post on file with author).

property (IP) law from each of my three case study cities – a total of over 1,000 published judicial opinions.[25] In observance that "personal" judicial autonomy is a prerequisite for "decisional" autonomy, that is, the ability of judges to decide cases "in accordance with law and without (undue inappropriate, or illegal) interference from other parties or entities" (Peerenboom, 2010, p. 71), I assess the frequency of citation to statute in this sample of IP judicial opinions. The number of publicly issued opinions covering the relevant period is relatively high in IP-related matters, and IP law had also become a primary component of an impartial and commercialized zone of judicial practice in reform-era China (Dimitrov, 2009; Y. Wang, 2015), rendering published judicial opinions and mediation statistics a sound empirical base for assessing decisional autonomy among China's local judges during the period under study. In Chapter 5, I first analyze the content of a sample of judicial opinions across my three cases; in recent years, Chinese courts have generally taken more seriously the observation that decision-makers who are required to give reasons will make fewer arbitrary judgments and will be more transparent in their actions (Shapiro & Stone Sweet, 2002, p. 229). However, there are no unified standards regarding the content of judicial opinions, resulting in local variation in opinion writing that can be discerned through analysis of a larger sample of written judicial decisions. In examining IP-related judicial opinions published by PRC courts, I have focused on several metrics including opinion length and the frequency and character of statutory citation.

Further, because lower mediation rates suggest that judges are confident in their abilities to apply law to facts and issue reviewable decisions in specific cases, the willingness of judges in a given court to adjudicate cases rather than to allow parties to broker mediated settlements suggests judges' confidence in their political leeway to issue potentially sensitive opinions and in the likelihood of avoiding reversal by a higher court (while judicial decisions can be reversed on appeal, mediated settlements cannot).[26] Hence, I assess the rate of mediation across my three case study localities, and Chapter 5 provides data regarding the frequency of judicial mediation in selected trademark disputes, which varies between cases. Shanghai exhibits the lowest rate of mediation in these three cases (20 percent of cases mediated) relative to Shenzhen (nearly 40 percent)

[25] The opinions were obtained from the Rouse Corporation, and more information regarding their analysis and collection of judicial opinions is available at www.ciela.cn/

[26] *PC2013-53, judge, Shanghai, May 2013.*

and Chengdu (over 40 percent), supporting the finding that Shanghai judges are the most decisionally autonomous in the sample. Although it would be unwise to rely in isolation upon mediation rates as a measure of judges' decisional autonomy, these trends corroborate patterns regarding changes to judicial selection and promotion in my case study courts, and mediation has been used elsewhere as a rough indicator of judicial professionalism. For example, in "work-unit" courts, which Ng and He find are characterized by top-down interference and personnel decisions valuing social connections over professional expertise, mediation is "the primary method of judging," largely because it is a way to avoid adjudication (Ng & He, 2017, p. 125). In similar fashion, others have argued that court mediation in the Chinese context is a revival of "pre-1978 Maoist-style" practices (C. Minzner, 2011a).

Case Studies: The Interrelated Spatial and Temporal Aspects of Courts in Urban China

The basic local-level puzzle analyzed in this book brings into question the spatial characteristics of a largely uniform court system – although Shanghai, Shenzhen, and Chengdu are all relatively similar urban localities within China's unitary state, the emergence of variation in these cities' courts reflects that the jurisdictions laid out by the central government cannot simply be reduced to subunits of a homogenous whole (see Valverde, 2015). Rather, as is implicit in Santos' concept of interlegality and allusion to the different perspectives presented by cartographic mapping scales, quite heterogeneous modes of governance can often "appear to coexist without a great deal of overt conflict" (Santos, 1987; Valverde, 2009, p. 141). In urban China between 1992 and 2016, particular local characteristics of local legal development and legal actors' attempts for career growth have interacted to produce locally specific results where the PRC's formal court structure would tend to minimize such differences.

To more systematically illuminate the relationship between economic development and judicial autonomy, I employ a focused, comparative case study approach based on in-depth interviews, multiple documentary sources, and official statistics that identifies and explains patterns in the evolution of the institutional design and functioning of China's urban court system over at least the past two decades (cf. Whiting, 2000). As such, my study is situated firmly in the realm of theory generation, like much of the scholarship in the emerging comparative judicial politics research program (Ginsburg, 2003; Hilbink, 2007; Kapiszewski, 2012, p. 5;

Trochev, 2008), while also building on previous scholarship documenting the growth of China's legal profession and the association between economic development and court autonomy. Hence, in recognizing the explanatory limitations of the case study method, my framework is more modest than Van Evera's theory-testing, "crucial case study" approach (King et al., 1994; Van Evera, 1997). Instead, this study focuses on a small sample of case studies that is not intended to be representative of Chinese courts as a whole yet still allows for the formulation of hypotheses regarding the evolution of judicial institutions in the specific context of urban courts in China (Whiting, 2000, p. 30), with an overall aim of creating new theories using a controlled comparison case study (see Van Evera, 1997). This research design examines cases for "associations between phenomena and for testimony by people who directly experienced the case (actors in the case, for instance), and their motives and beliefs about the case. These associations and participant accounts offer clues on cause and effect"; the research task, then, is to frame cases and effects in general terms for later testing against other evidence and cases (Van Evera, 1997, pp. 67–68).

I narrowed the selection of cases to the specific urban court systems of Shanghai, Shenzhen, and Chengdu to focus directly on differences in judicial autonomy associated with levels of economic development identified in previous research (Michelson & Read, 2011; Y. Wang, 2015). I selected cases based on variation in local models of reform-era economic development, and accordingly, all three of my cases exhibit above-average levels of development but differ regarding the economic model that produced that development, narrowing the range of variation regarding social, economic, and cultural factors that could also serve as explanatory variables for the emergence of differing levels of judicial autonomy (see Tsai, 2007, pp. 152–166).

Consistent with a "similar systems" research design, all three of the case study cities in this book are court systems located in large, populous urban centers within China. These three case study cities had resident populations (*changzhu renkou*) over 10,000,000, with Shanghai's population exceeding 23,000,000 (Chengdu Bureau of Statistics, 2011; Shanghai Bureau of Statistics, 2011; Shenzhen Bureau of Statistics, 2011). Each case study locality's economy is characterized by well-developed secondary and tertiary sectors: in Shanghai and Shenzhen, the primary sector comprised less than 1 percent of the local GDP, and in Chengdu, it comprised only 10 percent of the local GDP during the period under study (Chengdu Bureau of Statistics, 2011; Shanghai Bureau of Statistics,

2011; Shenzhen Bureau of Statistics, 2011). All three case study cities have similar "imprints" of the state sector on the local economy, as measured by the percentage of fixed capital investment (*guding ziben touzi*) undertaken by the state-owned sector: in Shanghai and Shenzhen, the state sector accounts for 37 percent of fixed investment, and in Chengdu, the figure is 30 percent (Chengdu Bureau of Statistics, 2011; Shanghai Bureau of Statistics, 2011; Shenzhen Bureau of Statistics, 2011).

Because local idiosyncrasies and situated knowledge can alter legal and regulatory governance (Valverde, 2009, p. 142), however, these three large urban centers also differ on several factors related to economic development and judicial politics, including the development of private markets for legal services and geographical location. Especially after 2001, variation regarding the developmental models found in each of the three case study localities has led to different patterns of local legal services markets across urban China, by which Shanghai and Shenzhen have resembled "high-end" legal services markets, whereas Chengdu has become characteristic of a "battleground" urban market (S. Liu, 2011a, 2011b). For example, ranges of annual "entry level" and "experienced" lawyer salaries reported to me in 2013–2014 by attorneys in each case study location reflected a higher end of the market in Shanghai at 120,500–473,333RMB and Shenzhen at 65,000–247,500RMB, with salaries resembling more of a battleground market in Chengdu at approximately 45,000–150,000RMB. Figure 2.1 shows that Shanghai, Shenzhen, and Chengdu span coastal and interior geographies of mainland China.

Although the three selected case studies are largely similar urban localities relative to the whole of China, they differ regarding specific socioeconomic factors linked to the emergence of more professionalized judicial designs in China's urban court systems – in particular, the size and diversification of the local legal profession. In this way, studying differences between courts in China's larger urban centers avoids documenting empirical differences between urban and rural localities already established by other scholars (Balme, 2009; Hurst, 2011) while also illuminating the factors that are associated with local judicial autonomy in China's understudied urban courts. This research design and the case selection protocol reflect that local and national laws can "create different legal realities" and "reveal the existence of different legal spaces and their correspondent forms of law" (Santos, 1987, p. 287), while also avoiding the conflation of the "urban" and the "local" that can occur when differences between urban cases are obscured (Valverde, 2009, p. 144). Chapters 3 and 4 explore these specific variations between

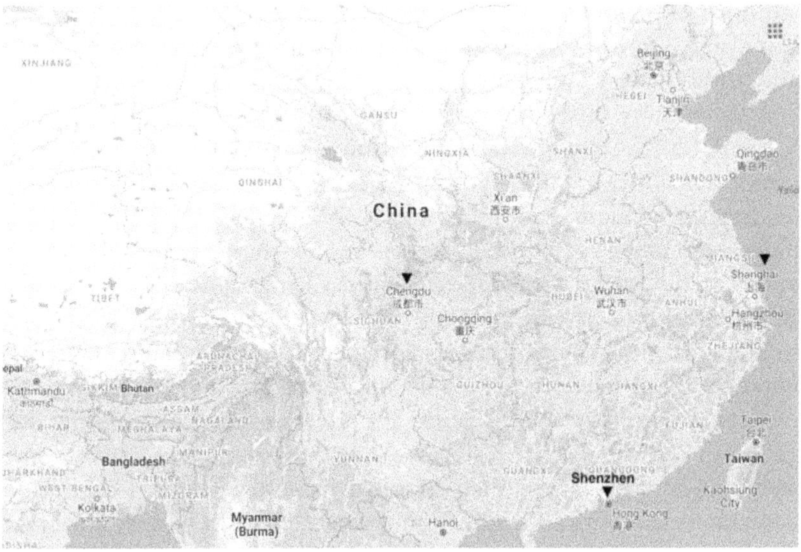

Figure 2.1 Map of primary case study cities.

three largely similar case studies and link them to outcomes in greater detail, employing a middle-range level of analysis useful for identifying causal mechanisms linking development and courts (Bennett & Elman, 2006, p. 459).

This research is based on 15 months of in-China fieldwork, conducted between June 2012 and July 2014, during which a substantial portion of this time I was affiliated with East China University of Political Science and Law (*Huadong Zhengfa Daxue*, or ECUPL) in Shanghai and traveled primarily to Shenzhen and Chengdu to conduct interviews, library research, and court hearing observation. I also made supplementary research trips to Beijing, Foshan, Wenzhou, and Wuxi to obtain more detailed information concerning judicial performance evaluation across localities (discussed further in Chapter 3). I returned to China during June and July 2014 for additional fieldwork and maintained contact with several interview subjects after returning to the United States. In all of these localities, I conducted a total of 130 interviews, including 61 total interviews with judges and 52 total interviews with lawyers. I selected judicial interviewees from as broad a cross section of courts in my cases as possible. Despite the difficulty of obtaining access to courts and judges, I conducted 49 interviews with judges across my three cases, and 12 interviews with judges in other Chinese cities.

Employing a broad conception of "jurisdiction" to frame the relationships and actions of lawyers and judges in a rapidly institutionalizing and authoritarian political context, and recognizing the role of space and temporality in shaping jurisdictions and legal forms (Santos, 1987; Valverde, 2015), I interviewed judges from a variety of court levels; however, the majority of my judicial interviewees worked at the Intermediate Court level, including nine interviews with Shanghai Intermediate Court judges, eight interviews with judges in the Shenzhen Intermediate Court, and eight interviews with judges from the Chengdu Intermediate Court. Regarding judges at the District Court level, I conducted 7 interviews in Shanghai, 11 in Shenzhen, and 6 in Chengdu. I also interviewed one Supreme People's Court (SPC) judge in Beijing and several lawyers who explained aspects of their practice and their experiences handling litigation in each local court system. Although most attorney interviewees were reluctant to discuss their personal income with me, I conducted eight interviews with attorneys from separate law firms regarding average incomes for entry-level associates, experienced associates, and partners.

I generally obtained introduction to judges via mutual contacts, fostered through my affiliation with ECUPL, then used snowball sampling to gain introduction to more interview subjects (Solinger, 2006). With the help of mutual social contacts, I would usually arrange a meeting with each interviewee for tea, coffee, or dinner in an informal setting away from the courthouse, with interviews ranging in duration from 20 minutes to 4 hours. On rare occasions, judges brought me to their offices for discussions over tea and even gave me a tour of courthouses and courtrooms. Although I prepared extensive lists of possible questions and discussion topics, I did not employ a predetermined interview questionnaire, but instead conducted "focused interviews" that allowed me to pursue particularly useful lines of thought and gave interviewees the opportunity to teach me how courts are managed in China (see Hurst, 2009; Merton et al., 1990).

Given that my interviewees represent but a small sample of all PRC judges, I rely on interviews in conjunction with various written and online sources to support my research findings. These other documentary sources include primary source documents, Chinese media publications, within-court publications available at the main library in Shanghai (e.g., *Shanghai Shenpan Shijian, Sichuan Shenpan*), Chinese and English secondary literature, and official government statistics. Triangulating interviews with written sources is crucial for research findings drawn from interviews with a small number of subjects who might not always be entirely forthcoming, especially given political and social sensitivities. I also spent a substantial amount of time personally observing court hearings (*pangting*) and shadowing lawyers in their offices as they went about their daily business, allowing for a greater understanding of the informal aspects of litigation in urban China. Although not capable of theory testing in the strict sense, using such methods in conjunction with each other can produce both testable claims that advance our understanding of Chinese judicial politics and modest generalizations regarding legal and political phenomena across time and space. Ultimately, this book finds that courts as governing institutions, when examined closely, turn out to be much more hybrid and complex than previous research might suggest (see Valverde, 2009, p. 142).

The leveraged analysis of carefully identified local similarities and differences is presented here within a delimited temporal structure, both to sharpen the analysis of local court systems and to acknowledge that the spatial and temporal dimensions of law are often intertwined (Valverde, 2015, p. 33). Court variations between similar urban localities in China have appeared in sharpest relief during the important period after liberalizing trajectories were resumed in 1992 and sweeping judicial reforms separated judges from the civil service bureaucracy in 2016. As noted above, differences and stratification between high-end and battleground local legal service markets have only become influential (and perhaps only truly appeared) in the wake of privatization and growth of the legal profession, especially after 1992, which accelerated as part of China's 2001 WTO accession.

Taking this approach is also consistent with both the approach of historical institutionalists and socio-legal scholars who prioritize the interrelated spatial, temporal, and processual elements in explanations of legal change (Hall & Taylor, 1996; Kinkel & Hurst, 2011; S. Liu, 2015; Ng & He, 2017; Thelen, 1999; Tsai, 2016). The ecological approach to the social forms of law, in this way, calls for an explanation of the temporality of socio-legal processes and their structural effects (S. Liu, 2015, p. 19), resulting in a synthesized ecological framework that presents an original, modestly positivist application of a theory of social forms to the incremental changes to personal judicial autonomy in China since 1992 (see, e.g., Hannan & Freeman, 1977, 1989; S. Liu, 2015; S. Liu & Emirbayer, 2016; Ng & He, 2017; Wang, 2015).

In measuring judicial selection and promotion mechanisms, court transparency, and judicial decision-making in three similar urban court

Table 2.2. *Review of variation in judges' decisional autonomy across urban court case studies (2012–2014)*

	Merit-based judicial promotion and court transparency	Compliance with "Giving Reasons" requirement and frequency of mediation
Shanghai	High competition; high routinization of competitive promotion: used for every opening and streamlining reforms implemented; high transparency levels	High frequency of citation to statute; low rate of mediation
Shenzhen	Medium competition; high levels of routinization, used for every opening and streamlining implemented; medium transparency	Medium frequency of citation to statute; medium rate of mediation
Chengdu	Low competition; low routinization, sporadic use; no streamlining implemented; low transparency	Low frequency of citation to statute; low rate of mediation

systems – Shanghai, Shenzhen, and Chengdu – this book pinpoints the differences between these cases in hopes of illuminating more general factors that lead to judicial autonomy in China. In so doing, this research design highlights the features of economic development most salient to the material and professional motives of lawyers and judges, i.e., revenues, remuneration, and labor markets for legal professionals in developing areas, which in turn affect the institutional, professional, and, in many ways, material, incentives of lawyers and judges. These data suggest that the urban court system with the most autonomous judges, determined by measures of judicial selection and promotion, as well as judicial decision-making, is Shanghai, followed in descending order by Shenzhen and Chengdu (Table 2.2).

During fieldwork, I learned that each city's courts were advised to implement "competitive promotion" systems for its mid-ranking judges, but surprisingly, the degree of competition and the level of routinization of these judicial promotion procedures varied distinctly between localities. Shanghai's court institutions were the most competitive and routinized, with mid-ranking judicial vacancies throughout the court hierarchy open to competition from any judicial applicant within the city. For instance, when Shanghai courts hosted "all-city" competitions, local CCP authorities' ability to directly pack the courts and influence promotion outcomes was fragmented and diminished by the results of exams, interviews, and performance evaluations used to select promotion candidates; furthermore, a streamlined process has in recent years allowed larger candidate pools in judicial promotion competitions. By contrast, judicial promotion competitions in my other two case study sites, Shenzhen and Chengdu, only included applicants within each individual court, and in Chengdu, competitive promotion procedures were sometimes ignored. Keeping promotion competitions internal to each specific court allows court leaders and local political elites to exert more direct, personal influence on promotion decisions, and when the courts simply do not use competitive procedures on a routine basis, local political elites, such as CCP Committees, have greater leeway to appoint friendly judges as they see fit.[27]

As noted above, the extant literatures on comparative courts and Chinese judicial politics do not explain this local variation in judicial autonomy between similarly developed localities in an authoritarian setting. Additionally, even the most systematic research on the emergence of judicial autonomy in China still relies on "perceived judicial corruption to measure the actual level of corruption" (Y. Wang, 2015, p. 60); conversely, this book uses information taken directly from courts and judges themselves to identify the factors responsible for local variation in Chinese judicial autonomy, cast light on the broader dynamics of judicial autonomy in China, and contribute to emerging debates in comparative politics, Chinese studies, and socio-legal research.

Conclusion

This book adopts an ecological approach to the explanation of court reform in urban China that helps uncover how significant changes can occur over time in the social forms of law, even despite limited mobilization by legal professionals for these changes. It also describes a middle path between an explanatory framework that finds that the top-down effects of the CCP or the demand-side pressures of interest groups or companies exercising political leverage end up affecting outcomes in

[27] *PC2013-1, judge, Shenzhen, January 2013; PC2013-3, judge, Shenzhen January 2013.*

judicial policy like those observed in Shanghai. To explain increases in judicial autonomy, I employ a socio-legal theoretical framework based on the interaction between social forms and processes of law, which are also conditioned by social structures of law, to produce changes to state institutions in a context of political ambivalence regarding specific aspects of the legal system. The interaction between the state and a class of professions – in China's case, a rapidly expanding corps of lawyers – appears to occur in the wake of economic growth but does not require a democratic political framework to take shape. The interaction of these state and societal factors becomes a broadly influential component of the legal system that operates at the boundary of state and society (S. Liu, 2011a). The particular features of the state-led reform projects designed to monitor bureaucratic performance present judges with their baseline incentive structure, under which judges assess whether changes brought by the expansion of the legal profession and the legal complex render a judicial career more or less desirable.

Underlying this main argument is a theoretical approach to the social forms and substance of law that can downplay the role of mobilization and power dynamics while still accounting for macro- and micro-level changes in the legal system. The reason for adopting this approach is not to avoid the very real conflicts and power struggles in some parts of the Chinese "legal complex" (see S. Liu & Halliday, 2016; Stern, 2013); instead, it is to apply a mode of analysis that can capture the dramatic changes in authoritarian courts that also occur over time, despite entrenched regime stability, state repression, and the limitations of grassroots political and social mobilization. Although it is not predicated upon mobilizing behavior on the part of the legal profession, this argument nonetheless underscores a subtle point made by scholars of the "legal complex," i.e., that "the emergence of a substantial market for legal services often stimulates the expansion of a private bar, which in turn multiplies centres of power outside the state" (see also Foucault, 2008, p. 149; Halliday et al., 2007, p. 28).

Although this research framework shows promise for explaining a wide range of legal and professional reforms, it has not been widely deployed in existing socio-legal scholarship on China. "One reason for this research vacuum is … Social scientists' intellectual preference for universal structural patterns," which often "undermines the discovery of contingent events that trigger or transform the processes of mobility in the legal profession…" (Liu, 2015). However, several important law and society works have relied on such an approach (Abbott, 1988; Galanter, 1974), and in its application to the PRC legal system, lawyer–judge interaction within the professional ecosystem can form a symbiotic relationship "through negotiated and reciprocal exchanges between lawyers and judges, which shapes the social structure of the Chinese legal services market as a whole" (S. Liu, 2011a). As mentioned above, new and varied opportunities for judges and lawyers in China have been the result of professions becoming interactional spaces for actors to engage in competitive cooperation with one another and "constitute various jurisdictional settlements" (Liu, 2015).

This approach might also be particularly helpful in analyzing the changes to the legal system in an authoritarian context like China, in which many observers argue that dramatic changes have occurred in the legal system since Dengist reforms began in 1978 (see, e.g., Peerenboom, 2002), even though such changes have seemingly occurred without the social mobilization of lawyers or other professional classes. Instead, the theory underlying these claims contemplates intense and widespread interaction between legal actors that, while itself largely apolitical, nonetheless wields substantial medium- to long-term influence on political and legal elements of the state. Factors operating at a subterranean level, rooted in an ecosystem of interactions and competitive cooperation of myriad legal actors, can accumulate to produce institutional change in socio-legal forms like judicial promotion hierarchies, especially when the ruling regime exhibits at least a halfhearted interest in expanding the legal profession and court system to serve organizational functions and attract foreign investors.

Despite the differences between the ecological approach presented in this book and the mobilizational approach taken by scholars of the legal complex, the development of local pockets of judicial autonomy in urban China shows that the impetus for greater legal and judicial autonomy, in a rapidly developing authoritarian context, can stem not from the leadership's conscious realization that autonomous law is needed for development, but from the more immediate life choices of legal professionals who find themselves in an expanding market for their services. As I argue in the following chapters, court leaders moved to retain judges by offering more competitive, transparent, bureaucratic careers to clarify the path to a secure, long-term existence in exchange for judges' fulfillment of their professional obligations to the state. These dynamics have led to the changes and differences in social forms of law in the urban case study localities that are examined throughout this book.

3

The Judicial Cadre Evaluation System

Foundational Institutional Incentives Undergirded by "Intra-state Legibility"

The Case Quality Assessment System (CQAS), examined in this chapter, provides the baseline institutional incentives for Chinese judges and determines the stakes for judges' career-related decisions, setting up dynamic interactions between the process, form, and substance of law in urban China. As described in Chapter 2, social processes of law can bridge the micro-level interactions of judicial, legal, and nonlegal actors, shaping macro- and meso-level changes in the ecology of court reform (Liu, 2015, p. 15). The positions of court leaders and mid-career judges, as defined by judicial performance evaluation systems like the CQAS operating in urban China during the period under study, lead to dynamic, competitive interactions between these two strata of judges (Park & Burgess, 1969). In the terms of ecology-based socio-legal theory, judges in these distinct strata act to enhance their own survival in a process of "competitive co-operation" (Hannan & Freeman, 1977; S. Liu & Emirbayer, 2016; Ng & He, 2017; Park & Burgess, 1969). Judges' navigation of the CQAS is also critical to understanding the influence of stratified local legal markets in urban China (described in Chapter 4) on judicial selection institutions and personal autonomy.

Judges, like other cadres and officials in China's political system, are regularly assessed according to rigid, quantitative performance metrics, and scholars have addressed similar topics in recent decades. Some have focused on judicial supervision and independence, arguing that Chinese Communist Party's (CCP) intervention into individual judges' decision-making can help promote the autonomy of China's judicial system (Peerenboom, 2010; Zhu, 2010), whereas others have maintained that previous expansions of extrajudicial influence in the legal system are a sign of the state's downgrading of – or "turn against" – law and judicialized dispute resolution (C. Minzner, 2011a). Finally, others have maintained a longer-term focus on policy targets and the quantification of assessment and political oversight in China (Edin, 2003; Kinkel & Hurst, 2015; O'Brien & Li, 1999; Whiting, 2004).

An understudied yet important element of performance evaluation involves court leaders' responsibility for the collective performance of their courts, as well as their reputational concerns within and among the judiciary, all of which play important roles in shaping judicial behavior. Based on my field research, I find that court leaders' professional survival is tethered to their courts' collectively assessed performance on quantitative indicators, which itself is tied to the retention of mid-career judges capable of deciding cases quickly and accurately. The globally unprecedented growth of the Chinese legal profession in the past two decades has made it difficult to stem the attrition of mid-career judges and avoid the court instability that judicial "brain drain" (*liushi renyuan*) creates (X. Liu, 2014). Under these conditions, mid-career judges pursue professional survival and career growth as lawyers – an action conditioned by competitive tensions with judicial colleagues, attorney acquaintances, and their court supervisors that can lead to cooperation as well as conflict. Court leaders' decisions to strategically reform judicial selection and promotion mechanisms can be seen as interactive responses to these dynamics in the hopes of preserving court leaders' hierarchical privilege and the basic organizational structure of their courts, all in an environment of competitive cooperation.

The emergence of these patterns has been facilitated by increasingly sophisticated reporting of performance scores regarding formal, quantitative evaluation indices, creating an overlapping interaction between written rules and practical implementation that exerts much stronger effects on judicial decision-making and behavior than either formal or informal factors alone. The result of this quantitative, highly visible supervision by central state principals of their local judicial agents constitutes what I call "intra-state legibility" (cf. Scott, 1999); in light of scholarship on judicial behavior in other countries, it should not be surprising that judges' decision-making is influenced by social concerns, such as their professional reputations, the esteem of their peers, or the lawyers who practice in their courts (Baum, 2006; Brinks, 2008; Miceli & Cosgel, 1994). However, such a perspective is largely new in the study of Chinese law.

Scholars have, however, previously addressed judicial evaluation and decision-making in China more broadly, resonating in several respects with recent accounts of the post-Soviet judiciary (Hendley, 2012, 2013). Stanley Lubman was among the first to note that burgeoning caseloads, bureaucratic incentives, and quotas have pressured judges, since at least 1984, to emphasize mediation instead of adversarial adjudication in the resolution of private disputes (Lubman, 1999). Randall Peerenboom sees formal bureaucratic supervision and evaluation promoting higher standards of professionalism through the manipulation of judicial salaries, alongside other rewards and punishments (Peerenboom, 2002, 2006). Though not directly incorporating the effects of judicial cadre evaluations, Rachel Stern suggests a model of civil judicial decision-making in one-party states based on her research on environmental litigation in the PRC, in which tensions between judges and nonjudicial elites (as well as between formal and informal norms) threaten the integrity of the judicial process (Stern, 2010). Carl Minzner also examines courts' evaluation of judicial cadres against the backdrop of China's overall cadre evaluation system, finding that bureaucratic control of the judiciary undermines the integrity of the PRC legal system even more clearly than in Stern's analysis (C. Minzner, 2011a, 2011b; C. F. Minzner, 2009). No authors in this growing literature, however, draw on in-country fieldwork and documentary analysis to explain just how contemporary judicial cadre evaluation (known as the Case Quality Assessment System or CQAS) is implemented at the level of individual judges and courts.

This chapter is based on interviews and documentary evidence focusing on the period from 2012 to 2014; it examines how court leaders (e.g., court presidents and vice presidents) are motivated to boost their courts' collective CQAS performance scores, not only through institutional incentives but even more so through informal discipline and shame-based motivational mechanisms.[1] Rather than judicial evaluations seamlessly constraining judges to mediate more cases or to avoid appellate reversal, informal practices emerge as responses to such quotas and ultimately exert a greater influence on judges' professional activity.

In addition to illuminating judicial behavior, the CQAS helps us better understand where Chinese judges stand in relation to their colleagues in other areas of the political system and bureaucracy. Unfortunately, prior work by legal scholars on Chinese courts' assessment of judicial performance has mostly refrained from engaging directly with broader social science research on cadre evaluation in China. Chinese judges are still considered "cadres" (*ganbu*) in the PRC political system – a term that has historically referred to revolutionary credentials of cadres as the leaders of

[1] By "ordinary judges," I refer to "Judges" (*shenpanyuan*) and "Assistant Judges" (*zhuli shenpanyuan*) under the Judges Law of 1995. Although higher-ranking judges at the Associate Division Chief (*futingzhang*) level and above can hear and decide cases, their duties are usually focused on the administrative work of running the court and assessing judicial performance. For a similar typology of the within-court hierarchy of Chinese judges, see Ling Li's typology of "Party Leaders," "Leader Judges," and "Frontline Judges" (Ling Li, 2012).

the revolution and the masses the followers (Brødsgaard, 2012, pp. 71–72). Although "cadre" has developed a less ideological and more bureaucratic meaning in contemporary China (Brødsgaard, 2012, p. 72), an implicit understanding persists that cadres like judges must be committed to the CCP and subject to the bureaucratic discipline of performance evaluation systems like the CQAS. The evaluation, reward, and discipline of judges, therefore, must be viewed against this backdrop.

Still, Chinese judicial work and judges' understandings of their professional roles differ from those of other cadres with more characteristically political identities and general responsibilities, for example, county-level mayors or CCP secretaries (Landry, 2008). In their study on village cadres, O'Brien and Li found that "particularly important tasks such as birth control may … be granted 'veto power'," where failure on that task means a failed cadre evaluation, "no matter how well the other targets have been met" (O'Brien & Li, 1999, p. 172; Whiting, 2004, p. 102). Although judges are also incentivized to do their jobs efficiently and without mistakes, my interviewees did not report the implementation of draconian performance metrics like "priority targets with veto power" (*yipiao foujue*), described in the literature on political cadres at the village, township, and county levels (Edin, 2003; O'Brien & Li, 1999; Whiting, 2000).

Rather, judicial and court evaluations primarily emphasize the analysis of predetermined targets on quantified indices (*zhishu*) (Edin, 2003, p. 39; Whiting, 2000, p. 207; Whiting, 2004). Court presidents generally do not face individual "veto targets" that can lead to the failure of ordinary judges' or court leaders' performance evaluations. Rather, court leaders and their subordinates are assessed using a litany of crucial indices and target performance rates that vary in importance based on trends within each particular locality. While judges' complaints resonate with those of other cadres in China's political–legal system (Scoggins & O'Brien, 2016), Chinese judges face a significantly different set of standards and challenges than their counterparts in local governments and CCP committees, whose evaluations have recently focused upon increasing industrial profits, industrial output, livestock revenue, the rate of family planning compliance, and even the reduction of environmental pollution (Su et al., 2012; A. L. Wang, 2013; Whiting, 2004, p. 107).

To address these issues and explain the implementation of the CQAS, this chapter is organized into four sections: (1) a brief history of the emergence of the CQAS, (2) a detailed accounting of the within-court tension between judges who manage courts (i.e., court presidents, vice presidents, and other court leaders) and ordinary judges who decide cases, (3) an explanation of how quantified performance assessment has supplanted judicial rewards and punishments, and (4) a section explaining that the CQAS goes beyond traditional concepts applied to principal-agent problems[2] and constitutes a new phenomenon that I call "intra-state legibility."

The Emergence of Unified Judicial Performance Evaluation, 1980–2014

Similar to judicial bureaucracies in other countries that fit the traditional model of a civil law system (e.g., pre-WWII Italy, pre-1978 Spain, Chile between 1964 and 2000) (Hilbink, 2007, pp. 224–234), employment as a judge in the PRC is intended to be a career position, with judges starting on the bottom rung and gradually moving up the hierarchical ladder. The reformed CQAS, which mediates the movement of judges within this hierarchy, is a systematic, multiple-index performance evaluation system that uses quantitative indices to evaluate the efficiency and accuracy of judges' and courts' work performance over time.

The cumbersome implementation of judicial evaluation has historically been masked by its straightforward description in the PRC Judge's Law: "Appraisal of judges shall be conducted by the People's Courts the judges belong to … The result of appraisal shall be taken as the basis for award, punishment, training, [or] dismissal of a judge, and for readjustment of his or her grade and salary."[3] These formal norms of judicial evaluation reflect the post–Cultural Revolution re-instatement of performance evaluations for use in resolving principal-agent discontinuities in China's political system (Manion, 1985, pp. 204–205). In a speech to the Politburo in 1980, Deng Xiaoping called for drastic changes to systems of organizational and personnel management within the Party–State bureaucracy (Manion, 1985, p. 206). A national work conference in 1983 pushed for greater emphasis on the assessment of concrete achievements rather than political attitudes or style in the cadre management system, and the CCP Organization Department issued official guidelines for the annual evaluation of party secretaries and government executives in 1988 (Whiting, 2004; Zhuang, 2010).[4]

[2] See, for example, the discussion of principal-agent dilemmas, "police patrols," and "fire alarms" (Gauri & Brinks, 2008; McCubbins & Schwartz, 1984).

[3] Judges Law of the PRC (*Zhonghua renmin gongheguo faguanfa*), Articles 19, 22.

[4] Whiting cites Organization Department Document No. 7 (1988), Central Organization Department Circular Regarding Trial Local Party-State Leading Cadres' Year-End Work Performance System (*Zhonggong zhongyang zuzhibu guanyu shixing difang dangzheng lingdao ganbu niandu gongzuo kaohe zhidu de tongzhi*).

In 1993, the National People's Congress (NPC) formulated general performance criteria for employees in all departments, levels, and areas in the country: political integrity, competence, diligence, and achievement (*de*, *neng*, *qin*, and *ji*). Local courts had already begun implementing cadre responsibility systems based on work targets before the State Council issued an "Outline on Deepening the Reform of the Cadre Personnel System" in June 2000 (C. F. Minzner, 2009, p. 66; Whiting, 2004, p. 105).[5] Soon thereafter, national policymakers began discussing the unification of the judicial cadre evaluation system.

The Supreme People's Court's (SPC's) second Five-Year Plan ("the Plan"), published in 2005, calls for reforming and "perfecting" (*wanshan*) the organizational structure of courts, judicial adjudication management, and judicial personnel management.[6] In Section 7, the Plan supports "establishing a scientific, unified system of assessing adjudication quality and efficiency" that "institutes scientific standards of assessment."[7] Other sections of the Plan demand "reforming the evaluation systems for judges and other court personnel," "scientifically designing evaluation items," "perfecting evaluation methods," "unifying judges' achievement evaluation standards and processes," and establishing a robust system of judicial punishment (*chengjie*).[8] Clause 32 of the Plan specifically seeks to reform judicial statistics so that courts can establish a system of indices capable of reflecting the work situation in every court level consistently and objectively.

Implementation of these aspects of the Plan was neither launched nor unified nationally until 2008, when the SPC launched a pilot project to formalize a national system of judicial performance assessment and to standardize the various subnational judicial performance evaluation institutions.[9] In March 2011, the SPC gave final approval to this pilot, publishing a decisive Guiding Opinion to launch a national system of the "case quality" assessment of China's courts and judges.[10] According to

[5] Whiting cites the Outline on Deepening the Reform of the Cadre Personnel System (*Shenhua ganbu renshi zhidu gaige gangyao*).

[6] The Second Five-Year Reform Plan of the Supreme People's Court of China (*Renmin fayuan erwu gaige gangyao*), SPC Document No. 18 [2005].

[7] Second Five-Year Reform Plan of the SPC, Clause 41.

[8] Second Five-Year Reform Plan of the SPC, Clauses 42–43.

[9] In the SPC's 2008 Provisional Opinion on this issue, this pilot project was referred to for the first time as "case quality assessment work." *See* Circular on SPC Publication of the "SPC Provisional Guiding Opinion Regarding Launching Case Quality Assessment Work," SPC Document No. 6 [2008]; J. Zhang (2011).

[10] "SPC Guiding Opinion Regarding the Launching of Case Quality Assessment Work," (*Guanyu kaizhan anjian zhiliang pinggu gongzuo de zhidao yijian*); Ying (2011); SPC Doc. No. 109 [2012], "Circular Regarding the 2011 National Courts Case Quality Assessment Situation"; *PC2012-23, judge, Shenzhen, September 2012.*

this Guiding Opinion, courts should emphasize "establishing a scientific and unified system of court evaluation" in accordance with the SPC's second Five-Year Plan.[11] Additionally, the Guiding Opinion states that judicial evaluation systems should be based on assessment indices (*pinggu zhibiao*) that establish a "quantified model of assessing judicial quality."[12]

The specific details of each locality's implementation of the system can vary, but a persistent pattern surfaced in interviews: Judges' primary motivation is to obtain promotion, which requires high scores on the CQAS evaluations; to obtain high CQAS marks, judges must not only demonstrate efficiency by resolving cases quickly, but they must also demonstrate accuracy by posting low levels of reversal on appeal.[13] Not surprisingly, this dual emphasis on both speedy and accurate dispute resolution can put judges in a bind such that one desideratum must be sacrificed to attain the other. The pressures inherent in the CQAS affect both court leaders, whose primary task is managing and organizing courts, and ordinary judges, whose primary responsibility is to resolve legal disputes through the litigation process.

In the words of a Shanghai judge writing for a court newsletter, the CQAS can be thought of as a "health check form" (*tijian biao*) for courts, and the cumulative (*zonghe*) indices that evaluate courts and court divisions as collectives can be thought of as a "conductor's baton" (*zhihui bang*) (J. Zhang, 2011). Although "every level court can, according to the major points emphasized, adjust the weight given to their specific assessment indices," the SPC consolidates its duty to unify judicial evaluations by maintaining broad authority to adjust the content and relative importance of each index "when appropriate" (*shishi*).[14] Additionally, the Guiding Opinion stipulates that judicial evaluations under the CQAS are administered via "one-level down" principles: "the court at one level above is responsible for organizing and leading the court one level below in assessment work, and can, regarding their own court and the courts in their jurisdiction, advance case quality assessment work."[15]

[11] 2011 Guiding Opinion, Article 1.

[12] Ibid.

[13] *PR2013-53, judge, Shanghai, May 2013; PR2013-5, judge, Shenzhen, January 2013; PR2013-51, judge, Chengdu, May 2013.*

[14] 2011 Guiding Opinion, Articles 13–14.

[15] 2011 Guiding Opinion, Article 16. Several scholars have discussed the operation of "one-level down" principles in greater depth (e.g., Landry, 2008, pp. 48–53; O'Brien & Li, 1999, pp. 171–176).

The Boundary between Boss and Worker: The Collective Nature of Court Leader Performance Evaluation in China Prior to the 2014–2016 Judicial Reforms

Within-court tension between court leadership and the judges who decide the vast majority of legal disputes in China has shaped the institutional incentives affecting judicial decisions in the overwhelming majority of legal disputes heard in Chinese courts. Court presidents (*yuanzhang*) and vice presidents (*fu yuanzhang*) have been responsible for court management, with their chances for promotion calibrated by the CQAS scores collectively produced by the judges and court divisions under their direction. The CQAS has incentivized court leaders to obtain the highest production and efficiency from each judicial worker within their courts.

The formal source for these incentives is the Guiding Opinion, which states in Article 1 that court leaders are evaluated by aggregated indices regarding the performance of their court and the subordinate judges and units within that court's jurisdiction.[16] Aggregating the performance scores of individual judges under the CQAS allows political elites to assess the performances of individual court divisions and courts as collectives by comparing similar units across jurisdictions and broader localities.[17] Indeed, the comparative rankings are explicitly mandated by the SPC Guiding Opinion: "For every half-year and year-long period, the SPC will engage in analysis of assessment statistics and indices and publish an 'All-Country Case Quality Analysis Report'; engage in summarization (*zongjie*) of Higher-Level Courts, Intermediate-Level Courts, and Basic-Level [i.e., first-instance] People's Courts' case quality situations, and at regular intervals provide feedback (*fankui*) regarding every level court's case quality assessment situation."[18]

Further, Section 4 of the Guiding Opinion informs courts that "Case Assessment Computer Management Software is issued in unified fashion by the SPC," and every level court should use this software to publish documents, reports, and statistical reporting sheets at regular intervals and according to SPC requirements.[19] Using the CQAS software, the SPC

[16] 2011 Guiding Opinion, Article 1.

[17] Examples of similar, comparable courts would be all first-instance District Courts in a municipality or all Intermediate Courts in a given province or region.

[18] 2011 Guiding Opinion, Article 24.

[19] 2011 Guiding Opinion, Articles 20, 23. In the wake of the Guiding Opinion, local courts have issued their own local Guiding Opinions implementing the SPC Opinion (e.g., Zhejiang High Court, 2013).

and High Courts throughout China distribute cumulative court and divisional index results, upon which lower levels of the court system should rely to "guarantee the objectivity of the assessments." CQAS assessment results thus become "the cumulative reflection of People's Courts' adjudication work situation."[20]

CQAS reports, court newsletters, and interviews with judges reveal how the CQAS is interpreted and implemented for several local research sites, pressuring court leaders and ordinary judges in those localities. For example, spreadsheets in Zhejiang province and Shanghai list the CQAS performance ranking for each court – from the Basic Level to the High Court – on specific indices.[21] In Shenzhen city (Guangdong province), the Guangdong Provincial Court's Analysis of the 2011 CQAS Primary Index Situation was drafted in response to cross-provincial analysis and "feedback" provided in the SPC's 2011 report regarding the 2011 case quality assessment situation for courts throughout the country. The Analysis in Guangdong High Court's report, as approved by the president and vice president of the Guangdong High Court, explicitly discusses Guangdong province's cumulative CQAS in comparison with other court systems throughout the country.[22]

Consistent with the spreadsheets from Zhejiang and Shanghai, court leaders in Guangdong are particularly cognizant of their own court's relative CQAS ranking relative to other similar courts. In Shanghai, court-specific publications note the importance of comparing indices that have met targets, that nearly met targets, and those that displayed a clear disparity with targets to understand an overall court's combined quality and efficiency (*zhixiao*) (Zhou, 2011). With the CQAS providing greater variety and comparability of statistical feedback, higher-level principals possess more detailed information regarding lower-level agents' performance, increasing the overall bureaucratic capacity of the court system (He, 2009; McCubbins & Schwartz, 1984; Scott, 1999).

Although "priority targets with veto power" that are used in other government units (c.f., O'Brien & Li, 1999) are not a prominent feature of judicial performance evaluations, other aspects of the CQAS reflect more general patterns of PRC bureaucratic management. Instead of an

[20] 2011 Guiding Opinion Article 17, 27.
[21] *PC2013-67, judge, Shanghai, July 2013 and PC2012-30, judge, Wenzhou, October 2012.*
[22] *PC2012-23, judge, Shenzhen, September 2012.*

isolated focus on limiting reversals of judgments on appeal (see, e.g., Minzner, 2011a), local court performance evaluation systems under the CQAS have instead informally emphasized a specific set of indices, similar to the practice of "hard targets" (*ying zhibiao*) observed by other scholars of China's bureaucracy. As Whiting describes, "hard targets" are a by-product of the excessive number and variety of tasks evaluated through performance-based measures, which force higher-level officials to identify the primary sets of targets that leaders actually consider critical to success during appraisal (Y. Wang, 2015; Whiting, 2004). In Chinese courts, the term for "hard target" seemed to vary by locality, as Guangdong judges used the term "core targets" (*hexin zhibiao*), whereas a judge interviewee referred to "first class targets" (*yilei zhibiao*) when discussing similarly important indices.[23] Generally speaking, mediation was emphasized strongly during the 2008–2013 tenure of the former SPC President Wang Shengjun,[24] yet general imperatives to resolve cases quickly and correctly operate in a complementary and combined fashion, without one or the other establishing fundamental priority (cf. Minzner, 2009, 2011a).[25]

Table 3.1 summarizes the important indices that were most frequently identified by interviewees as equivalent to "hard targets" under the CQAS.

Consistent with a finding that a limited number of CQAS indices serve as hard targets in Chinese courts, judges stated during interviews that although some CQAS indices listed in the 2011 Guiding Opinion appear to have equivalent weight *on paper* with indices listed in Table 3.1, they are unimportant in the overall scheme of the CQAS. For example, an index labeled "Degree of Public Satisfaction" is listed in the Guiding Opinion alongside the other "Impact" indices in Table 3.1. The Guiding Opinion notes that the "Assessment of the degree of public satisfaction can be collected according to needs from survey questionnaires given to people's congress representatives, members of consultative committees, clean government supervision personnel, parties to litigation and their legal representatives, which are administered by court organizations

23 *PC2013-70, judge, Shanghai, October 2013; PC2012-23, judge, Shenzhen, September 2012.*

24 *PC2013-56, judge, Shanghai, June 2013; PC2013-51, judge, Chengdu, May 2013.*

25 *PC2013-22, judge, Shanghai, March 2013; PC2013-56, judge, Shanghai, June 2013; PC2013-1, judge, Shenzhen, January 2013; PC2013-38, judge, Chengdu, April 2013.*

Table 3.1. *Selection of indices deemed important in Chinese lower courts' Case Quality Assessment System (2008–2013)*

Case quality index type	Case quality system index name	Effect of higher scores on index
"Fairness"	"Rate of First-Instance Cases in Which Judgment Corrected on Appeal (mistake)" (*yishen panjue anjian bei gaipan fahui chongshenlü*)	Negative
	"Rate of First-Instance Cases Reversed and Remanded" (*shengxiao anjian beigaipan fahui chongshenlü*)	Negative
	"Rate of Judgments Corrected on Cases in Effect at First-Instance Level" (*shengxiao anjian gaipanlü*)	Negative
"Efficiency"	"Average Cases Cleared Per Judge Per Year" (*fayuan nianrenjun jie'an shu*)	Positive
	"Rate of Cases Resolved within Statutory (Normal) Time Limits" (*fading (zhengchang) shenxiaonei jie'an lü*)	Positive
	"Rate of First-Instance Cases in Which the Simplified Procedure is Used" (*yishen jianyichengxu shiyong lü*)	Positive
	"Index of Resolving Cases in Balanced Time throughout a Year-Long Work Cycle" (*jie'an junhengdu*)	Positive
"Impact"	"Rate of First-Instance Cases in Which Neither Re-trial nor Appeal Are Sought" (*yishen fupan xisulü*)	Positive
	"Rate of Mediation" (*tiaojielü*)	Positive
	"Rate of Case Withdrawal" (*tousulü*)	Positive
	"Rate of Citizen Petitioning against Court" (*xinfang tousulü*)	Negative

Sources: PC2013-57, judge, Shanghai, June 2013; PC2013-67, judge, Shanghai, July 2013; PC2013-51, judge, Chengdu, May 2013; PC2013-66, judge, Shenzhen, July 2013; PC2012-23, judge, Shenzhen, September 2012; 2011 SPC Guiding Opinion.[26]

[26] Interviewees indicated that the "impact" category evaluates whether judicial decisions have resulted in social or mass instability. Additionally, this table refers to "hard targets" or quotas related to rendering judgments in legal disputes and does not include targets for other functions assessed in Chinese courts, for example, enforcement of judgments.

at every level and entrusted private civil research organs."[27] However, judges indicated that court leaders did not consider this "public satisfaction" index critical in judicial evaluations because it has proven impossible to measure "public satisfaction" reliably using the methods spelled out in the Guiding Opinion.[28] Similarly, the index for "rate of immediate enforcement of judgments" is listed in the 2011 Guiding Opinion as an Impact index, but judicial interviewees stated that the "rate of immediate enforcement of judgments" has little value and is never relied upon by court leaders under the CQAS because judgments are so rarely "immediately enforced."[29] Thus, even in a recently unified system like the CQAS, informal norms have emerged to distinguish between the indices suggested by the SPC and those that "really matter" at the local level.

More informally, the spreadsheets and reports that comprise the formal system's ranking of courts, judges, and court leaders make explicit which courts are performing well in the eyes of the system. These practices of discipline and shaming can be even more powerful influences over judges' lives than formal factors alone.[30] Because the court system publishes unvarnished quantitative rankings of the performance of each court in a jurisdiction and each judge in a court, unsuccessful court leaders can be shamed by poor showings on the rankings and become motivated to improve their courts' and their own individual performance. Court leaders are constantly interacting with each other through judicial conferences and various other social networking events; as one of my interviewees mentioned, travel to administrative meetings can keep court leaders away from their "home" courts for more than 200 days per year, leading to the oft-repeated criticism within courts that court leaders "should hold fewer meetings and instead handle more cases" (*shao kai hui, duo ban'an*). Under these professional circumstances, CQAS rankings become important status markers in the social lives of court leaders.[31] Further, when SPC rankings are particularly favorable for a given local court system, the results often find their way to the public press. For example, an article entitled "Shanghai Courts' Judicial Fairness Index and Transparency Level Are Highest in the Country" was published in the *Liberation Daily* (*Jie'fang Ribao*) and then reprinted in People's

[27] 2011 Guiding Opinion, Article 18(2).

[28] *PC2013-49, judge, Shanghai, May 2013; PC2013-56, judge, Shanghai, June 2013.*

[29] *PC2013-53, judge, Shanghai, May 2013; PC2013-56, judge, Shanghai, June 2013*; 2011 SPC Guiding Opinion, Article 10.

[30] *PC2013-65, judge, Foshan, July 2013.*

[31] *PC2013-62, judge, Wenzhou, July 2013.*

Court News (*Renmin Fayuanbao*), stating, "According to SPC statistics, Shanghai Courts' Judicial Fairness Indices have for five consecutive years ranked first among all the country's courts" (Guo, 2013). In this way, courts – and court leaders – at the high, intermediate, and basic levels are continuously and visibly compared using the CQAS, affecting their professional and personal status.

Quantified Assessment of Ordinary Judges and the Salience of Intrastate Legibility

Ordinary Judges' Perspectives in Urban China

Individual Chinese judges exhibit reservations regarding the trend toward quantification, perceiving a discrepancy between measuring company bottom lines and acts of governance. Still, the true power of quantitative assessment lies in its influence on subjectivity itself, as judges tend to accept CQAS performance scores as legitimate assessments of their own professional merit, resonating with the expansion of quantitative assessments in various professional contexts around the world (Merry, 2011, p. S88). Individual judges suggested in interviews that it is not merely the CQAS evaluation itself that creates professional pressure; rather, individual judges' self-evaluations against peers motivate them to obtain better scores. Every judge's annual evaluation score (*niandi kaohe chengji*) relies on broad aggregations of CQAS measures, referenced during within-court competitions between colleagues for promotion to vacancies within courts.[32]

It was telling, then, that an interviewee emphasized the importance of "pretty" (*piaoliang*) quantitative scores in their work and for judicial promotion prospects.[33] A different judge, when asked whether the court leaders post rankings to encourage everyone to work harder, replied, "No, you can't call it encouragement (*guli*), it's actually pressure (*yali*), and we feel the pressure because it's embarrassing to be ranked lower. Of course we know it doesn't really have much of a material impact, but lower performance is just embarrassing and makes us want to do better."[34]

Conversely, ordinary, case-deciding judges frequently complain that the system assumes all aspects of judicial performance can be quantified

[32] *PC2013-3, judge, Shenzhen, January 2013.*

[33] *PC2013-62, judge, Wenzhou, July 2013.*

[34] *PC2013-65, judge, Foshan, July 2013.*

and measured. As one judge from Wenzhou put it: "We are not workers in a factory, nor are we workers in a company, so a judge's performance cannot simply be measured by production metrics. There are many aspects of judicial performance that cannot be measured."[35] Courts' limited abilities to make sense of a morass of quantitative indices has also led to a noticeable shift toward adjudicating cases quickly, rather than avoiding reversal on appeal (*see* Minzner, 2011b). A judge from Shanghai explained that by focusing primarily on the speed of adjudication, the CQAS distorts the reality of judging, in which many factors including the technical or legal complexity of a case, or scheduling difficulties, can influence the time needed to resolve a dispute.[36] As observed elsewhere, Chinese judges perceive the tensions inherent in applying numerical measures to complex phenomena, glossing over context in pursuit of comparability, classification, objectivity, and scientific assessment (Merry, 2011, p. S85).

Not surprisingly, judges were fond of discussing the pressure of the system on their daily lives. One judge was eager to share a parody song, circulating at the time on Chinese social media (e.g., *Weibo* and *Weixin*). Sung by an "Entire Corps of Judicial Cadres," the song is set to the melody of a popular Chinese song called "Because of Love," and the song opens with the lyrics, "I give you the whole court report/Look at last month's rankings/My dreams are interrupted/By thoughts of cases, left/unresolved…" Continuing with the judge-singer pledging "to go crazy working hard" and bemoaning work that makes "young judges age beyond their years," the parody concludes with hyperbole: "When the deadline comes, some lie on the battlefield/Not quite dead, but surely injured *∧_∧*."[37]

This song parody, complete with a concluding emoticon signifying stress or tension, captures the pressures Chinese judges face: Heavy caseloads, under increasingly strict surveillance, with one's CQAS scores laid bare on the "whole court report." By contrast, the parody does not mention any desire to obtain performance bonuses or avoid fines. Indeed, even some court leaders have recognized problems in focusing too heavily on statistical indices. Some local court leaders in Shanghai have urged courts to avoid problems created by "too easily fluctuating numbers" (*fuzao shu*) or relying only on numbers to determine professional merit (Zhou, 2011, pp. 14–15).

[35] *PC2013-62, judge, Wenzhou, July 2013.*

[36] *PC2013-22, judge, Shanghai, March 2013.*

[37] *2013-63, judge, Wenzhou, July 2013.*

Beyond Police Patrols and Fire Alarms: "Intra-state Legibility" and the Principal-Agent Dynamic

Even as lower-ranking judges bristle at its stripping away of the complexities of judicial work, the CQAS remains a powerful disciplinary tool because, as noted above, judges fold their own self-reflexive assessments of their professional worth into its highly visible results. As these lived experiences of Chinese judges are distinct from state principals' use of "police patrols" or "fire alarms" to monitor the performance of local agents, the CQAS goes beyond grand projects to quantify, rank, and compare governance and civil society programs (Gauri & Brinks, 2008; McCubbins & Schwartz, 1984; Merry, 2011). Many modernizing states have used similar tactics to render "legible," and exert greater political authority over, subject populations (Scott, 1999). Notably, however, the PRC central government and the SPC are employing this system to govern the behavior of actors working *within and for* the state, rather than among a subject population. Indeed, more than anything else, the CQAS showcases the center's desire to command and control its unruly bureaucracy through quantitative and visible mechanisms of supervision.[38]

Whereas in the past, courts simply reported aggregate numbers from lower levels (and individual indicators could easily be ignored), there has been an abrupt and extensive clarification and quantification of the system since the SPC Provisional Guiding Opinion on the CQAS was issued in 2008.[39] A Chengdu judge stated that before 2008, there were hardly any quantitative indices, and the system mainly used a single metric – whether cases were reversed on appeal – to assess the quality of courts and judges (cf. Minzner, 2011b).[40] Another judge in Guangdong noted that in his court, as opposed to the near-constant surveillance under the unified CQAS, quantitative reports on courts' and individual judges' performance used to come only once per year, much like the work reports given by local courts to NPC branches at corresponding levels throughout the country. Court leaders have also become more focused on the CQAS

[38] This conceptual effort here aims to distinguish as well from Foucault's related concept of panopticism, which, although it bears a resemblance to intra-state legibility, seems most applicable to disciplining subject, even marginalized, populations for which "[v]isibility is a trap" (Foucault, 1977, p. 200). Although, in some sense, many of the Chinese judges described here appear to be trapped, they are not necessarily subjects of Foucault's panopticon, as they themselves are also agents of the state whose own power can continue to grow even as they are subjected to discipline.

[39] *PC2013-63, judge, Wenzhou, July 2013; PC2013-57, judge, Shanghai, June 2013.*

[40] *PC2013-60, judge, Chengdu, July 2013.*

because it gives them specific numbers that can be referenced in pressuring subordinate judges.[41]

Judges in basic and intermediate courts have in recent years received monthly internal newsletters assessing the relative performance of individual judges, court divisions, and courts as a whole.[42] Individual judges' and court divisions' scores are also readily available to all court personnel via computer software on each court's intranet (*neibuwang*). In a Shenzhen court, for example, a grid on the court intranet displays a "Frontline Soldier Report" for every internal court unit, which shows performance statistics across several courts and within-court divisions and allows all court personnel to have constant, almost real-time information regarding the performance of court divisions and individual judges.[43] These reports detail whether judges and internal court units meet predetermined values on CQAS index targets, with scores calculated under a parallel system, the Target Management Responsibility System (TMRS). A specific target score is assigned for each CQAS index, with indices on which the court fell short highlighted in red. Each division in the Shenzhen court was assessed over a six-month period regarding the rate of cases that were reversed and remanded on appeal. The goal was to avoid exceeding 12 percent of cases reversed and remanded on appeal. In one particular period, 23.64 percent of cases resolved by this division had been reversed by the intermediate court. Given that the division's performance on this index was worth 9 points, the division's failure to meet the target resulted in their receiving only 7.81 out of a possible 9 points on the cumulative performance assessment system for their court.[44]

The TMRS rules constitute the mechanism by which hard-target indices are enforced upon individual, ordinary judges. A Wenzhou judge explained that in his court, points as calculated under the TMRS rules (*banfa*) determine judges and court leaders' promotion opportunities;[45] however, consistent with the lack of "priority targets with veto power" reported by interviewees, none of the hard-target indices is so important that a low score on that one measure results in automatic failure or termination of employment – especially if the mistake only occurred in a

[41] *PC2013-62, judge, Wenzhou, July 2013.*

[42] *PC2012-14, judge, Wenzhou, August 2012; PC2013-53, judge, Shanghai, May 2013; PC2012-23, judge, Shenzhen, September 2012.*

[43] *PC2012-22, judge, Shenzhen, September 2012.*

[44] *PC2012-23, judge, Shenzhen, September 2012.*

[45] *PC2013-62, judge, Wenzhou, July 2013.*

small proportion of cases handled.[46] As several interviewees indicated, judges only lose their jobs if they are investigated for a serious crime like bribery.[47] Instead, if a given judge's performance on a particularly important index is substantially lower than that of the other judges in the same court, it is possible that he or she may face a fine, a demotion, a loss of nominal bonus pay, or a transfer to a different position within the court.[48] Similar to courts in Russia, rising caseloads and increased deadline pressure raise the probability of judicial error when deciding complex civil and economic cases (Hendley, 2013, p. 1), prompting the PRC courts to continue including "reversal on appeal" among the many performance indices. Hard targets increase the pressure on Chinese judges, enhancing the self-evaluating character and intra-state legibility of the CQAS.

Intrastate Legibility Supplants Formal Rewards and Punishments

With quantified, highly visible performance measures and their embedded mechanisms of self-discipline taking center stage under the CQAS, the other nominal, performance-related bonus payments and fines designed to motivate judges have largely been rendered obsolete. In 2007, the SPC issued detailed rules designed to discipline, motivate, and reward judicial cadres:[49]

> Bonus standards shall be implemented, according to rank, for personnel-awarded judicial bonuses; for every level of judge, the following bonuses shall be awarded: for every Chief Major Judge (*shouxi dafaguan*), award ¥340 (approximately $54 at ¥6.3/US$); for every First-level Major

[46] *PC2013-64, judge, Shenzhen, July 2013; PC2013-51, judge, Chengdu, May 2013; PC2013-53, judge, Shanghai, May 2013; PC2013-4, judge, Shenzhen, January 2013.* Interviewees in Wenzhou and Shanghai both stated that "party style and clean government" (*dangfeng lianzheng*) evaluations are mere ritual, and the only evaluations that practically influence promotion opportunities are the "professional" (*yewu*) evaluations. *PC2013-62, judge, Wenzhou, July 2013; PC2013-69, judge, Shanghai, July 2013.*

[47] *PC2013-56, judge, Shanghai, June 2013; PC2013-67, judge, Shanghai, July 2013; PC2013-67, judge, Shenzhen, July 2013; PC2013-51, judge, Chengdu, May 2013.*

[48] *PC2013-56, judge, Shanghai, June 2013; PC2013-70, judge, October 2013.*

[49] Supreme People's Court circular sent to Personnel Department and Finance Department "Regarding the Circular Regarding the Trial Implementation of Judicial Adjudication Supplemental Pay" (*Zuigao renmin fayuan zhuan'fa renshibu, caizhengbu "guanyu shixing faguan shenpan jintie de tongzhi"*) of August 7, 2007 (SPC Doc. No. 26 [2007]); Personnel Department and Finance Department Circular Regarding Implementation of Judicial Adjudication Bonuses (*Renshibu, caizhengbu guanyu shixing faguan shenpan jintie de tongzhi*) of July 31, 2007 (Personnel Department Doc. No. 105 [2007]).

> Judge (*yiji dafaguan*), award ¥318; for every Second-level Major Judge (*erji dafaguan*), award ¥298; for every First-level High-level Judge (*yiji gaojifaguan*), award ¥278; for every Second-level High-Level Judge (*erji gaoji faguan*), award ¥262; for every Third-Level High-Level Judge (*sanji gaojifaguan*), award ¥246; for every Fourth-level High-level Judge (*siji gaoji faguan*), award ¥233; for every First-level Judge (*yiji faguan*) award ¥220; for every Second-level Judge (*erji faguan*), award ¥210; for every Third-level Judge (*sanji faguan*), award ¥200; for every Fourth-level Judge (*siji faguan*), award ¥190; for every Fifth-level Judge (*wuji faguan*), award ¥180 [approximately $28 at ¥6.3/US$].[50]

The Judges' Law of China states, "result of appraisal shall be taken as the basis for award, punishment, training, dismissal of a judge, and for readjustment of his or her grade and salary."[51] Interviewees indicated, however, that performance-based awards, fines, and categorization carry little weight outside of the quantified CQAS evaluation itself and take a backseat to within-group shame or pride arising from the visibility of scores. The bonuses – often seen as arbitrary and unrelated to performance – are paltry to begin with, like those referenced above, and others can go as low as ¥10 (approximately US$1.58). A judge in Shenzhen explained that even judges in his court who achieve high performance scores receive a modest year-end bonus that usually only adds up to ¥1,000 (approximately US$158) – so little that, "if you treat your friends to one dinner, then your bonus is gone, so the bonus is basically nothing."[52] Another judge was even more direct: "The reason we want good CQAS scores isn't because of money (bonuses). It's because of face" (*mianzi*).[53] Similarly, a Shanghai interviewee, who did not take fines for "mistake" cases seriously, was surprisingly concerned with the loss of face that came with a "mistake case." For him, one or two "mistake" cases bore no real consequences – except for the shame in interactions with colleagues.[54] Another judge concurred that reversals on appeal do not substantially affect judicial decision-making, as their pay usually will not get docked (or docked only a negligible amount). Rather, there are three difficulties when a case gets reversed: Loss of face, "bothersome trouble" (*mafan*) – which means a scolding or shaming by one's boss – and finally, getting reversed many times could ultimately affect future promotion opportunities.[55]

50 Personnel Department Doc. No. 105 [2007].

51 Judges' Law, Articles 19, 22.

52 *PC2013-66, judge, Shenzhen, July 2013.*

53 *PC2013-65, judge, Foshan, July 2013.* Many scholarly works describe the phenomenon of "face," which used here refers loosely to within-group or social status (see, e.g., Ho, 1976).

54 *PC2013-22, judge, Shanghai, March 2013.*

55 *PC2013-57, judge, Shanghai, June 2013.*

Judges consider the bonus system especially patronizing because their salaries are relatively low in comparison to lawyers in the burgeoning private sector. Before judicial reforms in 2014, civil servants' salaries had not been increased for at least five years (Xinhua News Agency, 2013).[56] Even at high or intermediate courts, court leaders cannot unilaterally increase base salary for good performance[57] as, "no locality … can adjust bonuses on their own."[58] As a recent Xinhua article noted, one of the benefits of working for the state, despite the higher wages available in some private-sector companies (*qiye*), is that "government workers' salaries are stable and not as though they have nothing to eat" (Xinhua News Agency, 2013). Still, as an SPC judge pointed out in 2013: "in some small countryside towns, yes, ¥70-80,000 is a comfortable salary, but it's extremely difficult in a place like Beijing with the rising cost of living. The fluctuation of housing, food, and child rearing is so rapid that it is hard to say whether this salary is enough today, let alone tomorrow."[59] As one Shanghai judge summed up his valuation of bonuses: "For example, in July and August, the Shanghai municipal government might give us some supplemental money to help civil servants deal with the summer heat, maybe to buy something like ice cream."[60]

Judges also did not particularly fear fines or the withholding of salary, as a judge's base pay (*jiben gongzi*) flows from a judge's status as a civil servant and remains unaffected by the evaluation system. As another Shanghai judge explained (highlighting the tension between enforcing standards of judicial "accuracy" and, at the same time, piling on judicial caseloads):

> Nobody can meet the caseload deadlines required under the CQAS. You could ask Chairman Xi to come and be a judge, he couldn't do it either … So, if the higher court reverses one of the cases I decided, it won't really affect my chances for promotion. Also, there is not that much pressure from the fines given for reversal on appeal—I will get fined ¥200RMB (approximately $30 USD) for a reversed case or a 'mistake' case, and it's a fixed-amount fine. But in my view, one mistake case is no problem. There are a lot of these cases.[61]

[56] *PC2013-56, judge, Shanghai, June 2013; PC2012-31, judge, Wenzhou, October 2012.* Judges have traditionally been considered equivalent to general civil servants in China, although reforms introduced in 2014 proposed a separate, parallel personnel management system for judges. In Chapter 7, I address these reforms in more detail.

[57] *PC2013-54, judge, Shanghai, June 2013.*

[58] Personnel Department Doc. No. 105 [2007].

[59] *PC2013-52, judge, Beijing, May 2013.*

[60] *PC2013-54, judge, Shanghai, June 2013.*

[61] *PC2013-22, judge, Shanghai, March 2013.*

Quantified assessment has also rendered several older categories of judicial performance superfluous. Although Article 22 of the Judge's Law of 1995 calls for courts to classify judges as excellent (*youxiu*), competent (*chenzhi*), or incompetent (*bu chenzhi*) based on professional performance, many interviewees indicated that the overwhelming majority of judges receive a "competent" classification, such that when opportunities for promotion arise, their chances can be determined by slight variations in CQAS scores. For example, according to interviewees in Foshan and Shenzhen (both in Guangdong province), approximately 10 percent of judges are rated "excellent" during annual evaluations and 90 percent are rated "competent"; unless someone is investigated for judicial corruption, usually no one is rated "incompetent."[62] In Wenzhou, Zhejiang province, a judge stated that he had "never heard of" an "incompetent" judge; instead, their court has a modified system by which another category is added to the "competent" status, which is called "relatively good," denoting an upper echelon of competence.[63] Some jurisdictions also create a further distinction between "competent" and "basically competent" (*jiben chenzhi*), a distinction that is designed to affect judicial promotion opportunities. Shanghai interviewees also indicated that judges generally tend to be categorized similarly (*mei yi ge ren chabuduo*).[64] Across the board, the quantified and visible CQAS, combined with informal discipline and shaming, provides a new and extremely powerful set of tools to pressure judges socially and institutionally to succeed professionally. They have been made legible actors within the state, and thus subject to far more intrusive and effective top-down control – in a way they never were before – through the application of this system. Crucially, this has happened because of the internalized and *subjective* appropriation of the CQAS as a measure of judges' self-worth, rather than through the state's use of it as an *objective* assessment measure.

Conclusion

Consistent with an ecological explanation of court reform in urban China, this chapter has identified the ways in which the CQAS acts as a bridge between the micro-level interactions of court leaders and mid-career judges and the macro social structures of the legal system (see

62 *PC2013-64, judge, Shenzhen, July 2013; PC2013-66, judge, Shenzhen, July 2013.*

63 *PC2013-62, judge, Wenzhou, July 2013.*

64 *PC2013-67, judge, Shanghai, July 2013.*

Liu, 2015, p. 15). These findings highlight court leaders' vested interests in their subordinates' performance, as well as the competing demands of bureaucratic evaluations at different levels of the judicial hierarchy within courts. This account moves beyond previous studies of cadre evaluation in China, which have focused on tensions between territorial leaders and citizens, and engages these studies by examining which features of cadre evaluation in courts and other bureaucratic units are similar or dissimilar (Edin, 2003; O'Brien & Li, 1999; Whiting, 2004). Accordingly, at least before nationwide reforms beginning in 2014, court leaders and ordinary judges in urban areas faced professional pressures not from a single source but from a variety of trigger points emanating from the CQAS, including rising caseloads, informal shaming and praising, and stagnant rates of judicial pay. Because the performance evaluation system established under the CQAS sets up different, opposing incentives for court leaders and ordinary judges, the strategies of court leaders are susceptible to change if societal forces influence the availability of productive, experienced judicial workers who are critical to the promotion chances of court leaders.

In other legal systems drawing heavy influence from the civil law tradition, judges are secretly supervised not only for their official performance but also for their private conduct, fostering "anxious dependence on the higher echelons of the judicial hierarchy" among subordinate judges (DiFederico & Guarnieri, 1988; Hilbink, 2007). In China, by contrast, ubiquitous *and highly visible* CQAS rankings, statistics, and scores create public and transparent markers of status within urban China's court system, largely desensitizing judges to the system's formal carrots and sticks. This does not indicate that judges ignore the CQAS or the performance evaluations lack influence in judges' behavior. But instead of judges steadfastly following formal rules, horizontal peer-group shaming relegates judicial ambition to a superficial pursuit of higher CQAS scores and within-group success, leading to an overall sense of professional apathy. While other states have used similar tools to achieve hierarchical control over subject populations, the quantification, hard targets, and rankings of the CQAS in China have instead been used to produce increased supervisory capacity *within the Chinese state* over the PRC's local court system (Scott, 1999). As I argue in the following chapters, these experiences under the CQAS removed the possibility of "modern officialdom" for many of China's urban judges, pushing many to consider alternative career options outside of their courts (Weber, 1946). In China's post-Mao history, court leaders have generally been able to maintain the status quo because their judicial subordinates had few other options than a career position in the judicial bureaucracy. Chapter 4 provides evidence that the "pull" factors introduced by the unmatched growth of China's legal profession in the early twenty-first century – in a context of rapidly increasing costs of urban living – have provided judicial cadres with plausible alternatives for professional growth and survival in other settings, especially law firms. This professional ecology represents a significant departure from that which conditioned judicial careers in previous eras.

4

High-End Demand for Legal Services and Local Pressure to Professionalize the Judiciary

The strategic judicial responses to the Case Quality Assessment System (CQAS), detailed in the previous chapter, provide necessary context for understanding how the stratification of local markets for legal services in urban China can affect court reform and the decisional autonomy of judges. Variation in the development of the legal profession in different urban localities is the focus of this chapter, which will also trace the major spatial and temporal shifts that have influenced lawyers' career choices, and in turn, judicial designs in urban China. A spatially informed explanation of socio-legal processes and their structural effects begins with the higher salaries, standards, and status available to lawyers in "high-end" local legal service markets; the temporal analysis concentrates on how these dynamics were made possible by national recommitments to liberalizing reforms in the late twentieth century and then accelerated in the early twenty-first century. More specifically, the primary impetus for changes to the legal profession can be traced to Chinese leadership's post-1989 recommitment to liberalizing reforms and the subsequent return of substantial foreign investment; the reforms most relevant to the legal system included the first regulations governing foreign law firms, the legalization of foreign firms' presence in China (Stern & Li, 2016, p. 190), and the resumption of efforts to privatize large swaths of the Chinese legal profession (Michelson, 2003). Given that the political advocacy of lawyers is substantially constrained in China (see BBC News, 2014; Hand, 2007; Pils, 2007), the ecological framework presented in this book helps uncover important factors (e.g., the unprecedented re-establishment, internationalization, privatization, and growth of the legal services industry, as well as the spatial differentiation of local legal service markets across urban China) that nonetheless influence institutional change in courts despite state repression that substantially limits lawyer activism and other mobilization of the legal complex (Halliday et al., 2007; Halliday & Karpik, 1997; S. Liu & Halliday, 2016; S. Liu & Wu, 2016).

A claim that career incentives can influence judicial behavior is not entirely new, as interdisciplinary research on legal professionals in other contexts has also examined this relationship from a variety of angles. US Attorneys' rates of resignation are influenced, in part, by salary levels, with US public sector employment more attractive in districts with low private-practice salaries (M. Black et al., 1990; Borjas, 1982; Boylan, 2004). In research that has been cited in the Chinese context with respect to government officials' strategic pursuit of promotion opportunities outside of the judiciary, remunerative adjustments have also been used within performance evaluation systems to influence cadre behavior (Whiting, 2000, p. 110). Drawing from theories of behavior within firms (Baker et al., 1988), this research analogizes the importance of internal organizational incentives in private companies to the behavior of governmental officials within bureaucratic units. Applying some of these insights to better understand the behavior of Chinese judges, I find that many mid-career judges are likely to defect to a law firm career if the public–private salary gap widens such that it erodes opportunities for professional survival and growth that public sector employment can bring, in the Weberian conception of modern officialdom. Absent transparent, merit-based opportunities to advance professionally, judges are likely to resign from courts and pursue more lucrative law firm careers, if given the opportunity.

The CQAS exhibits formal and informal features that render judicial performance legible, allowing political principals to systematically monitor judicial behavior; judges' behavioral responses to the CQAS incentive structure help explain the local variation in judicial autonomy that I describe in Chapter 5. This variation emerges from the interaction between the constraints of the CQAS and the potential alternatives to judicial employment provided by elevated, "high-end" demand for private legal services. With retention of top mid-career judges a priority for court leaders aiming to improve their courts' collective CQAS scores, court presidents and vice presidents have reformed promotion mechanisms so that they are more competitive, transparent, and routinized. Demand for legal services reaches high-end levels when civil lawyers have greater success in attracting companies rather than individuals as clients and in handling financial disputes as the primary type of service provision. High-end lawyer salaries have far outstripped – in some instances by threefold or more – local judicial salaries, placing meaningful pressure on court leaders to reduce judicial "brain drain" to local law firms. This influence of local legal services markets is a crucial link between local economic development and judicial autonomy that supports this book's explanation for the emergence of judicial autonomy in certain Chinese urban localities – despite the authoritarian political dominance of the CCP.

With court leaders lacking any parallel, unilateral authority to raise salaries for judges – much less for particularly successful or talented judges – providing more professionalized career trajectories is a viable strategy for retaining the core judicial personnel vital to a court's bureaucratic success as a whole (Jiang, 2013).[1] In essence, local court leaders fear "brain drain" in robust legal service markets like Shanghai, where the market for private legal services critical to commercial activity has boomed.

The claims made in this chapter are supported by interviews with Chinese judges and lawyers conducted during in-country fieldwork from 2012 to 2014, with quantitative evidence from industry reports and government statistics presented to triangulate and corroborate the claims of my interviewees. I also rely on other documentary sources and refer to secondary literature on sociology of the professional classes to sketch the historical development and regional variation of China's legal system.

The First Two Decades of the Post-Mao Legal Profession in China: From State Legal Worker to "Unhooked" Private Counsel (1979–2000)

Given both the dramatic changes in the legal profession in the past four decades and lawyers' extensive interaction with courts,[2] it should not be surprising that the legal services market has influenced the courts and the broader legal system in China. The lack of emphasis on developing an organized legal profession has been persistent in Chinese history, even as far back as late imperial China (Bodde & Morris, 1967), as well as at the end of the Republican era and the beginning of the PRC (V. Li, 1978). Some have attributed the diminished role of the legal profession in China to an historical tendency to address disputes "primarily through reliance upon morality, custom, kinship or politics, rather than formal legality, with the result that there has been relatively little need for individuals whose work lies in the law" (Alford, 1995, p. 1).

[1] Although court leaders have lacked meaningful authority to grant pay raises to individual judges, promotions can raise judicial income in line with the pay structure set by the larger civil service personnel system. *PC2013-55, judge, Shanghai, June 2013.* Further, the national government has feared that raising the salaries of government officials like judges could create significant public backlash. *PC2013-52, judge, Beijing, May 2013.*

[2] As other scholars and I have observed, a wide variety of legal services firms are located within a few blocks of the courthouse in any large- or medium-sized Chinese city, including "law firms" (*lüshi shiwusuo*), "legal firms" (*falü shiwusuo*) or "legal service firms" (*falü fuwusuo*), "legal consulting companies" (*falü zixun gongsi*), and "investigating companies" (*diaocha gongsi*) (S. Liu, 2011b, p. 70).

Despite this historical context, and in many ways repudiating it, the market for legal services has been rapidly expanded and privatized in the post-Mao era, generating increasingly diverse and lucrative opportunities to work as a lawyer in China that would have been impossible during the Mao era. The construction of the legal profession in China after the Cultural Revolution has been "the most concerted effort in world history to develop a legal system" (Alford, 2010, p. 48; see also Lubman, 1999), and in the early twenty-first century, the speed and magnitude of law firm growth in China have been "unprecedented in the global history of the legal profession" (S. Liu & Wu, 2016, p. 800). By 2009, total national legal service revenues had reached 32.45 billion Chinese *yuan* (approximately $5 billion USD), and by 2016, China's legal landscape had been dramatically altered, with the legal profession built into a corps of over 250,000 lawyers (J. Cohen, 2016; X. Li & Cheng, 2013, p. 64).

Detaching Legal Workers from the State (1978–1989)

Along with the commercial development of the legal profession, the formal status of China's lawyers was re-established after 1978, but lawyers were not revived as a class of private practitioners; rather, lawyers were first established as public sector employees before they could be "unhooked" from the state later in the reform era (J. A. Cohen, 1980; Lubman, 1999, p. 154).[3] In 1980, the Standing Committee of the National People's Congress promulgated the Provisional Regulations on Lawyers, which re-established an organized legal profession after a 23-year period of atrophy and decline; in these Provisional Regulations, lawyers are described as "state legal workers," (*guojia falü gongzuozhe*), shortly after which they became administrative cadres with status comparable to officialdom, with access to classified state materials among their privileges (Alford, 1995, p. 28; J. A. Cohen, 1980). During this period, lawyers as state legal workers were primarily employed in "legal advisory divisions" (*falü guwen chu*), which were affiliated with different levels of state agencies or work units (Alford, 1995, p. 28). By the time the Lawyers Law was promulgated in 1996, lawyers would formally transition from public sector employees into "professionals providing legal services to society."

Between 1979 and 1984, the names of legal services offices were changed from legal advisory divisions to "law firms" (*falü shiwusuo*), and by

[3] 1980 Provisional Regulations on Lawyers, Article 1.

1986, the majority of law firms had detached themselves from the state (Michelson, 2003). The accounting and management of lawyers and legal services organization also underwent substantial institutional innovation during this period, especially with "cooperative law firms" (*hezuosuo*) emerging in 1988. "The main difference between cooperative and state-owned firms was that the former were self-accounting and could hire and fire lawyers freely – they were not part of the state personnel allocation system (*guojia bianzhi*)"; however, all profits had to be returned to the state, and like "collective enterprises," they operated rather autonomously but retained a socialist view of property rights (Michelson, 2003, p. 64). The momentum for even this limited form of privatization of the legal profession was curtailed, however, by the large-scale departure of foreign investors from China following massive social unrest and state repression in Beijing and throughout the country in 1989; in the uncertain period before the fabled "Southern Tour" (1989–1992), foreign direct investment (FDI) inflows to China from critical locations including Hong Kong, the United States, and Europe dropped dramatically (Pan, 2003, p. 832).

Privatization Revisited (1992–2000)

As Deng Xiaoping revitalized economic liberalization in 1992, calling for both "deepening" of legal reforms and privatization of enterprises during his now-famous Southern Tour, the Ministry of Justice (MOJ) in 1993 circulated the Plan Regarding Deepening the Reform of Lawyers' Work, which "effectively stripped the bar of its former civil service character. The politically embedded status of law firms and lawyers as state personnel with administrative ranks was formally abolished.... Even most state-owned law firms were on the road to operational and fiscal autonomy" (Michelson, 2007, p. 372). As part of these directives, the partnership firm was also unveiled. In contrast to cooperative firms, which ultimately remained state property, partnership firms under the PRC Lawyers' Law (Article 18) would be solely responsible for their own finances (Michelson, 2007, p. 372). Standards for lawyer professionalization were also established during this period, as biannual national bar examinations began in 1986, annual exams started in 1993, and lawyer and judge exams were merged into the unified judicial examination in 2001 (Liu, 2011b, p. 27). Overall, these developments in lawyer regulation and firm type during the 1980s and 1990s indicate that the legal profession in China was first reconstituted as a public sector industry, and was then gradually privatized via the new institutional configurations of the cooperative and partnership law firm types.

On this foundation, privatization of the legal profession would continue to accelerate dramatically after 1992. During the 1980s and 1990s, the total number of legal service firms in China rose from 3,653 to 9,541, and the number of lawyers rose from 43,530 to 117,260 (Cai & Yang, 2005; see also Givens, 2014).[4] The official state goal was to license 150,000 lawyers by the turn of the twenty-first century, but because it was not feasible to expand the state payroll so drastically, privatization of the legal profession emerged as an appealing option (Alford, 1995, pp. 30–31). This period also witnessed top-down efforts to professionalize and "internationalize" the legal profession, as "rice roots legal workers" (para-professionals known as "basic-level legal workers" (*jiceng falü gongzuozhe*)) were stripped of their formal status as legal professionals. This development reflected the influence of Zhang Fusen (Minister of Justice from 2000 to 2005), whose overriding policy portfolio seemed to suggest that an "international" legal profession could not abide rice-roots legal workers who were "a relic of the past that ill-served a China wishing to demonstrate progress toward a rule of law and the establishment of a world-class legal services market" (Alford, 2010, p. 48).

It was in this context that the "unhook and restructure" campaign (*tuogou gaizhi*) was launched in 2000, a policy of privatizing the legal profession mandated by the State Council and carried out by the MOJ and its local units, converting all remaining state-owned law firms to partnerships – the culmination of over 10 years of privatization (Michelson, 2003, pp. 59, 66). This campaign to privatize the legal service industry was largely successful: whereas in 1991, the state possessed ownership over 98 percent of law firms, no more than 22 percent of firms were state-owned by 2002 (Michelson, 2003, p. 66).[5] State-led privatization of Chinese lawyers also rapidly increased the aggregate number of lawyer personnel (*lüshi gongzuo renyuan*) in China to 122,585 by the year 2000, although this number fell short of the central government's initial goal to license 150,000 lawyers by the turn of the century (Chinese Lawyers Yearbook Editing Committee, 2005, p. 107). Nonetheless, Stern finds that the total number of law firms in China had risen to 17,230 and the number of lawyers to 195,170 by 2010, likely the result of *tuogougaizhi* and similar efforts (Stern, 2013, p. 21).

[4] By comparison, Stern finds that there were 8,571 licensed lawyers in 1981 and 79 law firms in 1979 (Stern, 2013, p. 21).

[5] Liu provides a comparable ratio for partnership firms (64.46 percent of Chinese law firms in 2002), cooperative law firms (17.68 percent of firms in 2002), and state-owned law firms (16.68 percent in 2002) (S. Liu, 2011b, p. 26).

Hence, in the first two decades after Mao's death, the Chinese Party-State not only reconstructed its previous public sector legal services industry but also largely privatized the profession via both incremental policymaking at some times and swift policy implementation at others.

The Emergence of Localized Markets for Private Legal Services (2000–present)

As noted in Chapter 2, this book's ecological approach to the social forms of law not only explains the temporal dimensions of socio-legal processes and their structural effects, it also assesses spatial variation in legal forms. In this book, variations in judicial administrative hierarchies (e.g., judicial promotion mechanisms) across case study sites are explained by variation in local legal services markets – especially by the difference between "high-end" and "battleground" markets described later in this chapter. In a broad sense, this spatial differentiation in local legal services has been brought about by the opening of China's command economy to substantial foreign investment and interaction, especially after recommitment to these reforms in 1992. This post-1992 period and the lead up to World Trade Organization accession in 2001 are critical inflection periods for the judiciary and the broader growth of the legal profession in China; as foreign capital returned to China after 1992, the Party-State legalized some operations of foreign firms in China (Stern & Li, 2016, p. 190) and began a process of privatizing the legal profession that lasted through the 1990s and into the new millennium (Michelson, 2003, pp. 59, 66). These changes laid the groundwork for China's accession to the WTO and the continued expansion of the Chinese economy into the 2010s, in large part, by creating a pool of Chinese lawyers free to collaborate with foreign firms in a gray zone of lucrative legal practice at the blurred boundary of PRC regulations (S. Liu, 2008; Stern & Li, 2016). As a result, the development of spatial differentiation in local legal service markets (the focus of this chapter) and reforms to judicial selection procedures (documented in Chapter 5) have been intertwined in many urban localities in China.

Spatial Differentiation in the Market for Legal Services across China

China's post-Mao legal reforms have generated locally differentiated markets for legal services, especially since 1992. The overall institutionalization and privatization of the legal profession has progressed more swiftly in economically developed areas, consistent with associations between economic liberalization, socioeconomic development, and judicial autonomy (X. Li & Cheng, 2013, p. 61; Peerenboom, 2011). Additionally, since 2000, Chinese lawyers have concentrated in wealthier provinces and large urban centers with robust markets for legal services, such as Shanghai and Shenzhen (Peerenboom, 2011). This localized development has stemmed largely from policies designed to detach the legal services industry from the public sector, implemented in the late 1990s and early 2000s.

In 1999, the State Council addressed the disordered market for the various "intermediary organizations" (*zhongjie jigou*) for legal services that had emerged by that time, whose legal status, specialized functions, and professional levels differed greatly. When the State Council issued its opinion in 2000 on the Unhooking and Restructuring of Social Organizations Engaged in Economic and Appraisal Activities from Government Agencies, it formally "unhooked" (*tuogou*) intermediary organizations from their affiliated state agencies and "restructured" (*gaizhi*) them in terms of personnel, finance, work scope, and title (S. Liu, 2011b, p. 26). Several measures were also promulgated in 2001 to "cleanse and consolidate" (*qingli zhengdun*) the legal services market, further accelerating lawyers' privatization (S. Liu, 2011b, p. 26). By 2002, 64.46 percent of Chinese law firms, or 6,880 total firms, had become partnerships, another 1,887 (17.68 percent) were organized as cooperative law firms, and the number of state-owned law firms had declined to 1,780 (16.68 percent) (S. Liu, 2011b, p. 26; cf. Michelson, 2003).

Importantly, at the local level, the implementation of the "unhook" and the "cleanse and consolidate" policies varied with local levels of economic development: "Unhooking law firms from the state has been more difficult in the less developed parts of China where demand for lawyer services is lower and law firms are more reliant on support from the local government" (Michelson, 2003, p. 67). For example, in the Western provinces, located in China's geographical interior, law firm privatization policies had a much more diminished effect than those implemented in Beijing: In Jiangxi Province, 124 of 268 legal service firms (46.2 percent) remained state-owned; in Yunnan Province, 161 of 346 of legal service firms (46.5 percent) remained state-owned; and in Gansu Province, 95 of 191 legal service firms (49.7 percent) remained state-owned (Chinese Lawyers Yearbook Editing Committee, 2005, p. 333). Law firms in Shanghai implemented the "unhook" and "cleanse and consolidate" privatization reforms most thoroughly, effectively eliminating all state-owned law firms by 2001 (only 2 of 460 law firms were state-owned at that time). Firm ownership patterns in Guangdong (the provincial location of Shenzhen) and Sichuan (the provincial location of Chengdu) continued to reflect public ownership of legal service firms. Although both Guangdong and Sichuan gradually privatized law firms, Guangdong did so more quickly between 2001 and 2006 and was also home to the highest aggregate number of private partnership firms among the case study sites, with the number of partnership firms in Guangdong province rising from 584 in 2001 to 900 in 2006 (China Lawyers Yearbook Editing Committee, 2009; Chinese Lawyers Yearbook Editing Committee, 2005).

In the wake of this recent history, few scholars have documented the degree to which the legal services industry in China has become stratified[6]; however, I find that among at least five distinct subpatterns of the contemporary Chinese legal profession identified by Sida Liu, two types are highly relevant to developed, urban localities: A "High End" market, which serves company and global clients, and a "Battleground" market in which legal services provided to individuals comprise a substantial part of the legal services market (S. Liu, 2011a).

As a result, an income gap has emerged between lawyers and the public judicial and governmental sector, particularly in high-end localities. Pay scales organized by bureaucratic civil service hierarchies have governed income levels for judges, which fall below the median average for the top professions in China, mainly because these salary levels were not adjusted to account for rising standard of living costs (Xinhua News Agency, 2013), until at least the judicial and civil service reforms of 2014–2016. During interviews in 2012–2014, various mid-ranking judges provided figures for their annual income, ranging from ¥70,000 to 80,000 for an entry-level judicial position at the SPC, to ¥100,000 at the Shenzhen Intermediate Court, and ¥120,000 at the Shanghai Intermediate Court.[7] These judicial salary figures are consistent with other ranges of judicial salary reported during similar time frames, e.g., a county court judge from Guangxi province claimed in 2013 that judges in Beijing's wealthy Chaoyang District were among the highest paid in the country, possibly earning ¥8,000 per month (approximately $15,483 at ¥6.2/USD in 2013) (Jiang, 2013). Others have similarly found that "The income gap between lawyers in rustbelt regions and those in Beijing and Shanghai is astoundingly large.... A lawyer in Lanzhou ... [said] that a former partner of his

[6] There are some exceptions to this general pattern (see, e.g., Peerenboom, 2011, p. 132).

[7] *PC2013-52, judge, Beijing, May 2013; PC2013-70, judge, Shanghai, October 2013; PC2012-6, judge, Shenzhen, June 2012.*

law firm went to Shanghai in 2000 and became an associate in a local law firm, where his annual income doubled from 100,000 to 200,000 yuan … Meanwhile, the in-migration of lawyers has also strengthened the stratification of the local bar in the receiving places, particularly in Beijing and Shanghai" (S. Liu et al., 2014, pp. 176, 185). As an SPC judge told me in 2013, judicial salary levels failed to adequately keep up with the spiking costs of living in urban China:

> If you are a young judge and have a child, the cost of living is so high! For example, you know you can't trust the quality of Chinese infant formula, right? So, one should really buy imported formula, which is expensive … One child goes through about 3-4 canisters of formula per month and each can costs at least ¥200, so if you're already paying maybe ¥700 per month just on infant formula, and your entry-level judicial salary maybe is only ¥6,000 per month, it's really difficult to get by.[8]

By contrast, lawyer income in China has increased dramatically, particularly in local markets where serving corporate clients is the norm. Knowledge that the average income for experienced associates in domestic law firms far outstrips judicial salaries in China's high-end legal service localities was widespread among the judges that I interviewed. One interviewee described that she had previously served as a judge, but had left her court position because she had many other higher paying job opportunities in the Shanghai law firm market.[9] A different District Court judge from Shenzhen was more effusive:

> Even for higher-ranking positions, judicial salary is approximately ¥100,000 (approximately $16,130) per year, and has not recently been raised, despite the rapid rise in cost of living. I have a classmate from law school who works locally in commercial litigation and IP law. She makes twice my salary and doesn't have to deal with the pressure of case completion quotas and appellate reversal limits [under the CQAS].[10]

According to a 2006 survey of 183 Chinese lawyers conducted by LawInn HR Consulting Co., average income for a mid-level associate (3–5 years experience) working in a domestic firm and holding a PRC degree at that time was ¥248,000; for a high-level associate (6–10 years experience) working in a domestic firm and holding a PRC degree, average income was ¥305,000 (S. Liu, 2011b, p. 136).[11] A mid-level associate working as a "Legal Consultant" in a foreign firm made an average of ¥350,000, and

[8] *PC2013-52, judge, Beijing, May 2013.*

[9] *PC2012-34, lawyer, Shanghai, October 2012.*

[10] *PC2013-3, judge, Shenzhen, January 2013.*

[11] The currency exchange rate between the Chinese *yuan* and the US dollar was approximately 8:1 in 2006.

	"Battleground"		"High End"
	Chengdu	*Shenzhen*	*Shanghai*
Experienced Associate:	**¥150,000**	**¥247,500**	**¥473,333**
Entry-Level Associate:	**¥45,000**	**¥65,000**	**¥120,500**

Figure 4.1 Selected annual estimates of lawyer income across local legal services case study cities (as of 2014).

attorneys with foreign law degrees could earn more than five times that figure (S. Liu, 2011b, p. 136). My own interviews with lawyers suggest that these income levels are more consistent with what I call a "High End" locality, like Shanghai, where a small sample of experienced associate attorneys told me that their average annual income was ¥350,000. These data from lawyer interviews are summarized in Figure 4.1, as interviewees across localities reported that income was much higher at the experienced associate level in Shanghai and Shenzhen.[12]

Among at least five distinct subpatterns of the contemporary Chinese legal profession, I find two types are highly relevant to developed, urban localities: A "High End" market that serves company and global clients, and a "Battleground" market in which legal services provided to individuals comprise a substantial part of the legal services market (S. Liu, 2011a). The high-income levels described by my lawyer interviewees and in the LawInn survey are more likely found in a successful high-end corporate practice, whereas lawyers, basic-level legal workers, and other law practitioners face fierce competition for business in "Battleground" legal services markets (Liu, 2008, 2011b, pp. 70–75, 106–116). Commercial lawyers

[12] Sources for lawyer incomes presented in this table come from interviews with three lawyers in Shanghai, two lawyers in Shenzhen, and two lawyers in Chengdu, all of whom were employed at different law firms within each city in 2014. See the Appendix for more detailed information regarding these lawyers' statements regarding income; more recent data (e.g., the 2020 *Michael Page Salary Benchmark*, www.page.com/about-us), are also consistent with the overall battleground/high-end distinction described here, assuming some salary inflation between 2013 and 2020.

in a battleground market must scrape together a client base, as one lawyer practicing in a small Chengdu firm described, "In other places like Shanghai and Guangzhou, lawyers can do bankruptcy and commercial consulting kinds of cases, but here, the cases are … 'run-into-problem' (*pengdao wenti*) cases, where something happened and so you have to say, hey lawyer, come help me."[13] These conditions seemingly render demand for mid-level lawyers in battleground legal services markets much less robust.

Liu does not explicitly classify varieties of local law firm development, but I take Liu's typology and apply it to my three case study cities based on information regarding the local income and the revenue of associate attorneys and law firm partners (see Figure 4.1). I classify a "high-end" locality as that in which the corporate legal services sector has expanded such that a mid-ranking judge has an opportunity to double or triple her or his annual income by switching to a law firm career. A mid-ranking judge in urban China possesses professional experience commensurate with an experienced associate attorney in a domestic Chinese firm (over five years of experience) or a China legal consultant in a foreign firm. At this level of experience, there is a significant difference between the lawyers I interviewed in Shanghai, Shenzhen, and Chengdu: The average incomes reported to me by attorneys in each locality indicate that, at the experienced and entry levels, salaries are higher in Shanghai than in Shenzhen, and lowest in Chengdu; incomes for experienced, nonpartner level attorneys in Shanghai are highest among my three case studies, followed by Shenzhen, then Chengdu (see Figure 4.1).[14] At the experienced associate level, judges possessing 5–10 years of experience could compete for a high-end law firm position above the entry level that is usually reserved for new law school graduates, but they would not be considered for partner until establishing a revenue stream.[15] Instead, interviewees told me that it was more likely that a former judge could enter a law firm and work for a senior partner, eventually building a sufficient client base to be considered for partner within five years of beginning work at the experienced associate level.[16] This situation threatens the promotion chances of court leaders, who have been publicly quoted lamenting the

[13] *PC2013-32, lawyer, Chengdu, April 2013.*

[14] These figures represent averages of incomes reported to me by attorneys working in Chinese law firms (more detailed information on each interviewee's quoted income is found in the Appendix).

[15] *PC2014-10, lawyer, Shanghai, October 2014.*

[16] *PC2014-10, lawyer, Shanghai, October 2014; PC2014-11, lawyer, Shanghai, October 2014; PC2014-8, lawyer, Shenzhen, October 2014; and PC2014-5, lawyer, Chengdu, October 2014.*

large number of productive, "backbone" judges who resign and thereby exacerbate the judicial "brain drain" problem that diminishes court leaders' CQAS scores (X. Liu, 2014).

At the same time, low civil servant salaries might suggest a role for corruption in retaining personnel in local courts. Although the Chinese political system is far from corruption-free (Ling Li, 2012), it remains difficult and risky to engage in systematic and long-term corruption, as mid-ranking judges usually cannot expect to receive bribes habitually as a form of "income" for at least a few reasons. First, judicial corruption is not usually the unilateral act of a single judge, as bribery usually requires a "middle man" (*zhongjian ren*); second, a single judge also tends to lack the authority to award a lucrative civil damages award, as such cases would likely use the ordinary procedure under the Civil Procedure Law, which requires a majority ruling from a three-judge panel; additionally, the CCP's anti-corruption judicial penalties are highly visible and severe – historically including the death penalty (Sapio, 2010).[17] Perhaps more importantly, the pursuit of professional career paths, rather than opportunities for corruption, appear to be the main drivers of the majority of cadres' behavior (Burns & Wang, 2010, pp. 74, 76). Judges with some experience handling cases are competitive candidates for law firm jobs and can usually select an alternative career path in a law firm if they are unsatisfied with the pressures of judicial work, e.g., "Ms. Sun," a former judge in Shanghai who resigned her judicial post in 2014 for a "big multiple" of her judge's salary (*The Economist*, 2014). On the other hand, judges also indicated during interviews in 2013–2014 that opportunities for more professionalized judicial careers (e.g., competitive mechanisms of judicial promotion) were expanding and that careers within the courts were becoming more merit-based.[18] If these reports are accurate, then reforming court institutions to produce more autonomous judges would make sense. As one judge in Shenzhen put it, "Although lawyers and judges have similar training, judges are different. A lawyer usually works to make money; judges deal with directly with citizens to make society more just, giving you a sense of duty that you can't get as a lawyer."[19] Under these circumstances,

[17] *PC2013-56, judge, Shanghai, June 2013*; PRC Civil Procedure Law, Articles 42 and 157. Although it can be used, the use of the death penalty for nonviolent crimes has declined in recent years, even in the midst of a harsh crackdown on corruption (Amnesty International, 2018, pp. 20–21).

[18] *PC2013-57, judge, Shanghai, June 2013; PC2014-2, judge, Shenzhen, June 2014; PC2013-38, judge, Chengdu, April 2013.*

[19] *PC2013-64, judge, Shenzhen, July 2013.*

career-minded judges in reform-minded courts face two potentially fruitful and stable law-related career trajectories: Remaining in their judge positions with a realistic chance at a merit-based promotion (and the administrative salary raise that such promotions provide) or leaving their judge positions to join a local law firm with a chance at a higher salary handling commercial litigation. The multifaceted implications of rising costs of living, expanding professional opportunities, and heavy-handed performance evaluation metrics are consistent with an overall ecology of competitive cooperation within the law-related professional space in urban China (see Hannan & Freeman, 1977; Park & Burgess, 1969), suggesting that the significant costs to court leaders resulting from the attrition of highly capable judges have generated pressure on court leaders to create a more professional career trajectory as a strategy to retain the best judges in a given locality.

Local Law Market Revenues and Characteristics

To help corroborate statements made during interviews – especially those regarding lawyer salaries – and to support the finding of local variation in the "brain drain" problem across different urban localities in China, this section presents local statistics from 2004 to 2009 regarding markets for legal services across my three case studies. Recall from the previous section, the judge who resigned her judicial post for a law firm position that paid a "big multiple" of her judicial salary: Are singular data points like this consistent with the local variation in judicial design that I observe in my specific cases? On the basis of official statistics corresponding to the size of provincial-level legal markets and the amount of revenue from legal services earned in recent years, I find that leaders in the Shanghai court system face disproportionately more pressure to entice judges to stay in their court positions than those in Shenzhen or Chengdu. Revenues in the Shanghai legal services market are far higher than that in either Guangdong province (home to Shenzhen city) or Sichuan province (home to Chengdu city), and more revenue is derived from representation of enterprises than individuals in Shanghai as well. Although these provincial-level data should not be viewed in isolation or as equivalent proxies to be used for direct comparison between the three cases under study, they can nonetheless serve as helpful reference points for assessing consistency and credibility of salary numbers presented above from interviews with lawyers and judges, provided as part of a holistic account of the local legal markets in China.

Table 4.1. *Variation in revenue from legal services across selected Chinese provinces (2009)*

	Total revenue earned by lawyers from representing clients in civil litigation (¥)	Total revenue earned via consultation with companies (¥)	Total population, 2010	Legal services revenue per capita (¥)	Revenue from company consulting per capita (¥)
Shanghai	1,416,750,000	571,040,000	23,019,148	61.5	24.8
Guangdong	2,344,550,000	663,290,000	104,303,132	22.4	6.4
Sichuan	186,370,000	124,230,000	80,418,200	2.3	1.5

Sources: China Lawyers Yearbook Editing Committee (2011, pp. 200–201); to calculate per capita figures, I used population data from 2010 (National Bureau of Statistics of the PRC, 2011).

From Table 4.1, it is apparent from two perspectives that the legal services environment in Shanghai is the closest to the high-end model of high revenues and robust demand for legal professionals: Shenzhen is likely similar to a high-end market but less so than Shanghai; and Chengdu is much less a high-end market than either Shanghai or Shenzhen. First, when financial data are normalized for population, Shanghai lawyers earn far more revenue from civil litigation than those in Guangdong or Sichuan; importantly, civil litigation is both the least politically sensitive and the most financially lucrative type of lawyer work, making it a highly desirable form of legal practice (Cai & Yang, 2005). Second, Shanghai lawyers made far more revenue per capita from consulting work for companies than those in either Guangdong or Sichuan, and data regarding revenue earned by lawyers also show that Shanghai has been among the most lucrative places for lawyers to do business in China since at least the mid-2000s.

Tables 4.2 and 4.3 present statistics from 2004 to 2006 regarding raw income from lawyers' professional practice across my case study sites. Table 4.2 indicates that Shanghai was among the most lucrative places for lawyers to do business in China following China's WTO accession in 2001–2002, as measured by aggregate revenue earned by lawyers in each jurisdiction. Thus, not only aggregate revenues but also data specific to civil litigation support the finding that Shanghai was the most lucrative locality to practice law among my three cases.

Table 4.2. *Summary of revenue from lawyer practice (2004 and 2006)*

	Lawyer practice revenue, 2004 (¥)	Lawyer practice revenue, 2004, per capita (¥)	Lawyer practice revenue, 2006 (¥)	Lawyer practice revenue, 2006, per capita (¥)
Shanghai	2,242,220,000	97.4	3,129,320,000	135.9
Guangdong	885,930,000	8.5	3,515,940,000	33.7
Sichuan	266,360,000	3.3	359,690,000	4.5

Sources: China Lawyers Yearbook Editing Committee (2005); China Lawyers Yearbook Editing Committee (2009).

Table 4.3. *Distribution of case type across localities (2004)*

	Consults for large companies among all company consults	Cases representing criminal defendants	Cases involving administrative litigation
Shanghai	3,631	10,928	1,919
Guangdong	2,505	16,703	2,437
Sichuan	2,059	18,907	1,936

Source: China Lawyers Yearbook Editing Committee (2005).

The robust earning capacity of the Shanghai legal profession is not surprising when considering trends in the clientele of most firms in that municipality. As Liu notes, high-end markets are characterized by the representation of companies and financial disputes more so than the representation of individual clients and relatively low monetary damages awarded from litigation. Table 4.3 indicates that, in the early years of the twenty-first century, the proportion of cases in Shanghai skewed toward the representation of companies much more than it did in Guangdong or Sichuan provinces:

Whether measured by aggregate revenue, civil litigation, or cases handled for company clients, Shanghai is the most commercially oriented professional legal market, which also renders it the most lucrative locality on average in which to practice law among my three cases. These variations in local legal markets translate into much higher income for lawyers in high-end versus battleground localities (see, e.g., Liu, Liang & Michelson, 2014, p. 12), lending further support to the thesis that courts in high-end localities will feel greater pressure to attract and retain high-quality mid-ranking judges than will courts in battleground localities.

The Suitability of Judges for Law Firm Careers in Urban China

Higher levels of economic development in high-end legal services markets such as Shanghai have produced higher demand for qualified legal professionals in those localities. Accordingly, these circumstances have placed greater pressure on court leaders in high-end legal services localities to attract and retain qualified legal professionals to staff judicial positions in their courts. One assumption upon which this argument relies: Judges, especially those who have acquired several years' experience in the courtroom making decisions on commercial legal disputes, would be desirable candidates for law firm job openings. For several reasons, mid-career judges in China would make very competitive job candidates for law firm jobs in their localities.

First, mid-ranking judges are desirable candidates for experienced associate-level positions in law firms because the coursework for judges and lawyers in Chinese law schools is largely identical, the bar exam for judges and lawyers was unified in 2001, and judges must pass an additional civil service examination (launched in 1994 and regularized in 2002), giving judges a supplemental professional qualification that is a key selling point for legal professionals on the job market (S. Liu, 2011a, p. 27; Minzner, 2013, p. 362; Peerenboom, 2002, p. 291).[20]

Second, judges who work in the same court for several years obtain a variety of distinctly local advantages, including familiarity with applicable laws, deep knowledge of the litigation process, and social connections. During field interviews, judges stated that those in judicial clerk-like positions (*faguan zhuli*) must apprentice for at least five years before they can ascend to decision-making authority, and another promotion to mid-level cadre status takes at least another five years.[21] Hence, case-deciding judges were even better trained for a career in litigation than recent graduates holding a foreign JD or LLM degree. Judges' experience as state employees also gives them deep knowledge of applicable laws, local processes of litigation, and first-hand knowledge of the "Chinese way" to handle tricky

[20] *PC2013-57, judge, Shanghai, June 2013; PC2012-3, judge, Shenzhen, June 2012.*

[21] *PC2014-1, judge Shenzhen, June 2014.*

legal disputes (S. Liu, 2008, pp. 785–786; S. Liu, Liang, & Michelson, 2014; S. Liu, 2011b). Aside from finding informal solutions when the formal law is ambiguous, lawyers in high-end domestic law firms must frequently interact with government agencies in their work, suggesting that judges' "inside knowledge" of government and legal system operations is vital to successful corporate legal practice in urban China. Even in the highly formal issue area of securities law, successfully resolving a case for a client does not imply composing a well-reasoned legal brief, but instead requires improvisational legal work that is often situated in the public–private boundary between market and state, especially when applicable rules are ambiguous. For example, one lawyer arranged a symposium with legal experts at the Ministry of Finance to produce a provisional memo that the lawyer could subsequently rely upon to produce a favorable interpretation of the law for a client (S. Liu, 2011b, p. 125). Other than using improvisational tactics when the formal law is ambiguous, associates in high-end domestic law firms also generally have more responsibility than their foreign peers for performing nonresearch tasks, such as conference calls, meeting clients, and dealing with government agencies (S. Liu, 2011b, pp. 127–130). In short, the on-site training and "inside knowledge" that judges receive in their courtroom workplace environments regarding the inner-workings of state institutions are much more likely to suit the Chinese legal environment than is the more formalistic legal training commonly seen on the resumes of associates in China's foreign law firms. At the same time, mid-ranking judges also obtain experience in handling a wide variety of legal disputes, giving judges both the formal background and the informal expertise that are vital to a successful lawyer practice in contemporary China.

Moreover, recent research on the stratification and local diversity of the legal profession in China emphasizes specifically that local, rather than geographically diffuse, social connections are important influences on "brain drain" from local courts. Migrating from a frontier region to establish a legal practice in a high-end locality is a difficult, sink-or-swim proposition – lawyers who leave their local communities to start a legal practice in a new city "face the harsh reality of assimilation or attrition after struggling a few years in the receiving place"; further, even after several years of hardship, migrant lawyers can be pushed out of their new locality entirely (S. Liu, Liang, & Michelson, 2014, pp. 22, 24). Further, the influence of lawyer migration on high-end areas of law practice remains small, with the vast majority of new migrant lawyers specializing in low-end, riskier, and less profitable legal areas, "chasing the ambulance" to make ends meet (Liu, Liang, & Michelson, 2014, pp. 22, 24). At least during the period studied in this book, a multiyear lag between arrival and assimilation into a new locality would create a barrier to leaving judicial posts in frontier regions, which at least could provide a measure of job security (Xinhua News Agency, 2013).

By contrast, because local connections have been the key to establishing a new client practice (Liu, Liang, & Michelson, 2014, p. 16), career change from a local judicial post to a local law firm position handling corporate litigation would be much smoother. The judges who indicated during interviews that they were considering becoming lawyers indicated that they would only consider lawyer openings in the same city or province rather than migrating to a different locality to start careers, as their law firm opportunities came from within their local social networks.[22] The local nature of judge–lawyer mobility is also consistent with similar research documenting symbiotic exchange between lawyers and state officials, with judges and lawyers acting as important brokers between market and state (S. Liu, 2011a).

The spatially contingent nature of foreign investment – and the patterns of law firm activity that come with it – also influences local degrees of stratification in the legal profession. Foreign law firms, relegated to a legal consultant role in China because of the restriction against foreign lawyers practicing in China, also compete with domestic firms for professional staff, especially for qualified mid-career legal workers in high-end localities like Shanghai. Foreign firms concentrate on recruiting mid-level Chinese associates (i.e., lawyers with 3–5 years of professional experience) because these candidates are more willing to accept the nonpartnership track positions that foreign firms have generally offered in recent years. As foreign firms do not offer a partnership track, it is very difficult for them to recruit top senior associates or junior partners, setting up a fierce competition for mid-level associates among foreign and domestic corporate law firms in high-end local legal services markets (S. Liu, 2011b, pp. 133–138). Also, foreign firms have not been allowed to practice law in China or to employ licensed Chinese lawyers, relegating the status of Chinese legal professionals hired by foreign firms to legal "consultants" (S. Liu, 2011b, p. 114). Article 15 of the State Council's 2001 Administrative Regulation on the Representative Offices of Foreign Law Firms forbids foreign law offices from engaging in "Chinese legal affairs" but, at the same time, permits

[22] *PC2013-43, judge, Shenzhen, April 2013; PC2013-48, Shenzhen judge, Shanghai, May 2013; PC2013-49, judge, Shanghai, May 2013; PC2013-56, judge, Shanghai, June 2013.*

foreign firms to "provide information regarding the influence of China's legal environment" (S. Liu, 2011b, p. 116). Thus, a foreign law firm operating in China seeking to provide services like formal legal opinions or court representation must collaborate with local law firms, and in the past decade, local firms have even taken control over substantive aspects of corporate legal projects, with their foreign firm collaborators increasingly outsourcing their work to local Chinese firms (S. Liu, 2011b, p. 117–119). These foreign firm practices in high-end localities might provide a plausible mechanism for explaining local variation in judicial autonomy in China that tracks with patterns of FDI inflows (cf. Y. Wang, 2015).

Publicly reported statistical data regarding the number of judges who have left courts since the mid-2000s are also consistent with variations in law practice revenue across urban China. When local demand for legal services is higher, we should expect more judges to leave courts searching for alternative professional opportunities. When normalized for population, the number of judges leaving Shanghai's courts is approximately 20 percent greater than that in Shenzhen (X. Liu, 2014; Lü & Wang, 2014).[23] Comparable data at the city level are not available for Chengdu, but provincial-level data for Sichuan show that the number of judges leaving basic courts in Sichuan is 74 percent less than the number of judges leaving Shanghai courts (Min, 2006). A judge from Shenzhen provided context to these news reports: "These stories [of lawyers leaving their judicial posts for law firm jobs in Shenzhen] include us judges right now – many are thinking of going out and becoming lawyers. To tell you the truth, right now regarding salary, in Shenzhen, regarding the cost of living, our incomes are actually not sufficient"; the judge then stated that because she already passed the unified judicial exam, she also could have many possible opportunities to forge a career as a lawyer.[24] As another judge in Shenzhen described the problem, judges' material conditions have potentially wide-ranging effects:

> You probably already know, even among civil servants, a judge's salary is not particularly high; in Hong Kong, have you heard of the policy of 'higher pay for clean government' (*gaoxin yanglian*)? It is where government salaries are such that officials do not have to worry about being able to afford basic living necessities (*yishiwuyou*) … for example,

[23] When normalized as the number of judges leaving the city's courts per 10 million residents, 29.6 judges per year resign their posts in Shanghai, whereas 23.4 judges resign annually in Shenzhen.

[24] *PC2013-1, judge, Shenzhen, January 2013.*

> the problem is that if wages are too low, a judge cannot ensure the most basic standard of living, and in this situation, it will also be difficult to guarantee a clean (*lianjie*) government or to decide cases fairly [because of the possibility of bribery]. For judges in China, salary levels are not particularly high, and even social status is not that high anymore, but for judge's basic living, to avoid corruption problems, the judicial salaries should be raised ... currently, an overworked judge can easily leave the court, resign, and change occupations, so currently this is a very big problem, this "brain drain" ... Many people are not willing to serve as judges, because one, deciding cases is hard work, two, there's a lot of caseload pressure, three, the amount you get for the work is not proportional to the time and work that you put in.[25]

Conclusion

The influence of local economic development on the practice of law has led to a wide income gap between high-end lawyers and judges in China, which threatens the "brain drain" of highly qualified mid-ranking judges from local courts to local law firms. In high-end urban localities, conditions have produced high demand for mid-level associates in local law firms – positions highly suitable for mid-ranking local judges. Because China's judicial performance evaluation system quantitatively measures court leaders' management performance based on the productivity of their subordinates, court leaders are personally and professionally invested in retaining hard-working, mid-ranking judges who can efficiently adjudicate cases and raise courts' and within-court units' collective performance scores. When law firms in high-end legal services localities can lure judges into careers as lawyers, court leaders have faced greater pressure to introduce judicial reforms designed to retain qualified judges. Evidence from interviews with lawyers and judges, macro-level statistics on law firm revenues across localities, and accounts of lawyer incomes across cases indicate that lawyer remuneration at the experienced and entry levels are higher in Shanghai than in Shenzhen, and lowest in Chengdu. In localities exhibiting high-end demand for legal services, greater judicial autonomy should also be present because of the pronounced "brain drain" effect noted by many Shanghai and Shenzhen judges.

This chapter has also presented evidence that local legal services markets in China have developed in a highly uneven manner across

[25] *PC2013-3, judge, Shenzhen, January 2013.*

the history of the post-Mao reform era and across geographic localities in China. At the outset of the reform era, lawyers were state employees working in state-owned legal service units or directly within government agencies; during the past two decades, however, the legal profession has been rapidly "unhooked" from the state, and in today's China, a multibillion dollar private legal services industry has emerged, featuring private lawyers conducting business with individuals and corporate clients and navigating a hands-off regulatory environment in which foreign and domestic legal service firms compete for market share and qualified legal professionals. This rapid privatization and unmatched growth of the legal services market in the early twenty-first century (S. Liu & Wu, 2016) has also produced substantial variation and stratification across localities in China. In urban China, legal services markets differ primarily regarding whether they have developed into high-end local markets, where lawyers primarily conduct increasingly lucrative legal service work for corporate clients, or battleground legal markets, where lawyers struggle to piece together business from individual clients and some company clients. In this context, it is surprising that the extant literature on judicial politics in authoritarian regimes has not extensively explored the relationship between political decisions to reform judicial institutions and economic conditions highly relevant to the judiciary, such as the development of local legal services markets. Despite the repressive limits on the Chinese legal profession's potential as a mobilized, activist force for political liberalism (Halliday et al., 2007), this chapter suggests that structural changes to classes of legal professionals can create pressure for judicial reforms in particular circumstances.

Chapter 5 traces differences in local legal services markets to the politics of local court reforms in urban China, addressing recent changes to the mechanisms of judicial promotion, court transparency, the writing of judicial opinions, and styles of dispute resolution. I have found significant qualitative variation in promotion mechanisms between the cases of Shanghai, Shenzhen, and Chengdu – cities that have relatively similar levels of economic development. During fieldwork, I learned that each city's courts have been required to implement "competitive promotion" systems for mid-ranking judges, but the implementation of these judicial promotion procedures varies substantially between Shanghai, Shenzhen, and Chengdu. Similarly, Shanghai courts exhibit higher scores on judicial transparency rankings, greater propensity to justify their written decisions with statutory citations, and a lower percentage of disputes resolved by mediation.

Why would judicial promotion mechanisms differ across these cities in China? I find that the pressure from rapidly privatizing legal markets, and the potential careers in law firms that are more available in high-end local markets like Shanghai, has contributed to the openness and competitiveness seen in judicial promotion mechanisms. In China, there is negligible multiparty fragmentation or civil society autonomy to empower the judiciary. Nonetheless, if greater numbers of expert judges can easily quit their jobs and find lucrative local employment as lawyers, court leaders are more likely to strategically reform court institutions toward providing judicial cadres more professionalized work environments and career trajectories. In high-end markets, judicial promotion mechanisms for mid-ranking judges are more competitive and less susceptible to the influence of the local CCP, transparency mandates are more thoroughly implemented, and court opinions indicate greater decisional autonomy of judges, all of which indicate that local legal services markets, even in an authoritarian context, can combine with institutionalist factors to bring about increases in judicial autonomy.

5

Expansions in Competitive Promotion and the Implications for Judicial Autonomy

The changes to the legal profession documented in Chapter 4 began to influence the court system particularly in the lead up to, and in the aftermath of, China's 2001 accession to the World Trade Organization (WTO), when rising lawyer salaries in high-end markets began making it difficult for courts to retain qualified judges. In the post-1992 period, foreign investors recommitted to China's liberalizing reforms (M. Gallagher, 2005; Hsueh, 2011; Pan, 2003), foreign law firms began operating legally in China, especially in the realm of guiding inbound investment (Stern & Li, 2016, p. 190), and the Chinese government continued "unhooking" the legal profession from the state as part of a larger effort to internationalize and privatize the domestic legal services market (Michelson, 2003, p. 66). These moves created a pool of Chinese lawyers capable of marketing their skills to both foreign law firms and an increasing array of Chinese firms in a lucrative zone of legal practice emerging at the blurred boundary of PRC regulations in urban China (S. Liu, 2008; Stern & Li, 2016).

This chapter details the changes to courts and judicial autonomy that have been deeply intertwined with the stratification of living standards, dramatic growth of the Chinese legal profession, and emergence of significant income differentials for lawyers across urban localities, especially after 1992. This series of events is consistent with this book's ecological explanation of court reform, which posits that the structure and process of socio-legal forms have an interactive relationship. I also provide evidence in the second part of this chapter, suggesting that these dynamics in the social forms of law influence the substance of law, for example, the decisions of court leaders in urban China to increase the transparency of their courts and enhance the statutory basis of their judicial decisions (S. Liu, 2015, p. 7; Weber, 1978). These developments also indicate expansions in judges' overall decisional autonomy, as discussed in Chapters 1 and 2.

From several scholarly perspectives, the process of selecting and promoting judges has long been identified as a critical nexus through which political influence can seep into the judiciary. For instance, even when arguing that judicial independence is a hallmark of American politics, seminal law, and economics, research finds that "It is of course unrealistic to suppose the judiciary wholly independent of the current desires of the political branches," which can influence the judiciary through the manipulation of the procedures for personnel selection and promotion (Landes & Posner, 1975, p. 885). The judicial selection and promotion process has also of course been a point of politicization of court cases in China (see Lubman, 1999, p. 264). Taking inspiration from these scholars, this chapter takes changes to the procedures for judicial selection and promotion in China as a touchstone for judicial autonomy, beginning by analyzing changes to judicial selection and promotion procedures in urban China. In this book, the outcome variable is "personal judicial autonomy," which is found when judicial terms of office are "reasonably secure" and when judicial appointments and promotions are relatively depoliticized, fair, and carried out according to pre-established rules (Peerenboom, 2010, p. 71). As noted in Chapter 2, this conceptualization draws heavily from Peerenboom's concept of personal judicial "independence," but at the same time "does not unrealistically require courts to be completely unmoored from their political and social surroundings," while still speaking to "the normative ideal that courts exist to serve as neutral impartial third parties to resolve disputes" (Brinks & Blass, 2018, pp. 23–28). Ultimately, the outcome variable of "personal judicial autonomy" strikes a proper balance between the measurable aspects of "personal judicial independence" and the conceptually precise elements of scholarly concepts of "autonomy."

This chapter then examines other aspects of the decisional autonomy of courts and judges (see Peerenboom, 2010, p. 71), such as court transparency, the prevalence of judicial mediation across cases, and the extent to which judges provide legally grounded reasons for their decisions in adversarial opinions. In general, I find significant qualitative variation in judges' decisional autonomy between the urban court systems of Shanghai, Shenzhen, and Chengdu – cities that exhibit similar levels of economic development. Why would judicial promotion mechanisms differ across these cities in China? I find that court leaders' fears of judicial attrition and "brain drain" (*liushirenyuan*, *rencailiushi*, or *faguanliushi*) produced by the greater potential for careers in high-end law firms contributed to the openness and competitiveness of judicial promotion mechanisms during the period under study. Until recently, little had been publicly known about such procedures (Peerenboom, 2010, p. 77); hence, this chapter also contributes to our empirical understanding of these important political–legal mechanisms, contextualizing survey-based research that underpins much of the extant literature on Chinese courts, which, although systematic, assesses courts using indirect measures that rely on the perceptions of citizens who have not had contact with the legal system (see Michelson & Read, 2011).

Changes to Judicial Selection and Promotion Before and After 1992

Taking a cue from other studies that use judicial personnel decisions (e.g., procedures governing appointment, promotion, removal, and the use of "court packing") to gauge whether courts possess sufficient autonomy to serve impartially in the legal disputes before them (Chavez, 2004; Dahl, 1957), this section details changes to judicial promotion mechanisms and the bureaucratic context of the judicial hierarchy for mid-ranking judges in China. Changes to judicial selection and promotion in the early 1990s were generally limited to personnel reforms applied to the larger civil service bureaucracy, which is consistent with the theory of this book: At that early stage in China's reform-era history, it is unlikely that Chinese lawyers, as a growing professional class, would have had a substantial political or policy impact. As discussed in Chapter 2, many observers suggest that there was virtually no professional class of lawyers at the start of reforms in 1978, and even those who dive deeper and account for a variety of other types of legal professionals, formal lawyers only numbered in the few thousands in the early post-Mao years (Alford, 2010).

Before a series of reforms in the late 1990s, PRC civil service was characterized by central planning, allocation of jobs to new graduates through government-determined manpower plans, subjective performance appraisal, and position-based pay (Barnett & Vogel, 1967; Harding, 1981; Schurmann, 1971; Yung, 1991). Through much of the 1990s, a "nominated appointment" system for selecting mid-level judicial cadres was used, whereby local court CCP Core Groups directly selected all judges, regardless of rank. Under this promotion system, the relevant court's CCP Core Group, along with the local Organization Department (OD), would (in the ambiguous phrasing of Party jargon) "mull over" (*yunniang*) candidates, directly and unilaterally selecting personnel for promotion, essentially allowing for systematic and widespread court-packing (Wei, 2010).[1]

In 1993, new regulations extended the civil service system to government units including the courts and procuracy, and this change was followed

[1] *PC2013-1, judge, Shenzhen, January 2013.*

by a stronger focus on using organized, transparent competitions for the professional promotions of public service employees (Burns & Wang, 2010, pp. 61–62). Specific standards for judicial promotion are found in the Judges Law (*faguan fa*) of 1995, which grant formal authority for appointing and promoting judges to local people's congresses and local courts; however, the letter of the law masks the fact that the local Party, *via* CCP Core Groups (*dangzu*) and the Party Organization Department (OD), has largely controlled judicial selection and promotion, with local legislatures generally serving as rubber stamps (Peerenboom, 2002, p. 305).[2] As in other government units, the CCP core group in a Chinese court has tended to include the top few party members – for example, the court president, vice president, and a select few division chiefs – who first caucus as CCP officials, then "don their government hats" as governmental court officials to implement directions from above (Lieberthal, 2004, p. 240).

In 1998, the Central Organization Department and the Central Personnel Department of the CCP jointly issued an opinion on competitive promotion that called on CCP Committees, government departments, legislatures, discipline and inspection committees, procurators, and courts to use "transparent and competitive promotion" (*gongkai-jingzhengshanggang*) for both leading and non-leading positions.[3] Importantly, these central-level regulations did not mandate lower levels to implement competitive promotion; rather, they simply authorized lower-level government departments and organs "to use transparent competition to confirm the selection of cadres," leaving open the possibility that at the local level, some courts could disregard competitive promotion for judges.[4] Nonetheless, the 1998 opinion called on courts and other state bureaucratic units to use competitive procedures when vacancies occur, when institutions are adjusted, when institutions are reorganized, when personnel exceeds the limit, and when there is a need for personnel

[2] *PC2012-14, judge, Wenzhou, August 2012; PC2013-48, Shenzhen judge, Shanghai, May 2013.*

[3] CCP Organization Department and the CCP Personnel Department Notice on Issuing the Opinion Regarding Party State Organs Implementing Competitive Promotion (*Zhongzubu, Renshibuguanyuyinfa "guanyudangzhengjiguantuixingjingzhengshanggang de yijian" de tongzhi*) of July 23, 1998, Central Organization Document Number 33 [1998] (copy on file with author).

[4] Notice on Issuing the Opinion Regarding Party State Organs Implementing Competitive Promotion, Central Organization Document Number 33 [1998].

adjustment.[5] Additionally, although the opinion states that in principle, the use of competitive procedures is confined to the promotion of cadres within units, state units are allowed to host transparent promotion competitions open to candidates within a system, department, or the general public.[6] Not long after the 1998 opinion, the Law on Civil Servants (*gongwuyuan fa*) became effective (in 2006) and again encouraged more competition and monitoring, holding out the possibility of performance-based rewards for those who might comply.

Judges in the Context of the Chinese Civil Service Bureaucracy

Judges and the court system in the PRC have a complex relationship with "executive branch" government ministries, CCP units, and larger civil service system. In general, broader court personnel decisions and the competitive promotion of judges in China are managed within the nationwide Party–State civil service management system, but some characteristics have differentiated judges from other types of civil servants, even before judicial personnel reforms beginning in 2014.[7] At least during some periods of China's recent reform-era history, the overall number of hierarchical levels, which affects salary and promotion, have been structured differently in courts, as there are only 12 judicial ranking levels, whereas there are 15 corresponding State Council levels (Shen, 1998). Additionally, Chinese judges have traditionally worn several "hats": They are concomitantly judges (*faguan*), civil servants (*gongwuyuan*), and cadres (*ganbu*). As one judge noted, the term "civil servant" refers to a judge's personnel identity (*shenfen*), which emphasizes a civil servant's individual position within the system, whereas the term "judge" (*faguan*) refers to one's professional position (*zhiwei*), which emphasizes an employee's professional specialty, e.g., a judge's expertise in handling and making decisions regarding legal disputes (Z. Liu, 2014, pp. 3–5).[8] A key element of recent reforms, however, is recognizing that a judge (*faguan*)

[5] Notice on Issuing the Opinion Regarding Party State Organs Implementing Competitive Promotion, Central Organization Document Number 33 [1998].

[6] Notice on Issuing the Opinion Regarding Party State Organs Implementing Competitive Promotion, Central Organization Document Number 33 [1998].

[7] This section describes the judicial and civil service systems as they stood in 2012–2013. A host of new regulations and policies on the relationship between judges and the civil service hierarchy was introduced in 2014, and these are discussed in more detail in Chapter 7.

[8] *PC2013-4, judge, Shenzhen, January 2013.*

is not just another "official" (*guan*), as the *People's Daily* has pointed out (Lü & Wang, 2014).

Despite these differences, the PRC Civil Servant's Law has often been the basic legislation governing the duties, authority, and management of judges, procurators, and other civil servants in China.[9] At least before reforms in 2014–2016, overall policymaking authority regarding promotion standards pertaining to both judges and other civil servant personnel was controlled by the CCP OD, under the supervision of the CCP Central Committee and Politburo. The OD handles civil service management, and these policies are implemented by the Civil Service Bureau of the Ministry of Human Resources and Social Security (formerly the Ministry of Personnel) (Burns & Wang, 2010, pp. 60–61). Competitive judicial promotion refers not only to rankings and cadre status within the court bureaucracy but also to rankings within the administrative bureaucracy. Depending on the court, judicial promotions to mid-ranking cadre status have generally referred to promotions to levels as high as "department-level" (*chuji*) (Pieke, 2009, p. 31).

The complex and overlapping nature of the court and civil service system reflects that the meanings of seemingly simple terms such as "civil servant," "cadre," and "judge" have proven notoriously elusive, especially in the post-Mao reform era (Brødsgaard, 2012; Pieke, 2009, p. 28). Historically, in communist one-Party systems, the concept of "cadre" (*ganbu*) has denoted a person's role in the workers' revolution – the core components of a Leninist vanguard Party (Brødsgaard, 2012, pp. 71–72). In contemporary China, "cadre" has developed a less ideological and more bureaucratic meaning, although there continues to be an implicit understanding that cadres must be both "red" and "expert": that is, they must be committed to foundational CCP principles and be professionally capable (Pieke, 2009, p. 29). Leading cadres (*lingdao ganbu*) in particular must exhibit ideological commitment to the CCP, as approximately 95 percent of such cadres are CCP members compared to 38 percent of the general cadre population (Brødsgaard, 2012, p. 74). In this context, the competitive promotion of China's judicial cadres is particularly significant because it is the process by which entry-level government employees advance to "official" cadre status[10] and become an integrated part of "the backbone of the political system" in the PRC (Brødsgaard, 2012, pp. 73–74).

[9] PRC Civil Servant Law of 2006, Article I, Clause 3.

[10] *PC2012-14, judge, Wenzhou, August 2012.*

The Process of Competitive Judicial Promotion

The 1998 Opinion on competitive promotion calls for eight steps that "generally should be" used during competitions: (1) distribution of information regarding the vacancy and requirements for the open post, (2) promotion candidates personally signing up or receiving a nomination for participating in the promotion competition, (3) the inspection of the qualifications of each candidate, (4) an exam by which each candidate is tested regarding the basic knowledge necessary to handle the duties of the new position, (5) those who pass the exam provide a speech introducing themselves and explaining their qualifications for promotion, (6) a "democratic vote" is administered regarding the candidates who pass the exam, (7) an "organizational inspection" occurs, whereby the remaining candidates are inspected for their "ethics, ability, industriousness, and achievements" (*de, neng, qin, ji*), and (8) confirmation, whereby the Party Group makes promotion decisions regarding the final candidates.

The stated objective of competitive promotion of judicial cadres is to "encourage leadership" and produce a pool of talented cadres while making "expanding democracy" the reform direction (Deng, 2001; Wei, 2010). At the local level, the highest court in an urban municipality guides the basic structure of the competitive promotion system through one-step down oversight, with Intermediate and Basic-level Court core groups possessing leeway to tweak their competitive promotion plans subject to the approval of the Party OD at the corresponding local level.[11]

According to these guidelines, several steps should be used during promotion competitions, including basic human resource management standards, plus exams, "democratic" voting on candidates, speeches, and organizational inspections. Interviews revealed more specific information regarding each step of the process as practiced at the local level, including additional procedural steps (e.g., formulation of a specific plan to begin the competition), steps gradually phased out in some localities (e.g., candidate speeches), the methods by which the list of candidates is narrowed, and the content of organizational inspections and democratic votes. Before nomination, the relevant court formulates a specific plan (*fang'an*) each time it seeks to conduct a promotion competition.[12] Then,

[11] *PC2013-53, judge, Shanghai, May 2013; PC2012-49, judge, Shanghai, December 2012; PC2013-50, political-legal cadre, Chengdu, May 2013; PC2013-51, judge, Chengdu, May 2013.*

[12] *PC2013-3, judge, Shenzhen, January 2013; PC2013-17, judge, Shanghai, March 2013.*

the court's CCP Core Group, in conjunction with the court's Political Department (*zhengzhibu*),[13] drafts a plan for competitive promotion, which must be eventually approved by the Party OD at the corresponding local level before the advertisement of vacancies and the beginning of the competition.[14]

After the court has obtained approval to implement a particular competitive promotion plan, candidates for the vacancies can nominate themselves (*baoming*) for the promotion competition, then the court's internal Political Department (*zhengzhibu*) screens them for the satisfaction of eligibility prerequisites (*fuhe tiaojian*). There are three types of prerequisites: (1) experience, which usually refers to completing at least 2–3 years of work at one rank lower than that for which promotion is sought, (2) age, which prohibit those older than 50–55 years old from competing for mid-ranking cadre promotion, and (3) work performance and discipline, designed to screen candidates based on superlative work performance (*chengji*) and history of CCP or government disciplinary proceedings (Wei, 2010).[15] Thus, the "fulfilling prerequisites" stage of self-nomination acts less as a political filter and more as a perfunctory check to see whether the candidates have worked long enough (usually three years for mid-level cadres) to apply for promotion.[16]

Candidates who satisfy the prerequisites compete for promotion in three major ways: written exam (*kaoshi* or *bishi*), "assessment" (*kaoping*), and "inspection" (*kaocha*).[17] The written test requires the composition of a written judgment and case analysis, and primarily tests legal application and basic writing skills. Candidates are given either a passing or failing grade.[18] The "assessment" includes a mock hearing (*tingshen*) and panel

[13] This observation is based on interviews of judges and the descriptions of various intermediate-level courts including those in Shenzhen and Chengdu. Depending on the court, the Political Department might have a subdivision called the Cadre Office (*ganburenshi chu* or *ganbu chu*) that specifically handles competitive promotion matters. *PC2013-17, judge, Shanghai, March 2013.*

[14] *PC2013-4, judge, Shenzhen, January 2013*; Shenzhen Intermediate Court Division and Vice Division Leading Cadre Competitive Promotion Implementation Rules; (Deng, 2001).

[15] *PC2012-49, judge, Shanghai, December 2012; PC2013-18, judge, Shanghai, March 2013*; Opinion Regarding Party State Organs Implementing Competitive Promotion, Organization Department Issuing Number 33 [1998]).

[16] *PC2013-1, judge, Shenzhen, January 2013; PC2013-4, judge, Shenzhen, January 2013.*

[17] In other government units, competitive promotion procedures differ slightly, with "peer evaluations" (*minzhupingyi*) and audits of previous performance acting to shorten candidate lists (Edin, 2003).

[18] *PC2013-1, judge, Shenzhen, January 2013; PC2013-18, judge, Shanghai, March 2013.*

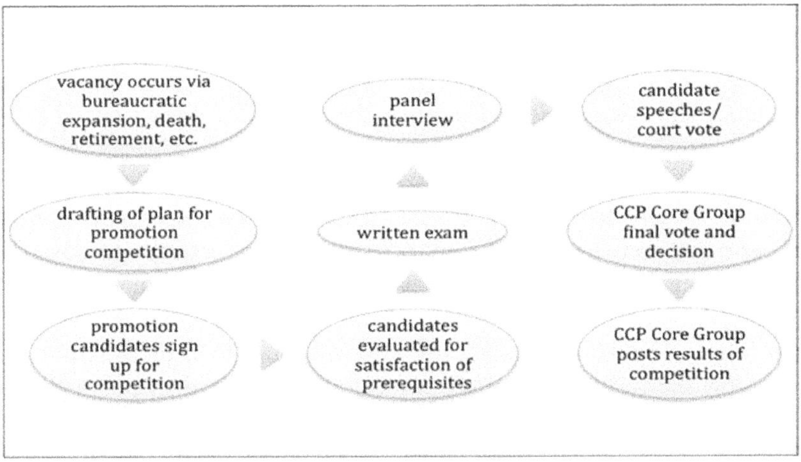

Figure 5.1 Summary of general procedure for promoting mid-level judicial cadres (2012–2014).

interview (*dabian*) with the court's CCP Core Group (Wei, 2010). The panel interview directly examines mid-level candidates regarding both adjudication (e.g., "What are some of the problems with this court's adjudication procedure and do you have any suggestions for resolving these problems") and administrative management (e.g., "If a member of your division has a family problem that begins affecting the division's work, how would you handle such a situation?") (Deng, 2001).

The "inspection" follows, in which candidates face a vote by all of their court colleagues based on several factors, which can include candidates' personal disposition, a 10-minute candidate speech to the court recommending oneself for promotion, or candidates' work histories (Wei, 2010). More specifically regarding the within-court casting of votes, the pool of "eligible voters" generally is all civil servants (*gongwuyuan*) in a particular court.[19] After the CCP Core Group wraps up the promotion process, the Court posts the results of the competition within the court (Wei, 2010). Figure 5.1 summarizes the general process of competitive promotion in China's courts, as of 2014.

The final stage of the promotion competition generally involves a selection from approximately 1.5–2 candidates remaining in competition for

[19] *PC2013-3, judge, Shenzhen, January 2013; PC2013-4, judge, Shenzhen, January 2013; PC2012-49, judge, Shanghai, December 2012.*

a single cadre position (i.e., "1½" means that if there are two vacancies, then there are three final candidates) (Ma, 2011).[20] The fundamental significance of the competitive procedures is that the competition, which includes the "democratic vote" (*minzhu ceping*) of one's judicial colleagues and a written examination, narrows the pool of promotion candidates, thus eroding the CCP Core Group and the local CCP's ability to directly appoint political favorites. Thus, the newer competitive promotion system increasingly employs merit-based selection methods, the pool of judges is evaluated using more formal and transparent means, and the local court CCP Core Group can only select the promotion winner after the candidate pool has already been winnowed to 1.5 or 2 finalists. By reducing the court CCP Core Group's ability to use overtly political criteria to appoint judges, competitive promotion procedures have diminished the overall influence of Party institutions and political leaders in the process of selecting mid-ranking judicial cadres.

As it relates to the hierarchy within each court, promotion procedures have varied between levels of the within-court judicial hierarchy (which I have simplified and listed in ascending order in Table 2.2). The promotion of judges to "mid-ranking" cadre status generally refers to the promotion of an associate judge to a division vice chief or a division chief position, which reflects a significant promotion from case handling to managerial duties, and corresponds directly with the competition in high-end legal labor markets for mid-level professionals with three to five years of experience mentioned in Chapter 4. Mid-ranking judicial cadres have tended to possess greater authority relative to ordinary judges; for instance, Division Chiefs possessed authority with Court Presidents to select the Chief Judge for judicial panels (*heyiting*) that hear individual cases under Article 10 of the Law on Organization of Courts.[21] The significance of this mid-level promotion is also reflected in the original Judges Law passed in 1995 (i.e., before the 2019 draft amendments to the law), which states that mid-level cadres should possess practical judicial experience (Article 12), and Division Chiefs and Associate Division Chiefs are situated in the mid-stratum of the court hierarchy, above "Judges" (*shenpan yuan*) and "Assistant Judges" (*zhuli shenpanyuan*) (Articles 3, 11, 12).

[20] *PC2013-3, judge, Shenzhen, January 2013; PC2012-48, judge, Chengdu, December 2012; PC2012-49, judge, Shanghai, December 2012; PC2013-17, judge, Shanghai, March 2013.*

[21] The reference here is to the version of the Law on the Organization of Courts effective during the period studied in this book (i.e., pre-2016); recent amendments to this law began in 2018.

Mid-ranking competitive promotion procedures are unique, as the process for advancing up the judicial hierarchy differs for judges who are not mid-level cadres. First, when promoting candidates from clerk (*shuji yuan*) to Assistant Judge and from Assistant Judge to Associate Judge (*shenpanyuan*), the votes of promotion candidates' colleagues were not considered in the overall candidate evaluation process.[22] However, candidates for these lower-level positions still participate in the nomination, exam, assessment, and inspection processes, after which CCP Core Groups directly select candidates.[23] Competitive procedures are not used, however, for promotions to court leadership positions such as Court President and Vice President.

Despite the similarities between the competitive promotion of Chinese judges and other civil servants, there are important differences between cadres working in State Council Ministries and in a Political–Legal bureaucracy (*zhengfa xitong*) like a court. Previous studies have found, for instance, that competitive promotion procedures exist primarily in central government bureaucratic units; in my fieldwork, however, I find that some variety of competitive promotion procedures are used throughout municipal, provincial, and district levels (Burns & Wang, 2010, pp. 66–67). Moreover, a few other studies discuss "mid-ranking" cadres, focusing instead on other cadre strata such as "basic cadres" (*jiceng ganbu*), "regular cadres" (*yiban ganbu*), "non-leading cadres" (*feilingdao ganbu*), "leading cadres" (*lingdao ganbu*), and "high level cadres" (*gaoji ganbu*) (Barnett & Vogel, 1967; Pieke, 2009, pp. 28–29). After bureaucratic reforms in the 1990s, high-level appointments like these appear to be principally determined via *kuai*-level authority, that is, by the CCP Committee one level above the court to which the president or vice president will be installed (Z. Liu, 2012). The court unit one level above that which the president will be installed (i.e., via *tiao*-level, vertical lines of bureaucratic authority)[24] provides administrative assistance to the judicial appointment process, and the CCP Committee at the same level of the new president's court provides suggestions on potential candidates (Z. Liu, 2012).

[22] *PC2013-4, judge, Shenzhen, January 2013.* For example, this interviewee could not remember casting a vote during a competition for promotion to an ordinary judge position, but clearly remembers casting votes on competitions for promotions from ordinary judge to cadre-level judge.

[23] *PC2013-4, judge, Shenzhen, January 2013.*

[24] Both Chinese and American scholars have discussed the importance of *tiao* (vertical) and *kuai* (horizontal) bureaucratic relationships (Liu, 2012; Lieberthal and Oksenberg, 1988).

The separate classifications for mid-level and high-level cadres reflect that the promotion of Intermediate-Level Court Presidents is subject to *nomenklatura* procedures (Peerenboom, 2002, pp. 284–285), which govern the highest stratum of China's Party–State hierarchy. Like other *nomenklatura* positions, Intermediate Court Presidents generally must be CCP members (Burns & Wang, 2010, p. 61; Manion, 1985); conversely, CCP membership is not generally required for promotion to mid-level judicial cadre status, similar to the treatment of other non-leading cadres (Brødsgaard, 2012, p. 74).

The Effects of High-End Demand on Judicial Selection and Promotion: Case Study Comparison

Local Variation in Competitive Judicial Promotion

As discussed in Chapter 2, I assess the degree of competition, routinization, and transparency to measure the concept of personal judicial autonomy and gain an understanding of the extent to which judicial terms of office are "reasonably secure" and when judicial appointments and promotions are relatively depoliticized, fair, and carried out according to pre-established rules (Peerenboom, 2010, p. 71). This method of measurement illuminates whether courts' implementation of competitive judicial promotion mechanisms can credibly disrupt the authority of CCP units and other political leaders from packing the courts with friendly judges – that is, directly and unilaterally selecting preferred judicial candidates – which was the standard practice throughout at least the 1990s under the "nominated appointment" system for selecting mid-level judicial cadres (Wei, 2010).[25]

During fieldwork, I observed that each city's courts are advised to implement "competitive promotion" (*jingzheng shanggang*) procedures for mid-ranking judges, but the degree of competition and the level of routinization of these judicial promotion procedures varied distinctly between localities. Shanghai's competitive promotion court institutions are particularly competitive and routinized, with mid-ranking judicial vacancies throughout the court hierarchy open to competition from any judicial applicant within the city. When Shanghai Courts host "all-city" competitions, local CCP authorities' ability to directly influence promotion outcomes is fragmented and diminished by the results of exams,

[25] *PC2013-1, judge, Shenzhen, January 2013.*

interviews, and performance evaluations used to select promotion candidates. A streamlined process has also arisen in recent years to allow larger candidate pools in judicial promotion competitions. By contrast, judicial promotion competitions in my other two case study sites, Shenzhen and Chengdu, were limited primarily to applicants within each individual court, and in Chengdu, competitive promotion procedures were sometimes ignored. Keeping promotion competitions internal to a single court allows local political elites to exert more direct, personal influence on promotion decisions.[26]

As covered in more detail in the case histories below, judicial promotion systems typically began to take on more local characteristics of acceleration and expansion starting in the early to mid-2000s. For instance, the competitive promotion system used in Shanghai, which has been distinguished by its expansive "all-city" promotion recruitment competitions first implemented in 2008, opens vacancies at the intermediate court level and above to any qualifying judge in the jurisdiction, i.e., basic court judges are authorized to compete for promotions to intermediate and high courts. In other intermediate courts like those in Shenzhen and Chengdu, competitions for promotion of mid-level cadres have been confined within each individual court, with division chief and vice division chief positions filled from the ranks of qualified assistant and associate judges. Participation levels in these promotion competitions have been robust, and competition for promotions has been particularly popular among younger, District-level judges. More retrospectively, it was only after 1992, when lawyer internationalization and privatization were rebooted and the legal profession developed more fully and unevenly, that the dynamics of the legal profession began pressuring courts to recalibrate various institutional practices related to judges' decisional autonomy.

If qualified, mid-level judges can easily quit their jobs and find lucrative local employment as mid-level law firm associates, court leaders are more likely to strategically reform promotion mechanisms in an attempt to retain these capable judges; after all, such judges can help improve courts' overall CQAS scores – and court leaders' own chances for further promotion. This argument links competition for mid-level legal professionals in high-end law firm markets and judicial designs in Chinese courts at the same level of the professional legal hierarchy. Examining specific patterns

[26] *PC2013-1, judge, Shenzhen, January 2013; PC2013-3, judge, Shenzhen, January 2013.*

of competitive promotion procedures of mid-level judges[27] between the cases of Shanghai, Shenzhen, and Chengdu, I find that the degrees of merit-based competition, transparency, and rule-based routinization of these judicial promotion procedures varied distinctly between localities.

The promotion of judges to mid-ranking cadre status generally refers to the promotion of an associate judge to a division vice chief (*futingzhang*) or a division chief (*tingzhang*) position, which reflects a significant promotion from case handling to managerial duties. Reaching this level usually requires between 5 and 10 years of judicial experience – similar to the experience of higher-paid associates or consultants in foreign firms located in high-end law firm markets (S. Liu, 2011b, p. 136). Mid-ranking judicial cadres possess greater authority relative to ordinary judges, as mid-level cadres should possess practical judicial experience,[28] Division Chiefs and Division Vice Chiefs are situated in the mid-stratum of the court hierarchy, above "Judges" and "Assistant Judges,"[29] and Division Chiefs have possessed authority with Court Presidents to select the Chief Judge for judicial panels (*heyiting*) that hear individual cases.[30]

Local court implementation of competitive promotion can vary on several dimensions, of which the following are the most significant: First, the degree of competition and transparency (i.e., in each locality, do lower court judges have the ability to compete for promotion to higher courts? How widely are promotion opportunities posted?); and second, the degree of routinization of rule-based procedures (i.e., is competitive promotion used for every mid-level judicial cadre vacancy? Have courts streamlined their promotion competitions to accommodate the participation of more candidates?).[31] Promotion procedures are less meritocratic and more subject to the influence of political leaders when the promotion procedures are contained within an individual court (e.g., Shenzhen and

[27] Promotion procedures have differed for judges who are not mid-level cadres. Before 2014, competitive procedures were not used for promotions to courts' top leadership positions such as Court President and Vice President, nor were they used for lower level appointments from Assistant Judge (*zhulishenpanyuan*) to Associate Judge (*shenpanyuan*). High-level judicial appointments have been primarily determined by the CCP Committee one level above the court to which the president or vice president will be installed with the court at one level above providing administrative oversight (Z. Liu, 2012).

[28] Judges' Law of the PRC (*Zhonghuarenmingongheguofaguan fa*), Article 12.

[29] Judges' Law, Articles 3, 11.

[30] Law on Organization of Courts of the PRC (*Zhonghuarenmingongheguofayuanzuzhi fa*), Article 10.

[31] *PC2013-3, judge, Shenzhen, January 2013; PC2013-4, judge, Shenzhen, January 2013.*

Chengdu), which allows CCP organs within courts to act more directly as conduits for local political leaders such as local Party secretaries, local mayors, or local governors (who often serve these posts simultaneously). By contrast, when Provincial High Courts and Intermediate Courts host "all-city" competitions (e.g., in Shanghai), each Court's Party organs and local political leaders possess fragmented and diminished authority to influence promotion outcomes. Party leaders would also seem to possess more authority over promotions when the courts simply do not use the competitive procedures on a routine basis.

Shanghai: Unique Opportunities for Promotion to Higher Courts

Among the three case studies analyzed in this book, Shanghai's court institutions are the most competitive and routinized, with mid-ranking judicial vacancies throughout the court hierarchy open to competition from any judicial applicant within the city, and competitive procedures used for every judicial vacancy. Because gaps remain between formal authority and local implementation of competitive judicial promotion systems even in urban areas exhibiting relatively similar levels of development, the important research questions at the local level involve whether and to what extent local leaders implement central directives to reform civil service promotion mechanisms.

The competitive promotion system used in Shanghai has been unique for its expansive "all-city" promotion recruitment competitions, which appear to have begun in 2008. Like other courts, candidates for promotion to mid-level judicial cadre posts in Shanghai's Intermediate Courts must participate in the competitive promotion process; however, unlike my other case study sites, vacancies at the intermediate court level and above can be filled by any qualifying judge in the jurisdiction, i.e., basic court judges are authorized to compete for promotions to intermediate and high courts. In other intermediate courts like those in Shenzhen and Chengdu, competitions for promotion of mid-level cadres are confined within each individual court, with division chief and vice division chief positions filled from the ranks of qualified assistant and associate judges. From 2010 to 2012, the Shanghai Intermediate and High Courts conducted several promotion competitions in which judges across the city competed (Wei, 2010).[32] Participation levels in promotion competitions were robust: For five advertised positions at the Intermediate

[32] *PC2012-49, judge, Shanghai, December 2012.*

and High Court levels in 2010, there were 106 applicants from courts across Shanghai – an average of 21 candidates for each position (Wei, 2010). Competition for promotions has been particularly popular among younger, District-level judges.[33]

Further, according to Shanghai High Court Party Core Group Member and Political Department Chief Wu Xielin, basic court judges can compete for open positions in the Shanghai Intermediate Court, and positions as senior as the High Court Department Vice Chief are also open to all-city competition (Wei, 2010). These "all-city" competitions were initiated by the Shanghai High Court, which pressured Shanghai's court party core groups to "broaden the horizons" of cadre selection, add competitiveness to judicial promotion, and invigorate the cadre selection system (Wei, 2010).[34]

Additionally, judges in Shanghai told me that competitive promotion procedures are used every time they have a vacancy for a mid-level judicial cadre position, suggesting that the use of competitive promotion has become routine in Shanghai.[35] Competitive promotion systems in Shanghai have also been streamlined, with candidates for promotion no longer required to present a speech in front of the whole court describing why they fulfill the conditions for promotion to mid-level cadre status.[36] Candidate speeches have been frequently cited by my interview subjects as repetitive exercises that provide little new information and waste valuable work time; accordingly, candidate speeches in other intermediate courts have also been eliminated in recent years, and several judges in those jurisdictions have suggested to me that the number of promotion candidates became so large that it was not feasible to hear a speech from each candidate.[37] Although this might limit the candidates' campaigning capacities, it also indicates that some courts have reformed their competitive promotion procedures to allow for the participation of a broader group of candidates than otherwise possible.

[33] *PC2012-49, judge, Shanghai, December 2012.*

[34] *PC2012-49, judge, Shanghai, December 2012; PC2013-49, judge, Shanghai, May 2013; PC2013-67, judge, Shanghai, July 2013.*

[35] *PC2012-49, judge, Shanghai, December 2012; PC2013-21, Shanghai judge, Shanghai, March 2013; PC2013-22, judge, Shanghai, March 2013.*

[36] *PC2013-21, judge, Shanghai, March 2013; PC2012-49, judge, Shanghai, December 2012.*

[37] *PC2012-49, judge, Shanghai, December 2012; PC2013-21, judge, Shanghai, March 2013; PC2013-22, judge, Shanghai, March 2013.*

Shenzhen: Reform with Limits

Unlike Shanghai, Shenzhen's Basic Court judges could not compete for mid-level cadre position vacancies at the intermediate or high court level; instead, the Shenzhen Intermediate Court filled such vacancies using within-court promotion competitions by which lower ranking assistant and associate judges competed for open division vice chief or division chief positions. Although Shenzhen's competitive promotion system has been used since the early 2000s and has undergone several reforms, some judges in the Shenzhen Basic Courts told me that they would welcome an opportunity to compete for promotion opportunities at the intermediate and high court levels, but these opportunities were not available to them (as of 2014). Additionally, these judges indicated that they have considered leaving their positions as judges to work in local law firms because they could probably have earned a higher income as a lawyer than as a judge.[38]

Regarding routinization and streamlining, the use of competitive promotion in Shenzhen began in approximately 2001, and since then, the Shenzhen Intermediate Court has used a similar competitive promotion system every time mid-level judicial cadre vacancies occur.[39] Although multiple-year intervals between mid-level cadre vacancies are possible, one judge guessed that on average there are about four vacancies per year.[40] Further, candidate speeches were eliminated in the early 2000s, as judges suggested that candidate speeches took too much time, provided colleagues with no information that they did not already know, and that eliminating speeches would allow competitions to accommodate larger applicant pools (see Deng, 2001, p. 17).[41] This explanation is consistent with transcripts of candidate speeches from Shenzhen competitions in the early 2000s: Out of 27 candidates for mid-level judicial promotion, all candidates spent a significant portion of their speech providing a personal and educational background, information which is already generally available to their colleagues during the whole-court vote; further,

[38] *PC2013-1, judge, Shenzhen, January 2013; PC2013-3, judge, Shenzhen, January 2013; PC2013-4, judge, January 2013.*

[39] *PC2013-1, judge, Shenzhen, January 2013; PC2013-3, judge, Shenzhen, January 2013; PC2013-4, judge, January 2013.*

[40] *PC2013-1, judge, Shenzhen, January 2013; PC2013-3, judge, Shenzhen, January 2013; PC2013-4, judge, January 2013.*

[41] *PC2013-1, judge, Shenzhen, January 2013; PC2013-3, judge, Shenzhen, January 2013; PC2013-4, judge, January 2013; PC2013-45, judge, Shenzhen, April 2013.*

several candidates indicated in their speeches that they were unwilling to discuss their positive personal traits despite such discussion being a primary objective of the speeches (Deng, 2001, pp. 81–82).

Chengdu: Sporadic, Outmoded Reform

The distinct model of the Chengdu court system's promotion competitions has been sporadic, nonroutinized use of competitive promotion mechanisms, without the expansive, all-city competitions found in Shanghai. Chengdu's lack of an all-city promotion system by which basic court cadres have opportunities to compete for promotions to higher-level courts reinforces Shanghai's uniqueness in this regard. In both the Shenzhen and Chengdu Intermediate Courts, judicial promotion of mid-ranking cadres has been confined to within-court opportunities, effectively introducing a promotion ceiling for the great majority of basic court judges in these localities. At least one judge in Chengdu commented to me that for a variety of reasons, she no longer seeks promotion opportunities within her own court.[42] At the same time, some judges in Chengdu's Intermediate Court felt that even the sporadic use of competitive promotion is preferable to the promotion system used prior to 2002.[43] Before then, the Political Department would unilaterally recommend the relevant promotion candidates to the court's Party Core group for a final decision on promotion, without conducting written exams, panel interviews, voting, or candidate speeches (similar to the direct nomination and appointment system described above).[44]

With respect to routinization, Chengdu's Basic and Intermediate Courts do not use competitive procedures for every mid-level cadre vacancy that occurs. Instead, a court's leaders in the Political Department and CCP Core Group have made case-by-case determinations whether to use competitive procedures to fill mid-level cadre vacancies.[45] Particularly if sudden vacancies in the Chengdu Intermediate Court occur, personnel of equal rank can be installed as "acting" (*daili*) Division Chiefs or Vice Division Chiefs for multiyear periods, in lieu of competitive promotion.[46] Other interviews suggested that, in general, competitive promotion for

[42] *PC2013-12, judge, Chengdu, January 2013.*
[43] *PC2013-8, judge, Chengdu, January 2013; PC2013-38, judge, Chengdu, April 2013.*
[44] *PC2013-7, judge, Chengdu, January 2013; PC2013-38, judge, Chengdu, April 2013.*
[45] *PC2013-12, judge, Chengdu, January 2013; PC2013-38, judge, Chengdu, April 2013.*
[46] *PC2013-7, judge, Chengdu, January 2013.*

Table 5.1. *Review of variation in competitive promotion across urban court case studies (2012–2014)*

	Merit-based competition and transparency	Routinization of rule-based use
Shanghai	High competition and transparency	High routinization, used for every opening and streamlining reforms implemented
Shenzhen	Medium competition and transparency	High routinization, used for every opening and streamlining implemented
Chengdu	Low competition and transparency	Low routinization, sporadic use; no streamlining implemented

mid-ranking cadres has not become a routine method of promotion in the Chengdu Intermediate Court.[47] By contrast, when I asked Shanghai and Shenzhen judges whether competitive promotion procedures were used for each mid-level vacancy, I received unequivocal affirmative responses.[48]

When the Chengdu Intermediate Court has conducted promotion competitions, all candidates for mid-level cadre positions have been required to present a speech, which as indicated above does not accommodate a large number of candidates for promotion competition.[49] Speeches in Chengdu's Intermediate Court have been designed to address candidates' judicial abilities and why they personally possess the skills of a mid-level cadre; at both the Chengdu Basic and Intermediate Court levels, candidate speeches were used as part of competitive promotion procedures, and judges noted that these speeches made it difficult to accommodate increasing numbers of promotion candidates.[50] Table 5.1 reviews the variation in competitive promotion procedures across my three case studies, describing how the practice of judicial promotion has been most competitive and routinized in Shanghai and least so in Chengdu.

[47] *PC2012-48, judge, Chengdu, December 2012; PC2013-7, judge, Chengdu, January 2013.*

[48] *PC2013-3, judge, Shenzhen, January 2013; PC2012-49, judge, Shanghai, December 2012; PC2013-17, judge, Shanghai, March 2013.*

[49] *PC2013-7, judge, Chengdu, January 2013; PC2013-38, judge, Chengdu, April 2013.*

[50] *PC2013-7, judge, Chengdu, January 2013; PC2013-38, judge, Chengdu, April 2013.*

Transparency Rankings: Case Study Comparison (2012–2013)

In addition to creating more merit-based promotion procedures, data from 2012 to 2013 also indicate that court leaders across China have attempted to render judges' career trajectories and work environments more professionalized by implementing transparency mandates, which judicial interviewees considered when contemplating their career options.[51] To assess courts' compliance with transparency guidelines, I examine transparency index scores from the Chinese Academy of Social Sciences (CASS), which assesses courts for the extent to which they provide timely information to the public via online websites – as ordered by the SPC (CASS: Chinese Academy of Social Sciences Legal Studies Department Rule of Law National Status Research Group, 2012). Rankings of the transparency levels of courts across my three case study cities are consistent with variations in the practice of competitive promotion in these cities. The 2012–2013 CASS Transparency Index ranks courts' compliance with transparency mandates across three evaluation issue areas: Online transparency regarding courts' general information (20 points), guidance regarding court procedure for litigants (15), judgment information (25), enforcement information (15), judicial/court (*sifa*) statistics (25), and measures which cumulatively yield a 100-point, composite transparency index (Li & Tian, 2013, p. 216). Although quantitative rankings can be susceptible to distortion in assessing transparency (see Michener, 2015), these rankings can serve as useful measures for corroborating this book's qualitative assessments of judges' decisional autonomy, and they are consistent with my findings regarding the competitiveness of mid-ranking promotion competitions. The degree to which a court prioritizes transparency in the administration of various court functions indicates the willingness of a court to act in accordance with pre-established rules and guidelines encouraging transparency handed down by the SPC. Although these CASS indices should not be viewed in isolation or as direct proxies for judicial autonomy, they can still serve a helpful triangulating function to assess the consistency and credibility of local accounts of competitive promotion presented in the previous section.

As the CASS researchers note in the report on the transparency rankings and indexes, judicial transparency "raises the level of judicial decision-making, protects judicial authority, protects public trust,

[51] *PC2013-64, judge, Shenzhen, July 2013; PC2013-53, judge, Shanghai, May 2013.*

prevents judicial corruption, and ultimately realizes the important meaning of realizing judicial justice" (Lin Li & Tian, 2013, p. 215). The CASS rankings also assess courts regarding the extent to which they provide timely information to the public via online websites, as ordered by the SPC (CASS: Chinese Academy of Social Sciences Legal Studies Department Rule of Law National Status Research Group, 2012). The CASS Legal Studies Research Department's Rule by Law Research Group conducted the data collection and analysis used to produce the transparency rankings, which reference publicly available court website information as a touchstone (Lin Li & Tian, 2013, p. 215). The Research Group is comprised of scholars from CASS as well as from the Chinese University of Politics and Law (*Renmin Zhengfa Daxue*) and received input from judges as lawyers in assembling the rankings (Lin Li & Tian, 2013, p. 215). According to the report, "judicial transparency" refers to every aspect of adjudication and information related to adjudication that is released to litigants and to the public, but also excludes information regarding state secrets, trade secrets, private personal information, and other information that might influence the normal judging of disputes in courts (Lin Li & Tian, 2013, p. 215).

During 2012, the CASS Research Group conducted a quantitative assessment of the judicial transparency situation of the high courts in 26 provinces and centrally administered cities, and in the intermediate courts of 43 relatively large cities (Li & Tian, 2013, pp. 215–217). The CASS analysis reveals that local courts' judicial transparency reflects the extent to which local courts are complying with central mandates from the State Council and the SPC to release public information and raise government transparency (Tian, 2012). For example, the Notice of the General Office of the State Council Regarding Improving and Strengthening Government Website Management Work and the SPC Rules Regarding Several Issues of Public Adjudication Government Information for Administrative Cases are both designed to push forward the efforts of courts and other government units to strengthen the meaning of transparency in government management (Tian, 2012). Thus, to the extent that the SPC has pushed courts to be more transparent, the CASS Transparency Indices can illuminate the extent to which local court systems prioritize compliance with central mandates; local variation between localities reflects differences in the degree to which transparency is emphasized in each locality (Tian, 2012).

Shanghai's court transparency index, which tracks consistently with the SPC's internal "national judicial fairness rankings," is higher than

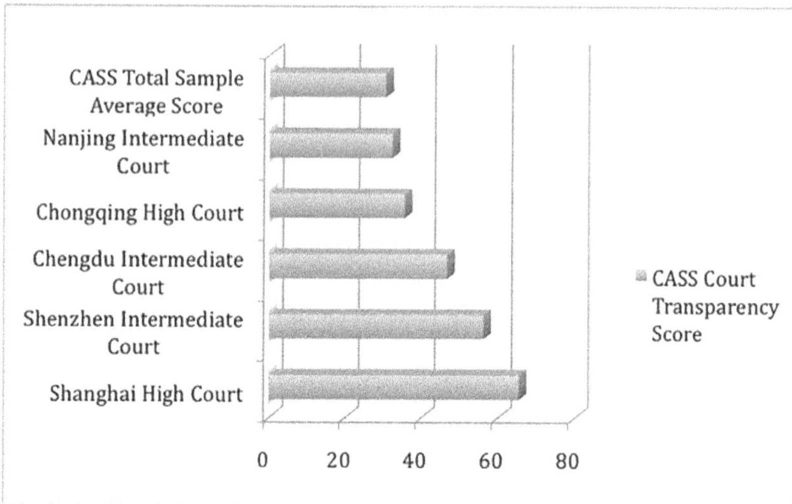

Figure 5.2 Local courts' scores on the 2012–2013 CASS Transparency Index (max score = 100).

those in Shenzhen and Chengdu. Figure 5.2 summarizes these 2012–2013 CASS Transparency Index scores for the highest court in each of my case study localities, providing a measure of local court compliance with the SPC's policies regarding transparency in court politics.

All three highest courts in the cases I studied were considered relatively transparent, judging by the results of the CASS study; however, Shanghai High Court's transparency score (65.5) was higher than that of Shenzhen Intermediate Court (56.25), and Chengdu Intermediate Court (46.75) (Lin Li & Tian, 2013, p. 216). For context, the CASS average score, as well as Nanjing and Chongqing's transparency scores, are included in Figure 5.2, as they are similar in size and national importance to my case study cities.

To synthesize the information regarding judicial transparency presented thus far, Table 5.2 reviews variation in competitive promotion procedures and court transparency, indicating that across my three case studies, the practice of judicial promotion is most competitive and routinized in Shanghai and least so in Chengdu. The competitiveness of Shenzhen's procedures falls between the two other cases. Consistent relative scores are reflected in the CASS Court Transparency Index, whose results are summarized in the right-hand column:

Table 5.2. *Review of variation in competition and transparency across cases (2012–2014)*

	Degree of competitive promotion	CASS transparency assessment
Shanghai	• High levels of promotion competition, with mid-ranking positions open to citywide competitions • Competitive promotion used for every mid-ranking vacancy; mechanisms in place for larger candidate pools	• Overall Transparency Score for Shanghai High Court: 65.5 (out of 100) • All-country top score for transparency of online litigation guide • Medium-high score for transparency of online information regarding the enforcement of damages • High score for transparency of statistical information related to court
Shenzhen	• Lower levels of competition; no ability for lower court judges to compete for promotion to mid-ranking positions at the intermediate court level • As in Shanghai, competitive promotion used for every mid-ranking judicial cadre vacancy; candidate speeches eliminated so as to enlarge the pool for competition	• Overall Transparency Score for Shenzhen High Court: 56.25 (out of 100) • High score for transparency of online litigation guide • High score for transparency of online information regarding the enforcement of damages • Medium-high score for transparency of statistical information related to court
Chengdu	• As in Shenzhen, relatively lower levels of competition; no ability for lower court judges to compete for promotion to mid-ranking positions at intermediate court level • Lower levels of routinization and streamlining; competitive promotion procedures sporadically used for mid-ranking judicial cadre vacancies	• Overall Transparency Score for Shanghai High Court: 46.75 (out of 100) • High score for transparency of online litigation guide • Medium-low score for transparency of online information regarding the enforcement of damages • Low score for transparency of statistical information related to court

Autonomy Reflected in Published Judicial Opinions (2006–2011): Case Study Comparison

The extent to which judges justify their decisions regarding legal disputes constitutes another aspect of Chinese court politics indicative of "judicial autonomy," that is, autonomy *vis-a-vis* the conflicting parties before a court in a given case (Shapiro, 1981). In a statement that can be applied to bureaucrats, administrators, and judges alike, Shapiro notes the importance of the basic requirement to "give reasons" for state actions: "A decision-maker required to give reasons will be more likely to weigh pros and cons carefully before reaching a decision than will a decision-maker able to proceed by simple fiat. In another aspect, giving reasons is a device for enhancing democratic influences on administration by making government more transparent" (Shapiro & Stone Sweet, 2002, p. 229). In this section, I discuss the process of civil litigation to provide necessary background before analyzing a sample of judicial opinions selected from a complete set of IP-related civil law judicial opinions (*panjueshu*) issued between 2006 and 2011 in each of the three case studies analyzed in this book. To gauge the extent to which judges comply with the "giving reasons" requirement and possess the ability to decide cases "in accordance with law and without (undue inappropriate, or illegal) interference from other parties or entities" (Peerenboom, 2010, p. 71), I assess the frequency of citation to statute in this sample of IP judicial opinions. It is not the intention of this study to view these data on judicial opinions by locality as independent proxies of judicial autonomy; rather, these empirical sources can serve a useful corroborating and triangulating role in assessing consistency and credibility of accounts of local judicial promotion reforms presented above from interviews with lawyers and judges.

Historically, political and socio-legal research on Chinese courts has assigned little empirical value to official judicial opinions, owing to their tendency to repeat facts with little legal analysis (Q. Zhang, 2003). Judicial opinions have also been criticized for their lack of authority in a system where the pronouncements of courts in discrete cases provide little precedential value or determinative interpretation of "what the law is" (Howson, 2010). However, things have changed in recent years: The SPC issued a notice in 2005 instructing lower level courts to include legal reasoning in judicial opinions – even those deciding cases in potentially sensitive legal issue areas such as environmental pollution – reflecting that "Even courts in single-party states are often compelled to offer public justification, however glancing, for their actions" (Stern, 2010, p. 80). Further, the Second Five-Year Plan of the SPC issued in 2005 called for establishing a "guiding cases system," whereby such cases would be selected and edited by the SPC to serve as a unifying standard for applying laws to specific factual scenarios. The Guiding Cases Provisions state that SPC guiding cases must be taken into account by lower courts when deciding similar cases (Ahl, 2014, pp. 1, 5). The 2011 SPC notice accompanying the first set of guiding cases indicated further that other higher-level courts within the PRC system can provide guidance on the trial work of courts within their respective jurisdictions by issuing "reference cases" (Ahl, 2014, p. 7).

Additionally, the SPC has required local courts throughout China to establish official websites that publish extensive information related to court work and the litigation process, including written judgments across a variety of legal issue areas (CASS: Chinese Academy of Social Sciences Legal Studies Department Rule of Law National Status Research Group, 2012, p. 33). The ambiguity of these court requirements can be useful from a research standpoint, as it helps identify courts that exceed the suggestions of nonbinding regulations aimed at enhancing transparency and providing the reasons and rationale for judicial decisions. In light of these developments, the analysis of judicial opinions issued by local courts can provide a window onto changes in the PRC judiciary over time, including increases in transparency, professionalism, and overall autonomy, especially in the realm of commercial litigation.

PRC Civil Procedure Laws Relevant to the Analysis of IP-Related Judicial Opinions across Localities

Some context regarding the procedural aspects of filing a civil lawsuit in China is necessary, as an initial matter, to clarify the analysis of judicial opinions across the three case studies discussed below. First, if a dispute that does not directly involve a PRC administrative organ arises between parties, a plaintiff can bring a first instance lawsuit in the civil court system. The plaintiff must be a citizen, legal person, or an organization. In the context of civil IP disputes, an individual citizen or a company with a claim to a specific IP right usually begins the lawsuit by suing the allegedly infringing individual citizen(s) or company/companies.[52] The plaintiff

[52] Civil Procedure Law of the PRC, Article 108. All references are to the version of the Civil Procedure Law as amended in 2012 unless otherwise noted.

must file a complaint with the court to commence a lawsuit, and the complaint must state claim of legal right to judicially ordered relief that can be resolved under the jurisdiction of the relevant court.[53] Jurisdiction in civil lawsuits attaches to the local court where the defendant has established "domicile" or "habitual residence"; in some IP cases, intermediate courts can possess first-instance jurisdiction instead of trial-level courts in situations where the case involves a foreign party, has a major local impact, or has been ordered to be first-instance intermediate court jurisdiction by the SPC.[54] If the complaint is procedurally and jurisdictionally sufficient, the court has 7 days to place the case on the docket, and the defendant has 15 days to file a defense to the plaintiff's complaint.[55]

First-instance civil cases in the PRC are tried either by a collegial panel comprised of an odd number of judges or judicial assessors, or by a summary procedure administered by a single judge.[56] In all of the IP cases analyzed in this chapter, disputes were handled by a collegial panel composed of three members, which included at least one presiding judge (*shenpanzhang*) and an assortment of other types of judicial personnel, including associate judges (*shenpanyuan*), judges "acting in their capacity as judges of disputes" (*daili shenpanyuan*),[57] or people's assessors (*peishenyuan*).

Consistent with the practice in an inquisitorial system of adjudication, the judicial officers on the collegial panel must "carry out investigations and collection of necessary evidence."[58] After evidence is collected or provided to the court, the case is tried in public, as long as the case does not "involve state secrets or personal privacy [and is] to be tried otherwise as provided by the law."[59] In such trials, the court holds a hearing in which the parties can make statements and the court can question the parties, witnesses can provide testimony, and the court can hear and discuss evidence.[60] In this sample of IP cases across Shanghai, Shenzhen, and Chengdu, all cases appear to have been "publicly tried" in this sense of the term. Finally, the court "shall publicly pronounce its judgment in all

[53] Civil Procedure Law of the PRC, Articles 108–110.
[54] Civil Procedure Law of the PRC, Articles 19, 22.
[55] Civil Procedure Law of the PRC, Articles 112, 113.
[56] Civil Procedure Law of the PRC, Article 40.
[57] For a more detailed explanation of the term "*dailishenpanyuan*," see the following blog post: http://blog.sina.com.cn/s/blog_4d9415d801000avo.html (copy of blog post on files with author).
[58] Civil Procedure Law of the PRC, Article 116.
[59] Civil Procedure Law of the PRC, Article 120.
[60] Civil Procedure Law of the PRC, Articles 124–127.

cases, whether publicly tried or not."[61] Ordinarily, courts must conclude cases within six months of docketing, unless an extension is granted by the court president of the court one level above.[62]

Regarding the substantive legal provisions related to the sample of IP-related manufacturing decisions analyzed here, basic guidelines are contained in the Patent Law (*zhuanli fa*) and the Trademark Law (*shangbiao fa*) of the PRC. Under the Patent Law, a person can apply for three different types of patent: (1) invention patent, which refers to "any new technical solution relating to a product, a process or an improvement thereof," (2) utility model, which refers to "any new technical solution relating to a product's shape, structure, or a combination thereof, which is fit for practical use," and (3) design patent, which refers to "any new design of a product's shape, pattern, or a combination thereof, as well as the combination of the color and the shape or pattern of a product, which creates an aesthetic feeling and is fit for industrial application."[63] Under Article 11 of the Patent Law, no entity or individual can benefit from the patent, for manufacturing or other business purposes, except for the patentee or licensees of the patentee. The Patent Administrative Department of the State Council has authority to examine and approve patent applications, and approved patents are valid for a period of ten or twenty years from the date of application, depending on the type of patent at issue.[64] If a dispute arises out of any exploitation of a patent without the permission of the patent holder, the patentee can bring a lawsuit in the court system or request settlement from the patent administrative department.[65]

Regarding trademarks, the Trademark Office of the State Administration for Industry and Commerce (SAIC) possesses authority over trademark registration and administration throughout the country.[66] Any natural person, legal person, or other organization can apply to the SAIC to register a trademark, and holders of trademark registrations have exclusive usage rights over a mark.[67] If any dispute arises regarding the infringement of the right to exclusively use a registered trademark, the relevant party can bring a lawsuit in the PRC court

61 Civil Procedure Law of the PRC, Article 134.

62 Civil Procedure Law of the PRC, Article 135.

63 Patent Law of the PRC, Article 2. (References to the Patent Law are to the version applicable to the period under study, i.e., as amended in 2008, unless otherwise noted.)

64 Patent Law of the PRC, Articles 34–35, 42.

65 Patent Law of the PRC, Article 60.

66 Trademark Law of the PRC, Article 2.

67 Trademark Law of the PRC, Articles 3–4.

system or it can request that the SAIC handle the dispute.[68] If an entity uses a registered trademark or an unregistered, well-known trademark as a trade name, with the purpose of misleading the public, the case can be handled as a claim under the Anti-Unfair Competition Law of the PRC.[69]

Analysis of Judicial Opinions from Civil Cases, 2006–2011

I obtained a comprehensive sample of civil IP-related judicial opinions from the Rouse Corporation, an IP consultancy firm in China, covering the period between 2006 and 2012.[70] Dating back to 2006, Rouse has collected judicial opinions published by courts throughout China, as the SPC encourages the publication of as many IP judgments as possible by courts with IP jurisdiction in China; however, not all IP judgments are published, and whether to publish a judgment remains in the discretion of the issuing court.[71] The Rouse database of judicial opinions was perhaps the earliest comprehensive compilation of judicial opinions across localities in China, making this sample a rich source for better understanding the operation of civil law courts in urban China during the period under study.

In an interview with a researcher at the Rouse Corporation covering the methods used to collect this sample of judicial opinions, I learned that their database of IP opinions and information is an attempt to centralize the collection of every publicly released IP-related court decision issued by local Chinese courts. Rouse used various print and online sources to collect judicial opinions, analyzed the content of the opinions, and provided statistical information regarding trends in IP-related adjudication, with some portions of these data available on their website without charge and other portions available for a fee.[72] Specific online sources that Rouse used to collect the opinions include the Chinalawinfo Company (chinalawinfo.com or lawinfochina.com, an online legal information service established by Beijing University and its Legal Information Center), the LegalStudio, a division of Lexis-Nexis that specializes in Chinese law

[68] Trademark Law of the PRC, Articles 57, 60.

[69] Trademark Law of the PRC, Article 58.

[70] For at least the period under study through the printing of this book, Rouse has provided data on IP-related disputes in the PRC via its website, www.ciela.cn/.

[71] Much of this information is available on the CIELA website, although a subscription is required.

[72] *PC2013-52A, law firm researcher, Beijing, May 2013.*

(legalstudio.com), and Westlaw.[73] According to my interviewee, Rouse's database was updated every day for the duration of my fieldwork.[74]

Across the three case study jurisdictions of Shanghai, Chengdu, and Shenzhen, I obtained a total of 1,452 first-instance IP-related judicial opinions, from which I culled a much smaller sample of 50 comparable cases.[75] To facilitate comparison and to limit the influence of extraneous factors that could influence the length, number of statutory citations, and writing style of the opinions, I focused only on cases dealing with IP disputes in the "Basic Manufacturing" industry, in which I included patent and trademark disputes in industries such as machinery for vegetable oil extraction, bathroom installations, stereo equipment, fabric looms, sewing machines, electric motorbikes, kitchen appliances, personal computer printers, and industrial electronics. Focusing on this type of manufacturing helps eliminate the influences that differences in technology might have on the ways in which judges might write opinions – for instance, judicial opinions on disputes in high-tech industrial sectors would likely require much more detailed explanations of technologies involved in disputes, greater potential for relying on expert witnesses, and greater variation in the need to cite specific legal provisions. Additionally, analyzing disputes arising from business at a specific industrial level such as basic level manufacturing allows me to analyze at least two of the major types of IP cases – patent and trademark infringement – providing coverage across at least part of the variation in different types of civil law commercial disputes.

Based on my reading of IP opinions across cases, there appears to be a common structure and uniform set of information contained in Chinese judicial opinions. The written opinions are generally organized into the following sections: Case title and case number, indicating the division of the court handling the case; identification of the plaintiff and defendant and their legal representatives, if any; the procedural history of the dispute, which begins the text of the opinion; a section outlining the plaintiff's claims and requests for damages; a section summarizing the defendant's response to the plaintiff's claims and any other claims the defendant might have; two sections summarizing the evidence, one each for the plaintiff's and the defendant's evidence; a section on the

[73] *PC2013-52A, law firm researcher, Beijing, May 2013.* More information on Law Info China is available at www.lawinfochina.com/ProductsServices/index.shtm.

[74] *PC2013-52A, law firm researcher, Beijing, May 2013.*

[75] *PC2013-52A, law firm researcher, Beijing, May 2013.*

court's discussion of the evidence presented; a section summarizing the court's decision, in which the facts that support the court's decision are recited (in the cases that I reviewed, statutory citations are usually found in this section); and at the end of the opinion, the court lists its holdings.

Variation across Cases Regarding the Extent to Which the "Giving Reasons Requirement" Is Satisfied

Table 5.3 presents data regarding the sample of first-instance judicial opinions regarding trademark and patent disputes in basic manufacturing sectors, divided across the three case study jurisdictions of Shanghai, Shenzhen, and Chengdu. Three different metrics indicate that Shanghai's judges exhibit the greatest fidelity to the "giving reasons" requirement in their judicial opinions. First, Shanghai judicial opinions exhibit a relatively high degree of citation to formal legal authority, suggesting greater effort to "give reasons" for the decisions made in the legal disputes at bar. As Table 5.3 indicates, first-instance IP-related opinions in Shanghai produce an average of 1.24 more citations per opinion than those in Chengdu, a difference of 20 percent; Shanghai court opinions in my sample cite an average of 0.72 more formal laws per opinion than opinions issued by first-instance courts in Shenzhen, a 12 percent difference. Second, this difference is even more striking when removing the relatively meaningless citations to Article 134 of the Civil Procedure Law, which states simply that cases should be heard publicly, subject only to a small number of exceptions inapplicable to the case opinions in my sample (e.g., "A people's court shall try civil cases openly, except those involving any state secret or individual privacy or as otherwise provided by law. Divorce cases and cases involving any trade secret may be tried in camera upon application of the parties"). Setting aside these citations, Shanghai judicial opinions cited 1.71 formal legal provisions more per opinion than did written opinions in similar cases issued in Chengdu's first-instance courts, a slightly more than 30 percent higher degree of formal citation than Chengdu's courts. The gap in the rate of citation was less prominent between Shanghai and Shenzhen, but first instance IP opinions from Shanghai courts that dealt with first instance disputes in the manufacturing sector nonetheless cited 0.41 more formal legal provisions per opinion than did first-instance Shenzhen courts, a 7 percent gap in citation frequency.

Perhaps the most direct measurement of the extent to which a court gives reasons for its decision in a case is the length of its opinion. Although this metric can fail to capture the quality of a judicial justification for a given decision, wide variation between courts and judges regarding opinion length suggests a lack of reasoning for a judgment for those cases with shorter opinions. In my sample, first-instance cases in Shanghai exhibit the most lengthy written opinions, but the variation between Shanghai and the other two case study jurisdictions is not large – on average only 200 characters separate an opinion written in Shanghai from an opinion written in the other two localities. Hence, according to the data on judicial opinions that I used to measure the "giving reasons" aspect of judicial autonomy, Shanghai courts provide the most statutorily grounded and lengthy opinions, followed by Shenzhen courts and Chengdu courts, which is consistent with the theory that high-end legal markets create pressure for judicial autonomy in local Chinese courts.

Variation in Mediation Rates across Localities

To measure judges' decisional autonomy, I also assess the rate of mediation across my three case study localities, and this section provides data regarding the frequency of judicial mediation in trademark disputes, which varies across Intermediate Courts in my three case study cities. Because lower mediation rates suggest that judges are confident in their abilities to apply the law to facts in a particular case, Shanghai's relatively low mediation rate also suggests that judges in Shanghai's Second Intermediate Court tend to have more confidence on average to issue a judgment despite the evaluation system's preference towards mediation and away from appeal (cf. Ng & He, 2017).[76] Although I note in Chapter 3 that judicial evaluations do not seamlessly constrain judges to mediate more cases or to avoid appellate reversal (C. Minzner, 2011a, 2011b), emerging informal practices ultimately exert a greater influence on judges' professional activity, as CQAS performance evaluation indices nonetheless still emphasized and encouraged mediated settlement. Historically, rising caseloads and bureaucratic pressures have compelled judges, since at least the early reform era, to emphasize mediation instead of adversarial adjudication in the resolution of private disputes (Lubman, 1999). Further,

[76] One of the major reasons that judges tend to mediate more cases is that such settlements cannot be reversed on appeal. *PC2013-17, judge, Shanghai, March 2013.*

Table 5.3. *Measures of "giving reasons requirement" (opinion length and citation count) and mediation rate across case study localities (2006–2011)*

Case study locality	Average number of citations to formal legal provisions contained in each judicial opinion	Average number of citations to formal legal provisions other than CPL Article 134, per judicial opinion	Opinion length, in average number of Chinese characters	The approximate percentage of cases mediated (instead of adjudicated) in selected IP disputes across case study locations
Shanghai	6.12	5.65	4,972	22%
Shenzhen	5.4	5.24	4,735	38%
Chengdu	4.88	3.94	4,785	42%

mediation was emphasized more strongly during the 2008–2013 tenure of former SPC President Wang Shengjun[77] (a period that overlaps significantly with that in which the cases in this dataset were decided), and was highlighted by a link between judicial mediation and policies designed to limit political dissent and produce social stability (Trevaskes, 2011). For these reasons, the use of mediation can serve as a useful measure for corroborating qualitative assessments of judicial autonomy provided earlier in this chapter, given that higher mediation rates tend to reflect a judicial tendency to avoid making decisions, to pressure litigants to resolve disputes for themselves and to comply with top-down political mandates aimed at preserving social stability.

The percentage of mediated cases presented in Table 5.3 reflects the extent to which mediation is emphasized in selected first-instance cases handled in the Intermediate Courts in each of the three case study cities of Shanghai, Shenzhen, and Chengdu. The publicly available data on the CIELA website provided by the Rouse Corporation provides both the number of judgments and the number of mediated settlements, from which calculations regarding the ratio of mediated to adversarial dispute resolution can be made. I restricted the sample of cases to IP disputes related to the manufacturing and machinery industry across cases to normalize the effect that differences across sectors might exert

[77] *PC2013-57, judge, Shanghai, June 2013; PC2013-51, judge, Chengdu, May 2013.*

on how courts handle disputes, that is, all three case study localities have comparable machine manufacturing capabilities, but dissimilar levels of development in the high technology sector. In general, the data indicate that Shanghai has the lowest mediation rate among my three cases, followed by Shenzhen and Chengdu, which is consistent with the thesis that high-end law firm markets tend to lead to greater judicial autonomy in local courts.

Conclusion

The evidence presented in Chapters 4 and 5 is consistent with the finding that public–private differences in professional conditions (e.g., wage gap, personal autonomy, and career trajectory) have been linked in part to design changes in China's authoritarian court system. Interview data, documentary evidence, and government statistics support the finding that the most competitive and routinized judicial career trajectories, the most transparent court information, the most active judges regarding the "giving reasons" requirement, and judges least likely to resolve cases with mediation are found in Shanghai, followed by Shenzhen and Chengdu. These findings suggest that when authoritarian regimes with rapidly expanding and liberalized economies grow alongside a downward pressure on formal compensation for public officials, imbalances between public and private salary fluctuations can interact with factors shaping the designs of courts. This research also draws attention to the entire class of legal professionals (i.e., not simply activist lawyers or judges) when discussing judicial reform, facilitating an analysis of how the choices of different actors within the legal profession and the wider forms of law in which they are situated contribute to the development of judicial autonomy in a given polity.[78] Joining other recent research that leverages subnational court variation to explain institutional change in the Chinese judiciary (Wang and Liang, 2019), this approach represents an alternative to other strands of the literature that examine judicial politics, even in more ambiguous political settings such as new democracies or transitional political systems, as affected mainly by activist legal mobilization (Epp, 1998; Pils, 2007) and competition between multiple parties (Chavez, 2004; Ginsburg, 2003). This book's ecology-based theoretical framework

[78] Other recent studies analyze processes by which the legal profession, using the framework of "fields" conceptualized by Bourdieu, influence authoritarian judges (Kisilowski, 2014).

illuminates a nuanced pattern: In high-end local legal markets in China, court leaders offer their judges better working conditions, including more professionalized selection and promotion mechanisms, which create conditions that appear to be at least partially responsible for greater judicial willingness to give reasons for their decisions and decide cases without resorting to mediation. This chapter provides empirical support for the thesis that institutional incentives and local legal services markets can act in tandem to influence courts, given that public and private sector labor markets for legal professionals are engaged in symbiotic development (S. Liu, 2011a). In this way, this book clears a path for researching the political and legal impact of a growing market for legal services that can apply to market-based national economies – authoritarian or otherwise.

6

Court Personnel, Bureaucratic Specialization, and the Limits of Top-Down Theory

The preceding chapters present evidence that dramatic changes to the legal profession, especially since 1992 and accelerating after the turn of the century, have pressured courts in urban China to revise mechanisms of judicial selection and promotion in the case study cities of Shanghai, Shenzhen, and Chengdu. In this chapter, I bolster this book's ecological theory of court reform by assessing an alternative explanation rooted primarily in top-down, state-centered logic – one assuming that leaders from the central CCP, state, or both have comprehensively determined the nature and extent of institutional change, consistent with the underlying assumptions of some scholars that judicial decisions are brought about by "the particular decision-making mechanism guided by the Chinese Communist Party's instrumental rule-by-law ideal" (Ling Li, 2012). Zhu's premise, for instance, is that the CCP is "the major force mobilizing, promoting, and implementing reform within the judiciary" in contemporary China (Zhu, 2010, pp. 52–53). While it is no doubt true to some extent that political power determines judicial outcomes in China – over 99 percent of criminal trials result in conviction – applying this premise to all judicial activities in China would mask significant change to China's courts in the last two decades.

Although it is often difficult, if not impossible to peel back the curtain and peer into the "black box" of the state, it is worthwhile to consider how a Party-led process of change might look. One mechanism by which legal forms like judicial selection and promotion mechanisms could change in top-down fashion would be the central Party-State's allocation of judicial personnel headcount (i.e., *bianzhi*) to local courts through the personnel management system. After all, in the early years of the People's Republic of China (PRC), personnel policy was at the core of the construction of the judiciary, which expanded rapidly across China in the early 1950s through central directives to local legal organs (Tiffert, 2015, p. 147). In the early post-Mao reform period, personnel policy remained important but was generally folded into a larger push to expand the courts via bureaucratic specialization (i.e., the opening of new court divisions and hiring of judges to address emergent legal issue areas) first in criminal, civil, and administrative law, then in particularly trending areas such as the "bright light" of the legal system – intellectual property law. In a context of ineffectual authority relative to police, procuratorial, and other branches of the political–legal state apparatus, China began to introduce geographically limited and issue-specific rationalized judicial enforcement in the early 1990s, a key component of which was the "creation of specialized tribunals … indicative of the state's resolve to invest scarce resources in an area of the law whose importance is on the rise, and to do so by adjusting the court system in ways that allow for the institutionalization of rationalized enforcement"; as part of this plan, important issue-specific court divisions "[emerged] first in the most developed cities in China" (Dimitrov, 2009, pp. 96–101).

Hence, it is plausible that the drive to specialize the courts in the "most developed" cities in China might have led to significant variation in the extent of bureaucratic expansion to the court division structure and judiciary in more economically developed urban centers like Shanghai. This chapter, however, presents evidence that this is not the case – despite differences in geography and development, court systems in Chengdu, Shenzhen, and Shanghai all demonstrated robust capabilities during the post-Mao era to expand and diversify their court and judicial structures, suggesting that top-down theories of court politics do not explain the local variation I describe in this book. In this way, this chapter provides an empirically rich account of bureaucratic reform in China's courts that demonstrates the limits of top-down theory and further supports the argument presented in previous chapters that the legal profession has generated significant pressure for urban court reform in recent years.

Personnel Policy and the Origins of the PRC Court System

With a morass of courts and other state organs searching for funding at the local level, a feasible theory of court reform in urban China could potentially rest on the premise that the more personnel (*bianzhi*) employed by a particular court, the greater its authority – as others have observed, "[p]ersonnel policy is the heart of power in a Leninist system" (Brødsgaard, 2012, p. 76). The courts have been no exception to this general dictum: In the early years of the PRC, in the midst of hurried reconstruction of the court system, personnel policy weighed heavily on the minds of judicial authorities who worked under the assumption that court staffing was a "high stakes battlefield" that "crystallized competing political and ideological visions of New China" (Tiffert, 2015, p. 147). Similarly, when competition for authority has emerged in more recent times between other local government units, the winner has usually been the unit with more personnel (Z. Liu, 2009; Mertha, 2006), and applying the often circular logic that can govern bureaucracies, previous *bianzhi* expansions can provide grounds for further expansions (Z. Liu, 2009, pp. 128–129). Loosely translated as "establishment of posts," *bianzhi* does not simply establish the *number* of persons employed in a bureaucratic unit, it also includes authority for the funding outlay to support the hiring of officials to fill the positions (Brødsgaard, 2002, p. 361). The concept of *bianzhi* differs from the *nomenklatura* institutions that apply to leading cadres in the Chinese bureaucracy: The *bianzhi* system encompasses millions of state-salaried employees, whereas *nomenklatura* only includes cadres in leadership positions from the central Party and government leaders to the local township leader (Brødsgaard, 2002, p. 362).[1] Despite the fact that *bianzhi* refers more to public sector personnel in general, rather than the key leadership posts, the issue remains critical to understanding how the "relevant Party leaders" could plausibly impact local court rules and norms by maintaining political control over bureaucratic authority – after all, *bianzhi* is ultimately managed by the Central Commission for Institutional Post Establishment (*Zhongyang jigou bianzhi weiyuanhui*), "which is placed directly under the Party's Central Committee and is thus managed and controlled by the Party" (Brødsgaard, 2012, p. 76).

Particularly since the mid-1990s, expansions of *bianzhi* have typically revolved around the extent to which courts can carve out institutional mandates in relation to emerging areas of law, often in the commercial realm. In this chapter, "Bureaucratic specialization" refers to the process of establishing issue-specific and bureaucratic management divisions in China's court system, including economic, intellectual property, administrative, and bankruptcy court divisions, among others. In this system, courts often lobby local governments and local CCP Committees for increases in personnel and resource expansions to establish new bureaucratic units, which can potentially reshape relations with local State and Party organs and offer a window onto court leaders' abilities to "coordinate" (*xietiao*) with local Party and government officials to open up

[1] Brødsgaard gives the example that "Peking University has several thousand people on the *bianzhi* of the educational system, but only the president and Party secretary of the university will be listed in the Central Committee's *nomenklatura*" (Brødsgaard, 2002, pp. 364–365).

new divisions and secure more funding (Z. Liu, 2009, p. 129). As recent research points out, a court's ability to secure funding might even reflect enhanced judicial efficiency and fairness (Y. Wang, 2015, p. 135).

Similarly, assuming that greater funding might be tied to more judicial efficiency, fairness, autonomy, and transparency, a top-down theory of court reform might posit an alternative to the main argument presented in this book, with the expectation that many of the changes to judicial selection and transparency discussed in Chapter 5 are the result of bureaucratic specialization and additional funding stemming from expanded *bianzhi* allocations over time. However, this chapter shows that these expectations are not consistent with the institutional history of courts in Chengdu, Shenzhen, and Shanghai; instead, all three court systems have had some measure of success in expanding personnel, resulting in negligible variation in the amount of bureaucratic specialization in these case study localities, even in the wake of the SPC's encouragement of court specialization ahead of and through World Trade Organization (WTO) and Trade-Related Aspects of Intellectual Property Rights (TRIPs) compliance in the mid-1990s and early 2000s. To the extent that increases in judicial autonomy and transparency could be based on expansions of institutional strength in courts during the beginnings of the commercialization of the court system in the early reform era (1978–1998), the top-down theory does not seem to hold up here, either – in fact, Chengdu has a well-established history of *bianzhi* expansion and bureaucratic specialization of its courts dating back to the start reforms in 1978, and Shenzhen has also expanded its judicial bureaucracy, despite its lack of a strong institutional foundation at the beginning of the post-Mao era. Because courts in all three case study sites appear to have had success in securing expanded personnel allocations in their courts during the reform era, the relative success of court leaders in expanding court hiring to meet the demands of growing caseloads does not seem to adequately explain the variations in judicial autonomy described in Chapter 5.

Before personnel allocation and bureaucratic specialization could become important elements of court reform in China, the court system had to first be re-established under Communist rule (i.e., after the CCP was victorious in the Chinese Civil War during 1946–1949) and then rebuilt to varying degrees during and after the Great Proletarian Cultural Revolution (1966–1976). The early period of PRC court bureaucratic politics immediately after 1949 focused on nationally uniform expansions of court institutions in which rural courts were largely rebuilt and urban courts reconstituted (Hurst, 2018, p. 57); the latter post-Mao reform period of court politics began to produce local variations in bureaucratic specialization as liberalizing economic reforms introduced new types of litigation to Chinese courts.

The Roots of Judicial Work: From Personnel Policy to the Beginnings of Bureaucratic Specialization under Mao (1949–1978)

From their inception, Communist courts and judicial work have been enmeshed in political bureaucracies. After the CCP defeated the KMT during the Chinese Civil War (1946–1949) and came to power in 1949, the Party faced the choice whether to incorporate parts of the Republican-era KMT legal and court system into the new Communist government. On January 14, 1949, the new leadership of the PRC announced that one of the eight fundamental conditions for the end of the Civil War between the Communists and the Republican *Kuomintang* (KMT) government led by Chiang Kai-shek (*Jiang Jieshi*) would be to abolish the Constitution of the KMT government as well as "all reactionary laws and decrees" (Chen, 2008, p. 44). The court system would start from a clean slate under a new constitution drafted by Mao Zedong and other CCP leaders and would become the new fundamental law of the Chinese people (Chen, 2008, p. 44; see also Shapiro, 1981, pp. 60–62). The rationale behind the abolition of KMT law is found in the "Instruction of the Central Committee of the CCP to Abolish the Kuomintang Six Codes and to Define the Judicial Principles for the Liberated Areas," issued in February 1949:

> The Six Codes of the Kuomintang, like bourgeois law in general, were framed in such a way as to conceal their class character … the Six Codes give the appearance the people are all equal before the law. But in reality, there can be no real common interests between … the exploiting classes and the exploited … Therefore, the Six Codes cannot be the applicable law in both the areas controlled by the Chiang Kai-shek and the liberated areas.[2]

Regarding judicial principles, these instructions explained to PRC judges how to operate in the legal vacuum created by the 1949 CCP edicts:

> Before the new laws of the people have been systematically promulgated, people's judicial work shall be based on policies of the Communist Party and various fundamental principles, laws, decrees, resolutions issued

[2] Instruction of the Central Committee of the CPC to Abolish the Kuomintang Six Codes and to Define the Judicial Principles for the Liberated Areas, Item 2, issued February 1949 (cited in Chen, 2008, p. 44).

> by the People's Government and the People's Liberation Army ... In the meantime, the judicial organs should educate and reform their judicial cadres through scorning and criticizing the Six Codes and all laws and decrees of the Kuomintang, all bourgeois anti-people's statutes and laws of Europe, America and Japan, through the learning of attitudes towards state and law of Marxism-Leninism and Mao Zedong Thought.[3]

The order implementing these instructions followed in March 1949, establishing and implementing the roots of a post-1949 Chinese judiciary that de-emphasized formal legality, and in which the institutional control of bureaucratic politics defined the role of courts (Chen, 2008, p. 45). Additionally, the Instructions make clear that at the outset of institution building in post-1949 China, the courts would largely start from a clean, Communist slate as politicized units under a new political–legal regime consisting of the CCP, the People's Government, and the People's Liberation Army.[4] Despite these revolutionary aspirations, however, the new nation-state recognized the dire lack of court institutionalization in the early years under Mao, as the effects of war, revolution, and intra-Party conflict had left the judicial system under-resourced and lacking a coherent jurisprudential corpus, making it difficult to tackle a growing case backlog; in response, the new government set out on new initiatives including the specialization of legal tasks – such as implementing the new marriage law – to spur judicial institution building (Tiffert, 2015, p. 148).

These efforts at spearheading new initiatives and specializing legal expertise were critical components of PRC courts' early struggles for institutional autonomy, and they have also emphasized separating courts from the revolutionary political bureaucracies to which "judicial work" was subordinated by the 1949 Instructions. As scholarship on the criminal courts has found, "...almost from their inception, criminal courts laboured to carve out a space for themselves independent of the public security apparatus – a labour that has shown much progress, but is certainly still ongoing" (Hurst, 2011, pp. 86–87). During the 1950s, there remained many geographic areas of China, particularly in the countryside, that had never been served by courts before, let alone newly established CCP courts. Instead, military commanders in many of these regions had set up adjudication divisions within

[3] Instruction of the Central Committee of the CPC to Abolish the Kuomintang Six Codes and to Define the Judicial Principles for the Liberated Areas, Item 5, issued February 1949 (cited in Chen, 2008, p. 45).

[4] Although the CPC's ascension to power brought dramatic changes in the judicial sphere, the Party was not able to eliminate all vestiges of the Republican-era justice system (Tiffert, 2011).

local public security bureaus rather than independent criminal courts to serve the social control function expected of modern states. After the revolution, grassroots courts began groping for institutional autonomy within the CCP bureaucratic apparatus by claiming this modest institutional role legitimizing criminal prosecutions and other actions of the state's social control machinery. Criminal law and the enforcement of new rules against forced marriages promulgated by the Marriage Law of 1950 became courts' trademark institutional functions during the Mao era; indeed, the 1979 Law on the Organization of the People's Courts stipulates that criminal case and civil case divisions could be set up at first-instance courts throughout the country, mainly for the processing of criminal and marriage-related legal disputes (Z. Liu, 2009, p. 125). From these beginnings, a substantial component of Chinese courts' struggles for institutional autonomy has been to establish a clearly delineated functionary profile distinct from police, procuracy, and military bureaucracies.

Aside from claiming a legitimizing niche within the state during this era, bureaucratically specialized courts also began efforts to demarcate divisions of labor between judges and other court workers. The first legal regulation related to courts, the Temporary Regulations Regarding the Organization of People's Courts (passed September 3, 1951), granted authority to divide cases according to legal specialty: "County-level courts that process many cases can establish separate criminal and civil law adjudication divisions" (Z. Liu, 2009, p. 125). This straightforward bureaucratic structure was replicated generally throughout the country, with national legislation (the 1954 Law on Organization of the People's Courts) formalizing local court authority at the Basic and Intermediate levels to establish criminal and civil adjudication divisions (Z. Liu, 2009, 125). During the 1950s and 1960s, the Party-State also established police, procuracy, and court institutions separate from the military apparatus. Bureaucratic specialization, among many other activities, was substantially disrupted during the Great Leap Forward (1958–1961) and the Cultural Revolution (1966–1976), and as a result, the PRC lacked national coherence and stability at the time of Mao's death. Although some scholars suggest that the court system was essentially destroyed during the Cultural Revolution (Lubman, 1999, p. 251), more recent research suggests that campaign mobilization had an uneven influence on court institutions in some areas during this period (Hurst, 2011).

At the outset of the post-Mao reform era beginning in 1978, courts were reconstituted on the foundations of their criminal and basic civil law dispute resolution bureaucracies. In Shanghai, Shenzhen, and Chengdu, caseload in the early days of the reform era was split between criminal and civil cases: From 1979 to 1981, criminal cases comprised 64 percent of the Shenzhen City Court's caseload (the remainder were civil cases); between 1977 and 1981, criminal cases comprised 40 percent of the total percentage of first-instance cases in the Chengdu City Court; and between 1966 and 1976, the total percentage of criminal cases among all cases concluded throughout the multileveled Shanghai court system was 47 percent (Chengdu Intermediate People's Court, 1997; Shanghai Judicial Gazette Editing Committee, 2003; Shenzhen City Local Gazette Editing Committee, 2006).

The Beginnings of Local Specialization (1978–1993)

In the turmoil following Mao's death and the end of the Cultural Revolution, reforms to rebuild Party legitimacy on a foundation other than Maoist campaign politics were prioritized for the purpose of undergirding a court system designed to resolve disputes arising from an expanding, internationalizing, and liberalizing national economy. Deng Xiaoping featured law prominently to help establish stability and order for economic development (Chen, 2008, p. 52); after the leadership transition in 1978, the state rapidly enacted myriad laws and regulations, most of which were aimed at regulating economic and commercial relations, based on the Party's perceived need for national economic development (Chen, 2008, p. 51). Closing the Third Plenum of the 11th Party Congress in 1978, Deng stated, "relations between the country and its enterprises, between enterprises, between enterprises and people should be confirmed via legal forms; contradictions between the same should also not infrequently be resolved through law" (see Foucault, 2008; Liu, 2009, p. 125). Thus, during the Deng era, the Chinese legal system was constructed around the premise that a market economy should aspire to some ideal type of formal rationality, which has led to a renewed focus on the ways in which personnel management, bureaucratic expansion, and issue-specific legal specialization could continue to be the hallmarks of Chinese court institutionalization (Chen, 2008, p. 61).

Court bureaucratization in the early Deng era began to assume a more local character as courts adapted to the new party line. Between 1978 and 1993, legal reforms resulted in the creation of four discrete issue areas, which mirrored the internal structures of PRC courts throughout the country: criminal law, civil law, economic law, and administrative law (cf. Hurst, 2018). For example, within-court Administrative Litigation Divisions began to specialize in handling administrative lawsuits against the state; in 1982, the Provisional Civil Litigation Law recognized the legitimacy of administrative lawsuits, leading some local courts to accept administrative cases in their Civil Divisions or Economic Divisions. In 1987, the SPC issued a rule on the establishment of Administrative Litigation Divisions effective across the country, and on January 14, 1987, it instructed local courts to establish standalone Administrative Litigation Divisions in local courts (Z. Liu, 2009).

In similar fashion, cases of an "economic nature" (i.e., disputes among persons or companies arising from contract breaches) were handled simply as "civil" cases before 1978 (Chengdu Intermediate People's Court, 1997, p. 166, 169); although such cases were heard in Chinese courts even during the Mao period, there existed no specialized bureaucratic court units specifically authorized to handle cases involving contract breaches. By the next year, however, courts at the high and intermediate levels in large- and medium-sized cities throughout the country were establishing "Economic" Divisions within courts to accept disputes that would be filed pursuant to the Economic Contract Law of 1980 (Z. Liu, 2009, p. 125). On September 2, 1983, the Law on the Organization of Courts was amended so that basic-level, first-instance courts could establish Economic Divisions and that intermediate-level courts could establish other specialized divisions in addition to Economic Divisions "according to needs" (Z. Liu, 2009).

Court leaders in Chengdu acted quickly to expand. Any first-instance or appeals cases that involved economic matters in Chengdu before 1980 were handled within the scope of general "civil" adjudication (Chengdu Intermediate People's Court, 1997, p. 166).[5] After the announcement of economic reforms at the Third Plenum of the 11th Party Congress in 1978, the Chengdu Intermediate Court, according to "relevant laws and regulations," and in accordance with the needs of development, formally established a standalone "Economic Division" in September 1980 specifically designed to handle legal disputes of an economic nature (Chengdu Intermediate People's Court, 1997, p. 166). By 1982, all of Chengdu's courts had established economic case adjudication divisions, pushing the *bianzhi* in Chengdu's Intermediate Court to more than 140 personnel, more than doubling the total number of court personnel in only four years. Between 1980 and 1989, Chengdu courts handled 11,905 cases that involved contracts or administrative cases of an economic nature (Chengdu Intermediate People's Court, 1997, p. 167). By the end of the

[5] After two decades of hearing "economic" cases separately from "civil" cases, Chinese courts eliminated the distinction around the year 2000 (Peerenboom, 2002).

1980s, administrative litigation and economic contract disputes had given local courts an institutional authority to handle specialized commercial and economic cases in addition to the general civil and criminal types of legal disputes that they inherited from Mao-era court institutions.

Accelerated Expansion of Local Court Divisions: Issue-Specific Bureaucratic Specialization (1993–2016)

In the early 1990s, local courts continued to enhance their bureaucratic specialization as economic disputes increased in number and complexity, and courts in all three of my case studies were no exception to this general trend. Accordingly, in the SPC's First Five-Year Plan (issued in 1998), then SPC President Xiao Yang called on local courts to specialize their internal court adjudication divisions, and other higher courts urged (*ducu*) subnational local courts that are not the explicit recipients of *bianzhi* expansions to lobby local government units for expansions of their own personnel (Z. Liu, 2009).[6] Following the Mao era, Deng focused on local experimentation to facilitate economic development and trade liberalization; by the early 1990s, in the wake of the success of many of these local economic experiments, Deng reinvigorated the construction of the legal system to mirror the intended gradualist character of economic policymaking: "...legal provisions will inevitably be rough to start with, then be gradually improved upon. Some laws and statutes can be tried out in particular localities and later enacted nationally after experience has been evaluated and improvements have been made" (Chen, 2008, p. 54).

The central government rolled out initiatives in several localities aimed at enhancing courts' ability to handle intellectual property disputes ahead of China's accession to the WTO and integration into the TRIPs framework. Localized court bureaucratization began with the rising prominence of intellectual property law around this time (Dimitrov, 2009; Shanghai High People's Court, 2011). On August 5, 1993, the Beijing High People's Court and the Beijing Intermediate People's Court became the first two specialized IP Divisions in China, with the NPC approval of the SPC's establishment of an independent IP adjudication division (*shenpanting*)[7] following soon after (Dimitrov, 2009, p. 101; Z. Liu, 2009;

[6] The First Five-Year Plan of the Supreme People's Court (*Renmin fayuan "yi wu" gaige gangyao*), 1999–2004; *PC2012-27, judge, Wenzhou, October 2012.*

[7] To clarify, I translate *shenpanting* as "divisions" located within China's general court system. In his work on IP Divisions in China, Dimitrov variously refers to these divisions as "courts," "divisions," or "tribunals" (Dimitrov, 2009, pp. 100–101). Referring

Yan, 2007). These IP-related reforms were followed by the SPC's Five-Year Plan in 1998 calling for the separation of divisions within the court (Z. Liu, 2009). The emergence of specialized IP Divisions then accelerated after 2000 but has generally proceeded gradually and locally over the past two decades, diffusing into several other legal issue areas. In the wake of IP-related reforms to China's court system, an increasing number of local Chinese courts have established specialized divisions in various other areas of law, including finance, loan default, juvenile-related affairs, company liquidation, bankruptcy, labor, and environmental protection (Dimitrov, 2009; Peerenboom, 2002; Shenzhen Intermediate People's Court, 2011; Stern, 2010; M. Zhang & Zhang, 2012).

To establish a new bureaucratic structure like a within-court division in the absence of direct allocation from the central government, it has been necessary for a local court to obtain approval from the local division of the Human Resources and Social Security Office (*Zhonghua renmin gongheguo renli ziyuan he shehui baozhangbu*), a State Council Ministry, as well as the local branch of the Commission for Institutional *Bianzhi*. This CCP unit would then need to approve (*pizhun*) the court's request to establish a new structure. For instance, in Shanghai, the Finance Division was established at the Intermediate Court level via application from the Shanghai High Court.[8] Personnel allocations would have then needed to be apportioned to the corresponding government institutions within the locality, and from the Shanghai High Court to the Basic Courts, based upon factors ranging from economic development, population size, and degree of technical development. (High courts oversee personnel allocations for all levels below it but strive to establish "one-step down" supervision of Intermediate Courts that usually govern municipal-level jurisdictions, instead of receiving ongoing supervision from *kuai*-level CCP Committees and branches of the Commission for Institutional *Bianzhi*.)[9]

The IP Divisions established in Chinese courts in the 1990s were concentrated mainly in the types of localities under analysis in this book – developed urban areas in China (Dimitrov, 2009, p. 101). The first specialized IP tribunals were set up in the Beijing High People's Court and in the

to issue-specific "divisions" in China's courts prevents confusion with other independent, issue-specific "courts" such as military courts, railway courts, and maritime courts, which are not discussed here. Not until August 26, 2014 did the National People's Congress began considering establishing standalone IP *Courts* in Beijing, Shanghai, and Guangzhou (X. Zhang, 2014).

[8] *PC2012-49, judge, Shanghai, December 2012.*

[9] The term "*kuai*" here refers to the concept of *tiao-kuai guanxi* (see Lieberthal, 2004; Lieberthal & Oksenberg, 1988).

Beijing Intermediate People's Court, and during the first decade or so of specialization, standalone IP Divisions were established in Beijing and Shanghai throughout the Basic (first-instance), Intermediate, and High Court levels (Dimitrov, 2009, pp. 101–102). At that time, Chengdu City in Sichuan province and Shenzhen City in Guangdong province also established IP Divisions in their Intermediate Courts. By 2000, several cities across Guangdong province had also established specialized IP Divisions, and Chengdu established a standalone Intermediate Court IP Division as well. In this way, establishing issue-specific court divisions would have indicated officials' resolve to invest institutional resources in an emerging area of the law (Dimitrov, 2009, p. 101).

Case Studies on Bureaucratic Specialization in Local Courts

Under a top-down theory of court reform in urban China, it might be plausible that greater funding for courts is tied to increases to personal judicial autonomy and court transparency. However, the history of bureaucratic specialization and court expansion during the reform era does not suggest that there is a relationship between top-down personnel reforms and the increases in judicial autonomy and transparency observed in Chapter 5. Instead, court systems with lower levels of judicial autonomy (e.g., Chengdu) have, nonetheless, also demonstrated a strong history of obtaining personnel allocations in the reform era, and court systems with higher levels of autonomy (e.g., Shenzhen and Shanghai) have also succeeded in obtaining *bianzhi* allocations and specializing their courts regardless of the strength of their institutional foundations at the start of the post-1978 reform era. These patterns appear to hold true even following the SPC's efforts to specialize courts ahead of WTO and TRIPs compliance in the mid-1990s and 2000s (1992–2016).

At the beginning of the reform era, both Chengdu and Shanghai were highly institutionalized court systems, both possessing established, well-defined duties resolving criminal prosecutions and simple civil disputes among private citizens (Chengdu Intermediate People's Court, 1997; Shenzhen City Local Gazette Editing Committee, 2006). Shenzhen, conversely, had only begun to urbanize at the time of Mao's death; however, as a result of its status as a local experiment for economic liberalization during Deng Xiaoping's reform era, its court system has grown substantially since then (Shenzhen City Local Gazette Editing Committee, 2006).

Chengdu

Chengdu, as an historically important trade center in Western China, experienced greater institutionalization of its court system during the Mao era than did many other localities, including Shenzhen. Chengdu remains a highly urbanized and developed locality, perhaps the most important thoroughfare from central China to the Western frontier regions, and Chengdu's courts were highly institutionalized – especially relative to Shenzhen – at the beginning of the reform era. At the outset of reforms led by Deng Xiaoping, caseloads were split between criminal and civil cases: Between 1977 and 1981, criminal cases comprised 40 percent of the total percentage of first-instance cases in the Chengdu City Court (Chengdu Intermediate People's Court, 1997).

Soon after, the Chengdu Intermediate Court experienced expansions in its court bureaucracy that reflected national trends: "In 1978, after the Third Plenum of the 11th Party Congress, Chengdu's two levels of court construction experienced democratic and legal institution strengthening, and internal units were perfected, with personnel allocation numbers rising each year" (Chengdu Intermediate People's Court, 1997, p. 67). In January 1980, Chengdu added an Economic Division and split the Criminal Division into Criminal Divisions 1 and 2. As noted earlier, after 1978, the Chengdu Intermediate Court formally established a standalone "Economic Division" in September 1980 specifically designed to handle legal disputes of an economic nature (Chengdu Intermediate People's Court, 1997, p. 166). By 1982, all of Chengdu's courts had established economic case adjudication divisions, pushing the *bianzhi* in Chengdu's Intermediate Court to more than 140 personnel, whereas just four years earlier, there were only 68 personnel in the Intermediate Court. Further, in 1983, the large Wenjiang District merged with Chengdu City, unifying the two jurisdictions' Intermediate Courts and creating the Chengdu Intermediate Court and local Chengdu court districts that remained in use at least through 2013. Additionally, in January 1987, Chengdu established its standalone Administrative Division (Chengdu Intermediate People's Court, 1997, pp. 29–36).

Beginning in the 1990s, however, bureaucratic specialization in Chengdu has been comparable to that of other similarly situated cities, even Shanghai and Shenzhen. Civil Division 3 of the Chengdu Intermediate Court handles a variety of IP cases, and the Sichuan High Court (located in Chengdu City) had five judges assigned to it as of 2012. As noted previously, in 2000, Chengdu was among the earliest localities to establish IP Divisions at the Intermediate Court level. Despite a lighter IP caseload over the past two

Table 6.1. *Chengdu Intermediate People's Court, internal structure (2012)*[10]

Court division	Scope of cases handled
Criminal Division 1	Criminal cases that are not economic, relevant to corruption, or drug crimes; guidance of basic courts' adjudication work
Criminal Division 2	Economic, corruption, and drug cases; supervision of basic courts
Juvenile Division	3-in-1 division for cases related to juveniles
Civil Division 1	Marital cases, inheritance cases, labor cases, and personnel disputes
Civil Division 2	Mortgage disputes; guidance of lower courts
Civil Division 3 (IP Division)	Unfair competition and monopoly cases, credit cases, and cases involving foreigners
Civil Division 4	Real estate disputes, development project contracts, and contracts for sale; supervision of lower courts
Administrative Division	First- and second-instance administrative disputes, adjudicated according to law
State Compensation Division	Disputes concerning claims of infringement in which damages against the state are alleged and/or confirmed

decades, the Chengdu Intermediate Court has established an IP Division in correspondence with the structure of the Sichuan High Court.[11]

Since 1998, bureaucratic specialization in Chengdu's courts has been largely on par with the personnel allocations seen there and in other developed urban localities. The bureaucratic structure of the Chengdu Intermediate Court as of 2013 indicates that internal court adjudication organs have been expanded and specialized to a significant degree (Table 6.1).

The internal bureaucratic units responsible for case adjudication in the Chengdu Intermediate Court are largely separated along types of commercial dispute, including mortgage, real estate, and antitrust. In other emerging legal issue areas, the Chengdu Intermediate Court was chosen by the SPC as a site for the city's first juvenile division – among the first

[10] The internal structure of the Chengdu Intermediate People's Court is available on the court's website, see http://cdfy.chinacourt.org/article/detail/2014/07/id/1355292.shtml (a copy of the court structure as of 2012 is on file with author).

[11] *PC2012-36, judge, Chengdu, October 2012.*

divisions specializing in juvenile issues in the country.[12] The Juvenile Division has helped Chengdu Intermediate Court increase its personnel allocations: After an initial apportionment of 10 personnel in 2006, the Chengdu Intermediate Court's Juvenile Division successfully lobbied for 4 more personnel; as of December 2012, the Juvenile Division employed 19 personnel, including 1 Division Chief, 2 Division Vice Chiefs, with several ordinary judges (*shenpan yuan*) and clerks.[13] A judge who worked in Chengdu Intermediate Court's Juvenile Division indicated that training seminars were conducted as a result of the juvenile division's establishment and that the general process of examination, selection, and hiring was sufficient for finding good juvenile judges in Chengdu.[14]

Shenzhen

At the beginning of the reform era in 1978, Shenzhen was not formally incorporated as an urban locality but was organized instead within the Bao'an County jurisdiction. It only became a municipal-level jurisdiction in January 1979 while serving as the first Special Economic Zone (SEZ) of the post-Mao reform era. At that point, the Bao'an County court was eliminated and Shenzhen City Court was established (Shenzhen City Local Gazette Editing Committee, 2006, p. 213). In just three decades of liberalizing reforms, Shenzhen's jurisdictional area has developed from a primarily agricultural and fishing economy into a postindustrial urban center, which is reflected in its within-court organizational structure (Shenzhen City Local Gazette Editing Committee, 2006).

When the Shenzhen City Court was established in March 1979, its primary function was to take jurisdiction over criminal and civil cases (Shenzhen City Local Gazette Editing Committee, 2006). As noted previously, caseload around the time that the reform era began was split between these two case types: From 1979 to 1981, criminal cases comprised 64 percent of the Shenzhen City Court's caseload (the rest were civil cases). Soon thereafter, the makeup of Shenzhen's caseload began to diversify, as the Shenzhen City Court's Administrative Division was established following national court reforms in 1987, and in 1989, the Real Estate Division was established. In 1993, Criminal Division 3 and the Bankruptcy Division were established, followed by the establishment of the IP Division in 1994.

12 *PC2012-48, judge, Chengdu, December 2012.*
13 *PC2012-48, judge, Chengdu, December 2012.*
14 *PC2012-47, judge, Chengdu, December 2012.*

Table 6.2. *Shenzhen Intermediate Court, internal structure (2013)*[15]

Court division	Scope of cases handled
Criminal Division 1	First- and second-instance criminal cases
Criminal Division 2	First- and second-instance criminal cases
Civil Division	Marital and family cases, unfair benefit, "traditional" civil cases; agricultural contract cases (*nongcun chengbao hetong*); contracts between natural persons, torts; guidance over lower courts
Commercial Division	Domestic disputes between legal persons, contracts; domestic securities, futures (*qihuo*), banknotes (*piaoju*), and stock equity (*guquan*) cases; responses to lower courts' requests for extensions of time in adjudicating cases
IP Division	Copyright cases that do not involve computer software; trademark cases; patent cases; technology contract; unfair practices; new plant material cases; responses to applications for time extension from lower courts
Foreign Commercial Cases Division	First- and second-instance cases involving disputes between legal persons, disputes between legal persons and other entities including company, liquidation, securities, contracts, and other cases
Real Estate Division	Cases involving real estate, include sale, rental, sale contract, land use, and other types of disputes
Labor Disputes Division	First- and second-instance labor disputes
Company Liquidation and Bankruptcy Division	Acceptance and resolution of bankruptcy and liquidation cases

Shenzhen has had success expanding its court system since the early 1990s, and since 2000, the Shenzhen Intermediate Court has added specialized internal bureaucratic units including a Labor Disputes Division and a division that specifically handles company liquidation cases (Shenzhen City Local Gazette Editing Committee, 2006, pp. 216–217). The institutional structure of Shenzhen Intermediate Court as of 2013, thus, reflects a largely specialized division of judicial labor, and in total, Shenzhen had established the following internal structures responsible for adjudicating cases (Table 6.2).

[15] The internal structure of the Shenzhen Intermediate People's Court is displayed on the court's website, www.szcourt.gov.cn/sfgk/kgjs/jgzn/2014/11/21145118509.html (a copy of the court structure as of 2013 is on file with author).

Shenzhen's success in bureaucratic specialization is surprising given the complex process of opening a new, specialized court division. A Shenzhen Intermediate Court judge told me that, during the period under study, personnel allocations in the Shenzhen courts were controlled by the court at each administrative level; thus, the Guangdong High Court wielded authority over personnel allocations for the whole province, and the Shenzhen Intermediate Court possessed control over personnel allocations for the city. As a result, each court was required to obtain the approval of the court one level above to open a new division, and the higher-level courts can informally suggest that specific lower-level courts apply for *bianzhi* expansions as opposed to allowing each court to apply directly to local Party or government institutions.[16]

Under these circumstances, Shenzhen's court system has become substantially specialized, and Shenzhen's courts have established themselves as capable court bureaucrats in the reform era. As noted in the previous section, Shenzhen's basic-level (primarily first-instance) courts had not established standalone IP Divisions by 2000, but Shenzhen Intermediate Court had successfully established an IP Division. Shenzhen's Basic Court level very quickly thereafter became an arena for IP-related bureaucratic specialization owing to its position as an important center for the internet services and social media industries and home to Tencent (*Tengxun*), Inc., whose headquarters are located in Shenzhen's Nanshan District. In 2006, Shenzhen's Nanshan District Court launched a "3-in-1" specialization plan modeled after the successful experience of Pudong a decade earlier (Shenzhen Intermediate People's Court, 2010, pp. 6–7); by 2010, in a span of just under four years, courts throughout Shenzhen's Intermediate and Basic levels had established specialized IP adjudication divisions (Shenzhen Intermediate People's Court, 2010; Sun, 2010).[17] In each new division in Shenzhen, usually at least Division Chief and two Division Vice Chiefs were employed, and in the Shenzhen Intermediate Court, one of the Civil Divisions had over 40 personnel, whereas the Bankruptcy and Foreign Disputes Divisions employed 10–20 personnel, including clerks.[18]

Independently established IP Divisions with specifically allocated personnel are perceived among judges in Shenzhen as a positive development that would likely yield greater professional opportunities for judges in their locality.[19] Specialized bureaucratic units such as IP Divisions

[16] *PC2013-1, judge, Shenzhen, January 2013.*

[17] *PC2013-1, judge, Shenzhen, January 2013; PC2013-3, judge, Shenzhen, January 2013.*

[18] *PC2013-1, judge, Shenzhen, January 2013.*

[19] *PC2012-7, judge, Shenzhen, June 2012.*

in courts allow judges to focus on handling IP cases, especially when a "3-in-1" Division has been set up so that IP judges can hear criminal, civil, and administrative IP cases.[20] Bureaucratic specialization has also spurred courts to develop training seminars for IP judges, which include annual conferences bringing together judges, university professors, and experts in IP law, which are organized by the IP Bureau (*zhishichanquan ju*) of the Ministry of Justice (*sifa bu*).[21]

Shanghai

In Shanghai, the court system was substantially institutionalized during the Mao era, and caseloads during the period immediately before Mao's death were split between criminal and civil cases: Between 1966 and 1976, the total percentage of criminal cases among all cases concluded throughout the multileveled Shanghai court system was 47 percent (Shanghai Judicial Gazette Editing Committee, 2003). After more than three decades of the reform era, Shanghai court leaders had exhibited a strong ability to obtain bureaucratic resources and personnel allocations via the opening of new courts and court divisions, particularly since IP Divisions began proliferating in the lead up to China's accession to the WTO in 2001–2002. As of 2013, the bureaucratic units that are designed to handle cases at the Second Shanghai Intermediate Court include the following adjudication divisions/units, exhibiting a focus on specialization by issue area (Table 6.3).

The division of labor in Shanghai's courts reflects that (as of 2013) it has been able to obtain substantial personnel allocations to handle an increasing variety of civil case types. For most of the different specialized areas of law practiced in China, including real estate, labor, bankruptcy, IP, and finance, Shanghai's Intermediate Courts have established specialized divisions for handling each type of case. Similar to interviewee accounts from Chengdu and Shenzhen, when a court within the Shanghai administrative locality seeks to establish a new bureaucratic division, it has generally needed to obtain approval from the local Shanghai branch of the Party Commission for Institutional *Bianzhi*, which is in charge of appropriating personnel allocations. For example, on January 2, 1994, this branch of the *bianzhi* commission would have been responsible for approving the Shanghai High Court and the Intermediate Court's establishment of IP Divisions (Shanghai Judicial Gazette Editing Committee, 2003, p. 46).

[20] *PC2012-6, judge, Shenzhen, June 2012.*
[21] *PC2013-48, Shenzhen judge, Shanghai, May 2013.*

Table 6.3. *Shanghai Second Intermediate Court, internal structure (2013)*[22]

Court division	Scope of cases handled
Criminal Division 1	Noneconomic criminal cases
Criminal Division 2	Economic and financial criminal cases
Juvenile Division	All cases to which a juvenile is a party
Civil Division 1	Traditional civil cases, e.g., marriage and family law disputes
Civil Division 2	Real estate cases
Civil Division 3	Labor disputes
Civil Division 4	Bankruptcy cases
Civil Division 5	IP cases and cases involving foreigners
Civil Division 6	Financial disputes
Administrative Division	Administrative and state compensation cases

These new bureaucratic divisions have expanded *bianzhi* personnel allocations in Shanghai's court system. In Shanghai's Second Intermediate Court, for example, the Labor Division employed approximately 20 personnel with 1 Division Chief and 1 Vice Division Chief; the Finance Division employed 12 personnel with 1 Vice Division Chief; the Real Estate Division had hired approximately 40 personnel as of 2013; the Commercial Division that handles non-finance cases employed approximately 40 personnel; the First Civil Division employed approximately 40 personnel; the Juvenile Division had 6 personnel; Civil Division 4 employed between 30 and 40 personnel; Civil Division 1 had approximately 40 personnel; and the IP Division had approximately 15 personnel. In total, the court employed over 400 personnel, of which approximately 200 were judges.[23] To establish a new division, local personnel institutions might provide several more Division Vice Chief position allocations, usually at 1 Vice Division Chief personnel allocation per every 10 ordinary, case-deciding judges.[24]

As noted previously, Shanghai and Beijing were the only localities in China in which standalone IP Divisions had been established throughout the Basic (first-instance), Intermediate, and High Court levels by

[22] The internal structure of the Shanghai Second Intermediate People's Court is displayed on the court's website, www.shezfy.com/page/ljfy/?lm=0a (a copy of the court structure as of 2013 is on file with author).

[23] *PC2012-49, judge, Shanghai, December 2012.*

[24] *PC2012-49, judge, Shanghai, December 2012.*

2000 (Dimitrov, 2009, pp. 101–102). Shanghai's Pudong New District, for instance, has topographically, socially, and financially transformed in only two decades from farmland to a global financial hub; the city's court system has also become a testing ground for new policies in the specialized handling of IP and Finance legal disputes. In 1996, for instance, Pudong District Court was chosen as a "3-in-1" pilot project for handling civil, criminal, and administrative IP adjudication exclusively within a single court's IP Division, symbolizing the high priority assigned to IP law (Shanghai High People's Court, 2011; Shanghai Judicial Gazette Editing Committee, 2003).

The experience of Pudong has also served as a catalyst for bureaucratic specialization throughout other courts within Shanghai itself, as Huangpu District Court has also established a specialized IP Division and the Shanghai High Court in 2008 further expanded the implementation of the "3-in-1" specialization strategy (Shanghai High People's Court, 2011). Two High Courts and nine Intermediate Courts throughout the country also started pilot projects (*shidian*) for Pudong-style IP court specialization, which later became goals listed in the national-level IP Strategy (*guojia zhishichanquan zhanlüe zhaiyao*) (Shanghai High People's Court, 2011).

In addition to suggesting a local court's positive relations with local political elites, the establishment of specialized court divisions within the court bureaucracy also creates more opportunities for the court to enhance its technical expertise. Shanghai Pudong District Court's experience with the "3-in-1" Model of specialized IP Divisions serves to consolidate the specialized function of IP Divisions in that court system, allowing judicial labor specialization of IP-specific judicial panels and IP as a substantive legal issue area to take precedence over previous distinctions between criminal, civil, and administrative law (Shanghai High People's Court, 2011).

Conclusion

Bureaucratic specialization has become increasingly localized since the beginning of the reform era, shifting priorities regarding court reform in China toward technocratic imperatives. Through an historical analysis of bureaucratic specialization in courts from the Mao era to the present, this chapter offers further support for the overall ecological theory of this book by examining a competing hypothesis that the CCP, and especially central leadership in Beijing, determines the nature and extent of institutional change in China's courts via allocations of funding and personnel, with little influence from outside factors. This theory is plausible but ultimately unpersuasive because there has been little variation in court specialization and personnel allocation among the case study cities, especially since 2003. Further, the case study localities where we would expect to see little bureaucratic specialization from the early reform era through the early twenty-first century, such as Chengdu, in fact demonstrate a strong degree of institutionalization during this period. Viewed as a whole, courts in all three case study sites appear to have successfully expanded personnel allocations in their courts during the reform era, and as such, the relative success of court leaders in expanding court hiring to meet the demands of growing caseloads does not provide a satisfactory explanation for the variations in judicial autonomy described in Chapter 5. Although this does not make the argument of this book a "theory-testing" case comparison or overall research design (Van Evera, 1997), it lends further support to the main argument that the interactive effects anticipated by an ecological theory of court reform in urban China, resulting from the unprecedented growth legal profession in recent decades, provide a more robust explanation of changes to decisional judicial autonomy (Peerenboom, 2010) since the turn of the century, rather than top-down, state-led mechanisms of bureaucratic specialization and personnel allocation.

7

Conclusion

In 1996, Chinese President Jiang Zemin endorsed "ruling the country in accordance with the law and establishing a socialist rule-of-law state" (*yifa zhiguo, jianshe shehuizhuyi fazhi guo*), concepts that were subsequently incorporated into China's Constitution. This decision followed a long debate among policymakers and government elites: In February 1996, Wang Jiafu, former head of the Law Institute of CASS, smoothed over the conceptual conflicts between legal constraints on regime activity, the centralization of power, and the leading role of the CCP, going so far as to find that *yifa zhiguo* could provide the legal basis for centralized power and continued leadership of the Party (Peerenboom, 2002, pp. 6, 59–60). Jiang described these as major policies of the CCP and integral parts of Deng Xiaoping's theory of socialism with Chinese characteristics.

Despite the prominence of the broad "ruling according to law" precept, however, proposals to professionalize and grant bureaucratic autonomy to the Chinese judiciary have historically been rejected, even well into the post-Mao "reform and opening up" (*gaige kaifang*) era. In 2000, for instance, the SPC requested that the Personnel Department and the Ministry of Finance separate the judiciary from the bureaucratic hierarchy governing other civil servants, a move designed to enhance the ability of courts to retain career judges by offering better benefits and higher salaries. Such reforms would have increased bonus pay for case-deciding judges to a level 20–25 percent higher than that of other civil servants, and they would have established a system of remuneration that would be controlled by "judicial levels" (*faguan dengji*) – a hierarchical ranking system separate from the civil service system (Z. Liu, 2014).[1] Alluding to a pre-existing PRC policy designed to raise the professional level of cadres, then SPC President Xiao Yang supported this request, which would

[1] Liu also refers to the SPC Report Regarding Implementation of Judicial Adjudication Bonuses (*Zuigaorenminfayuanguanyuluoshishenpanjintie de baogao*), of April 18, 2000, Supreme People's Court Document Number 46 [2000].

have required amending the Judges' Law to provide preferential (*congyou*) welfare benefits to judges, with an argument that judicial salaries in most countries throughout the world are higher than those of ordinary civil servants; the National Peoples' Congress (NPC) Standing Committee rejected these SPC proposals in 2001 (Z. Liu, 2014, p. 156).[2]

In a three-year period between 2014 and 2016, however, China's national leadership reversed course, embarking on significant nationwide judicial reforms that in many ways mirrored the judicial personnel reform proposal put forward by SPC President Xiao Yang in 2000 (Chin, 2014; Hernandez, 2018; Hernandez & Carlsen, 2017; Johnson, 2016; *The Economist*, 2014). The 2014–2016 reforms were much more substantial and wide ranging than the more limited 1996–2001 *yifa zhiguo* reforms and, ultimately, any other national judicial reforms before or since. Their official objectives, harkening back to Xiao Yang's 2000 proposal, were particularly important: distinguishing judges from other Party cadres and giving them better status and pay; breaking down or reconstituting some of the basic internal structures of the courts that have discouraged talented judges; and abolishing performance indicators that have been poisonous for judges and litigants alike (Finder, 2016). These reforms were no judicial pet project, either – during 2014–2016, the main government body that pushes reform in China (i.e., the *shengaizu*) met 18 times, and 13 of those meetings addressed the judiciary (Johnson, 2016). Following up the SPC's Five-Year Plan for the judiciary, the SPC issued a comprehensive official assessment of its reform efforts (which were cleared by the Party leadership), focusing on its achievements between 2014 and 2016, and it also released SPC President Zhou Qiang's work report regarding judicial reforms, a first for the SPC (Finder, 2016). During the reform effort, the issue of "rule of law" was taken up at the party's Central Committee meeting, comprising more than 370 leaders, in October 2014; leaders were to discuss ways of "Dealing with the disillusionment in the judiciary" and strengthening the rule of law, with President Xi Jinping saying that he wanted the courts to help him "lock power in a cage." The Central Committee meeting appeared to be "…the first time such a conclave has been devoted to the rule of law" (*The Economist*, 2014).

Although the argument put forward in previous chapters primarily details local courts, this book also provides insights into these nationwide

[2] This article references in support a document called the SPC President's Explanation to the Draft Amendments to the Judges' Law (*Faguanfaxiuzheng an [caoan] de shuoming*), of May 30, 2000, Supreme People's Court Document Number 88 [2000].

changes. Regarding the motivations for the 2014–2016 national-level judicial reforms, my argument is more suggestive than definitive; nonetheless, I find that that these national-level reforms were motivated by a constellation of similar local concerns including judicial "brain drain," rapid increases in the cost of living in urban China, and the major transformations of the legal profession particularly prevalent in high-end localities elucidated throughout this book, which is consistent with the particular timing of national-level judicial personnel reforms in 2014–2016. After China's leadership recommitted to liberalizing reforms in 1992, foreign investment inflows resumed and accelerated (M. Gallagher, 2005; Hsueh, 2011; Pan, 2003), and foreign firms began operating in China (Stern & Li, 2016, p. 190). China's moves toward accession to the World Trade Organization (WTO) in 2001 also helped consolidate the internationalization and privatization of the legal profession (Alford, 2010; S. Liu, 2008; Michelson, 2003; Stern & Li, 2016), setting the stage in the early 2000s and beyond for the intertwined spatial differentiation of local legal service markets and judicial selection reforms in China's courts documented in Chapters 4 and 5.

These developments, especially since 2001, seem to have been key elements for understanding institutional change in China's courts, especially those in urban areas. This institution building in the legal system, a crucial cog in China's economic expansion over the past four decades, placed intense staffing pressures on local courts. The high-end legal service markets that have proliferated in urban China since the turn of the century have offered judges potentially lucrative alternative careers, threatening court leaders' abilities to retain highly qualified and experienced judges. When young, talented judges can easily quit their jobs and find high-paying local employment as lawyers, court leaders have sought to retain these judges by resorting to one of the only methods at their disposal for stemming judicial attrition: strategically reforming promotion mechanisms and increasing overall court transparency. More competitive and transparent promotion clarifies the path to career success for ordinary, mid-ranking judges, providing ordinary judges with greater assurance of upward career mobility. Ultimately, the design of this study not only illuminates local mechanisms of change but also provides the contextual background necessary for understanding court reforms at the national level.

Consider as well that in 2014, when national reforms were announced – but before approval from national elites – courts in Shanghai had already begun implementing the reforms: "Party leaders … are expected to review and endorse a pilot program, already under way in Shanghai, that grants judges special bureaucratic status distinct from other civil servants, raises their salaries, and gives them more power over trials and decisions" (Chin, 2014). Pilot projects had already begun likely because Shanghai Court Presidents had started implementing competitive promotion and other reforms to judicial selection years before; seen in this light, national reforms seemed to mirror those pushed forward by judicial "policy entrepreneurs" in Shanghai in the previous decade, rather than national leaders (even those in the SPC) devising policy from the top and implementing it in Shanghai and other local jurisdictions (see Mertha, 2009; cf. Zhang, 2012).

During interviews in summer 2014, judges claimed that pilot projects for courts in localities such as Shanghai and Guangdong province were designed to address the problem of judicial "brain drain"[3] by removing judges' civil servant identities and hierarchical rankings, setting up an entirely independent hierarchical structure specifically designed for case-deciding judges.[4] Several judges and lawyers that I interviewed hoped that salaries for case-deciding judges would be raised above those of other civil servants and that judges who decide cases would also be automatically promoted after serving a certain number of years as a judge with case-deciding authority.[5] In addition to addressing these judges' concerns and advancing the core judicial reform measure of "treating judges differently from clerks and other support personnel and civil servants" (Finder, 2016), the 2016 reforms even emphasized the importance of judicial independence, phrased broadly in Article II of the White Paper as "Ensuring Independent and Impartial Exercise of Judicial Power Pursuant to Law":

> In accordance with the Constitution of China, the people's courts shall exercise judicial power independently pursuant to the provisions of the law, and are not subject to interference by any administrative organ, public organization or individual.... The local courts are not courts belonging to local governments but the judicial courts established by the State at the local level to exercise judicial power on behalf of the State. Since 2014, the SPC has been cooperating with other departments of the Central Government to ... uphold judicial authority, thus forming an institutional environment and social atmosphere that respects [the] judiciary, supports [the] judiciary and trusts [the] judiciary.[6]

[3] *PC2014-3, judge, Shanghai, July 2014.*
[4] *PC2014-3, judge, Shanghai, July 2014.*
[5] *PC2014-2, judge, Shenzhen, June 2014.*
[6] White Paper on Judicial Reform of Chinese Courts, March 3, 2016, available at http://english.court.gov.cn/2016-03/03/content_23724636.htm (copy of relevant section on file with author).

Viewed in this context, the preceding chapters of this book provide compelling evidence that the Party-State's decision to reverse course between 2001 and 2014, particularly with respect to the issues of separating judges from the civil service bureaucracy and recognizing the importance of judges' dispute resolution capabilities, grew out of local concerns over judicial attrition, which had been exacerbated by the rapidly growing status and remuneration of legal professionals. These dynamics were most prevalent in China's high-end local legal service markets, such as Shanghai, after China's accession to the WTO in 2001–2002 and the concomitant privatization of legal practice in China. Not until then did the growth of the legal profession and the resulting judicial attrition sufficiently pressure urban court systems such that national leaders were convinced to enact nationwide judicial selection and promotion reforms. By contrast, the widespread social and political unrest, state repression, foreign capital flight, and the stalling of liberalizing reforms between 1989 and 1992 likely sapped momentum for increased judicial professionalism ahead of the *yifa zhiguo* reforms that began in 1996.

Historical Perspectives, Post-2016 Realities, and the Limits of This Study

The historical perspective of this book emphasizes the period of the post-Mao reform era after Deng's 1992 Southern Tour, with a primary focus on explaining substantial changes to large, local, urban court systems during 2001–2014 and to court systems nationwide during 2014–2016. For a variety of reasons, it is difficult to draw reliable conclusions regarding how court reform in urban China applies to socio-legal phenomena after 2016. The Party-State appeared to reverse course on judicial reforms after 2016, which also coincided with several historically significant international developments, which introduced law-related shocks to Chinese judicial institutions whose broader import still remains unclear. These possible influences include at least the following: fraying relations between China and several nations, including the United States, which involved pressure from the Trump Administration for wide-ranging legal reforms associated with disputes over trade barriers; China's amendments to criminal extradition law involving Hong Kong, which triggered a mass protest movement historically unrivaled in scale, size, and persistence; and of course, the COVID-19 pandemic that swept the globe beginning in late 2019, which appears to have accelerated the application of the national security law in Hong Kong and legal restrictions on protest gatherings.

Combined, these factors muddy the waters substantially for those attempting to explain change in the PRC's legal politics and judiciary, as they present new causal dynamics and (especially in the case of COVID-19) have made in-depth fieldwork on these topics effectively impossible. For these reasons, little is known about how courts actually operate in China after the dramatic, nationwide reforms to China's judiciary in 2014–2016.

Legal Realities after 2016

The judicial reforms of 2014–2016 were followed by international shocks to Chinese reform-era trajectories that likely influenced court policy and the broader legal system in China. These international shocks are reflected perhaps most vividly by Donald Trump's election to the US Presidency in November 2016, which was followed a few weeks later with a much publicized conversation between Trump and Taiwan's President Tsai Ing-wen, which broke with decades of US policy: "It is believed to be the first time a president or president-elect has spoken with the leader of Taiwan since diplomatic ties between Washington and Taipei were cut off in 1979" (Paletta et al., 2016). Most importantly for the present discussion, Trump's election presaged the wide-ranging legal ramifications of the US–China "trade war," a hotly contested set of interwoven domestic and international policy and legal debates that formally began in January 2018.

As is widely known, the world's two largest national economies "have been locked in a bitter trade battle" since at least 2018, involving hundreds of billions of dollars' worth of tariffs on American and Chinese goods (BBC News, 2020a). The United States raised tariffs generally in January 2018, and in July of the same year, the United States applied $34 billion worth of tariffs specifically on Chinese goods, with China responding in kind with retaliatory tariffs (Schlesinger & Ailworth, 2018). A tit-for-tat tariff struggle ensued, interspersed with negotiations aimed at lowering tariffs and pledges by the Chinese government to commit to large purchases of US goods. On January 15, 2020, the United States and China agreed to a "Phase One" trade deal, which formally itemized several of the legal issue areas viewed as central to the trade dispute, including intellectual property rights, technology transfer, food and agricultural products, financial services, exchange rate matters and transparency, and expanding trade, with reference as well to bilateral evaluation and dispute resolution procedures (Donnan et al., 2020). Unlike other trade agreements, the US–China Phase One agreement essentially relied solely on bilateral negotiations rather than arbitration through multilateral bodies such as the World Trade Organization (Davis, 2020). As of the end of 2021, trade relations continued to be tense, despite the efforts of Chinese and US officials to reach a comprehensive agreement (Wong & Lo, 2021).

Although it is unclear the extent to which escalating international tensions may have played a role in retrenchment of China's domestic legal reforms after 2016, national-level court policy departed significantly from the trajectory set by the 2014–2016 reforms by broadly taking aim at "the West" and concepts like judicial independence that were tentatively praised in reforms passed just a few years earlier. In February 2018, the PRC Party-State signalled that just as it could briskly implement dramatic changes to the judiciary in 2014–2016, it could just as quickly undo them, as the CCP "cleared the way for President Xi Jinping to stay in power indefinitely" by abolishing term limits on the presidency, "a momentous break with decades-old rules meant to prevent the country from returning to the days when Mao was shown cultish obedience" (Buckley & Bradsher, 2018). This development is consistent with a "new post 2018 judicial order" that emphasizes the importance of Chinese judicial work to resolutely preventing and opposing "the eroding influence of mistaken Western thinking...."[7] The SPC issued a variety of judicial policy documents in April 2020, consistent with the court's commitment made in January 2020 to better serve the Party and State, which appeared to "signal the way that the Chinese judicial system will develop in the post-19th Chinese Communist Party ... Congress Fourth Plenum New Era" (Finder, 2020).

Instead of ensuring the "Independent and Impartial Exercise of Judicial Power" (as the 2016 reforms did), the post-2016 reforms unambiguously emphasize "political correctness" and "perfecting the comprehensive leadership of the Party ... the most important goal is to uphold and implement the Party's absolute leadership of the courts and persist in putting the Party's political construction first"[8] (Finder, 2020). China's post-2016 legal reform order also emphasizes "Socialist Core Values" and an "Ideological Responsibility System" aimed at "maintaining and improving the loyalty of the Bureaucracy, as well as maintaining their ideological unification" (Finder, 2020).

[7] Opinion of the Supreme People's Court on Thoroughly Implementing the Spirit of the Fourth Plenum of the 19th Party Congress to Advance the Modernization of the Judicial System and Judicial Capacity (*Zuigaorenminfayuanguanyurenminfayuanguancheluoshi dang de shijiujiesi Zhong quanhuijingshentuijinshenpantixi he shenpannenglixiandaihua de yijian*), issued April 1, 2020, Paragraph 5.

[8] *Ibid.*

China's new mainland judicial policies have also appeared alongside other changes – especially those related to Hong Kong – further demonstrating the historic nature of law-related changes in Chinese politics since the mid-2010s. In February 2019, the Beijing-friendly Hong Kong government proposed the "Fugitive Offenders and Mutual Legal Assistance in Criminal Matters Legislation (Amendment) Bill," which would have allowed the Hong Kong Chief Executive to decide, in *ad hoc* fashion, whether to extradite criminal suspects pursuant to the request of another government, including that of the PRC. Under this provision, it would have been possible for citizens of Hong Kong to be extradited to mainland China to face trial (BBC News, 2019; Council, 2019). The bill triggered a far-reaching protest movement in Hong Kong, which was initially buoyed by concerns that the extradition bill would upend the foundations of Hong Kong's autonomy under China's "One Country, Two Systems" Policy (Chan, 2019). The protests began in March, and just a few months later on June 11, 2019, protesters surrounded "the Legislative Council building in an effort to block the session" (Lague et al., 2019). Although the proposed extradition law was formally withdrawn on October 23, 2019, protesters evolved their strategies, demanding "…an independent commission of inquiry into police's handling of the unrest … amnesty for all arrested protesters, as well as universal suffrage … [and] disbanding of the police force" (Leung et al., 2019).

The onset of the COVID-19 pandemic in the subsequent months likely helped diminish the scale and size of Hong Kong protests. Aside from fears of virus transmission, Hong Kong authorities enacted a new regulation in April 2020 "banning public gatherings of more than four people … in an effort to combat the coronavirus pandemic," stoking fears that the measures "might be used to crack down on political dissent…" (Hui, 2020). In May 2020, China's legislature introduced "security legislation for Hong Kong which would make it a crime to undermine Beijing's authority in the territory" (BBC News, 2020b), which was passed by the NPCSC on June 30, 2020 (Press, 2020). In the wake of the so-called national security law, several countries including Canada, Australia, the United Kingdom, New Zealand, Germany, and the United States passed laws in response, including to suspend extradition treaties and special trade status with Hong Kong (Cheung & Ng, 2020; Reuters Staff, 2020). However, by the end of 2021, it appeared that Hong Kong's national security law and other crackdowns had essentially brought the pro-democracy social and political movements in Hong Kong to a halt (Wong & Lo, 2021), which will in all likelihood usher in a vastly new set of legal dynamics in Hong Kong and the mainland.

Building a Research Agenda

These developments since 2016 encapsulate why the application of historical parameters, as used in this book, can help advance research on judicial politics in China: First, it is not yet possible to gauge the effects of these wide-ranging, law-related, and often unexpected developments on China's domestic court politics, making it reasonable to limit the historical analysis of this study to the period up to and including 2016; moreover, the developments during the period of 1992–2016 are not only crucial elements of the broader post-Mao legal reform effort, but they are also critical for beginning to understand its new post-2016 realities.

In interviews conducted in 2012 and 2013, several case-deciding judges in China's urban courts expressed frustrations with heavy workloads, low pay, and overbearing performance evaluation systems that resonated with Xiao Yang's proposal to professionalize the judiciary over a decade earlier. It is important to acknowledge the role that the globally unprecedented growth in the Chinese legal profession since 1992 has had in generating local income gaps between lawyers and judges that are so substantial that they create pressure for judicial reforms – indeed, where the income ceiling for law firm partners can reach into the millions of Chinese *yuan* but judicial salaries barely keep up with rapidly increasing costs of living in urban China (S. Liu & Wu, 2016).[9] Other judges claimed that it is impossible to meet the deadlines for case resolution imposed by the judicial performance evaluation system in China.[10]

Interviews like these suggest that the local pilot projects designed to experiment with judicial personnel reforms of 2014 did not come out of nowhere – as noted earlier, this book shows that local urban courts essentially rehearsed these reforms in the years leading up to their official pronouncement in 2014–2016. Measuring judicial autonomy by analyzing the competitiveness and routinization of judicial promotion mechanisms, compliance with judicial transparency mandates, and the extent to which judges justify their case decisions with written reasons, this book finds that local demand for legal professionals influenced the material and professional incentives of lawyers and judges starting in the early- to mid-2000s. Enhancements to judicial autonomy in urban China during this

[9] *PC2012-49, judge, Shanghai, December 2013; PC2012-6, judge, Shenzhen, June 2012; PC2014-11, lawyer, Shanghai, November 2014; PC2013-52, judge, Beijing, May 2013.*

[10] *PC2013-22, judge, Shanghai, March 2013.*

period emerged from the interaction between local demand for high-end legal services provided by legal professionals in urban China and the institutional incentives for the promotion of China's court leaders. The local undercurrents pushing local reforms to judicial promotion, transparency, decision-making, and bureaucratic specialization, documented particularly in Chapters 4 and 5, cast light on the pressures that today's Chinese judges and lawyers face, which have likely informed the regime's approach to introducing and implementing policies in 2014–2016 aimed at rendering the judicial branch more professionally autonomous from the broader civil service system.

As a theory-generating study, this book takes a suggestive and provocative approach that is supported by extensive documentary, interview, and historical data. While I rely primarily on original data and explain subnational patterns in Chinese judicial politics, my overriding aim has been to generate defensible theoretical claims and spur further systematic research into the determinants of judicial autonomy, rather than to test the internal and external validity of causal claims. As a result of the comparative case study research design and employment of qualitative methods, the fieldwork in this book took place in only a small sample of courts, and thus, the possibility of selection bias limits the generalizability of the current study (Geddes, 1990).

To remedy this and other similar shortcomings, future scholarship should both expand research on judicial autonomy in other parts of China and build comprehensive datasets using new and emerging sources of information. For example, one potential limitation of this study that should be addressed in future research is urban bias. As noted in Chapter 2, all of my case study localities are large, urban centers that boast relatively large and diverse law firm sectors; although my "similar systems" research design necessitates this approach and it also tells us much about under-explored elements of China's urban courts, many parts of China are not served by high-end corporate clients or even "battleground" law firms, and this book does not necessarily specify whether and how mechanisms of demand for legal professionals would influence judicial institutions in less developed localities. Future research in peri-urban and rural localities could pinpoint whether the form or dynamics of local law firm markets shift across spatial types, or whether the findings of this study are limited to the cases examined or a different subset of court systems in China.

The use of documentary materials in the study of Chinese law and politics could be ramped up as well, which would ideally help track change between the pre- and post-2016 periods. Judicial opinions could help here – the China Judgments Online website[11] has opened new opportunities for research on judicial decision-making, which might be helped even further with text analysis.[12] In addition to traditional close readings of important documents, textual content analysis might be used to gain a machine-aided understanding of important data characteristics of judicial opinions and other texts, or these methods might perhaps also be used to select cases for close reading regarding particular questions (Liebman et al., 2020). Ideally, datasets could be constructed using judicial opinions as well as judicial selection and promotion announcements as primary source materials (which can be made from gazettes, yearbooks, and adjudicatory newsletters)[13]; future interviews with Chinese officials can also be more effective when questions and conversations can be better tailored around specific questions gleaned from these materials (Solinger, 2006).

Given that there have long been data limitations regarding the specific mechanisms of judicial promotion in China[14] and that this book has concentrated on creating theories, detailing complex causal pathways, and developing insights about the evolution of judicial promotion mechanisms and transparency policy in urban China (Geddes, 1990, p. 149; Whiting, 2000, p. 30), further subnational comparative analysis could attempt to confirm variations in judicial promotion mechanisms within and across rural, urban, and peri-urban contexts. Broader hypothesis testing and more in-depth individual case studies could further pin down fine-grained causal mechanisms and trace the exact processes at work on the ground in specific contexts.

To do this, future studies might consider beginning a theory-testing phase of the research cycle in at least two ways. First, it is certainly feasible that existing research, such as Yuhua Wang's (2015), is at the very least partially compatible with the main findings of this book, and it might be

[11] The China Judgments Online website is available at https://wenshu.court.gov.cn/.

[12] Danie Stockmann provides a helpful overview of this method on the website http://daniestockmann.net/research/content-analysis-of-chinese-texts/.

[13] During my fieldwork research, many local court newsletters have been accessible at Shanghai Library.

[14] As noted, previous scholarship has not detailed the criteria for becoming a judge and for being promoted (Peerenboom, 2010, p. 77). Stanley Lubman notes that CCP officials have historically selected judges using opaque, nonprofessional processes (Lubman, 1999, p. 256). Hurst's recent study is among the few that explore potentially fruitful approaches to incorporating China's legal system into cross-national comparative frameworks (Hurst, 2018).

possible to craft future research to resolve tensions between similar but competing claims. For instance, this book and Wang's both assume that there is a role played by foreign investment in China's domestic legal politics and that that foreign law firms compete fiercely with domestic firms for professional, local legal staff, especially for qualified mid-ranking legal workers in high-end legal markets like Shanghai (S. Liu, 2011a, 2011b; Y. Wang, 2015). In this way, both Wang's theory and this book posit that judicial reform outcomes (whether autonomy or partial rule of law) are determined at least in part by a root cause linked to foreign investment. A "crucial case study" approach (whether a single case or a small set of crucial cases) could investigate whether Wang's pathway (the demand-side exit-voice mechanism of asset-holding foreign investors/lobbyists) or the mechanism described in this book (internationalization and growth of the private legal service profession) leads to certain variations in outcomes related to China's judiciary (see Van Evera, 1997, p. 66). To illustrate, further research could verify whether causality works pursuant to the following "multiple chain of causality" mechanism:

```
      → p →
A → →       → → B
      → q →
```

In this schematic, "A" could represent the influence of foreign investment, with "B" representing judicial outcomes in China; it might be possible that in some localities, the "p" pathway (e.g., Wang's exit/voice mechanism) leads to changes in the judiciary, whereas in others, the "q" pathway (e.g., growth of the local legal profession) is activated. Accordingly, early theory testing phases of this research might follow a "pathway case" approach whereby causal hypotheses are not necessarily confirmed or disconfirmed, but rather clarified (Gerring, 2007). Otherwise, there is also potential to adjudicate between my and Wang's theories by analyzing a critical case in which court reforms occurred in a given locality that exhibits either a high-end legal service market or substantial numbers of foreign investors from outside the China circle, but not both.

Second, both the English- and Chinese-language literature on PRC courts have discussed the possibility that "pull" factors like increasing attorney salaries and "push" factors such as crushing caseloads and other workload burdens under the CQAS (detailed in Chapter 3) could create pressure for judicial promotion reforms (see, e.g., Hu, 2015). A potential research strategy for assessing the merits of push versus pull explanations could also form the basis for a potential "crucial case" research design by obtaining comparative and time-series data on crushing caseloads and other judicial workload burdens (perhaps measured by cases assigned or accepted per judge or per court division, or a more holistic measurement of judicial workload burden based on the different factors examined in Chapter 3), which could serve as a measurement for a variety of "push" factors in a given court or locality. These data could then be compared to similar information regarding local lawyer salaries to gauge the relative strength of "pull" factors. Cases could then be selected based on differences on these two potential explanatory variables to help judge the strength of push versus pull factors across localities in China. In these ways, a variety of alternative theories might either be tested for consistency with my theory or reassessed and clarified further in a broader theory-testing phase of the research cycle on Chinese courts.

Whether it is called "partial rule of law" (Y. Wang, 2015, pp. 18–19) or the circumscribed judicial autonomy described in Chapter 2 of this book, Party–State leaders in China are unlikely to grant full-fledged autonomy to PRC judges, much less establish a constitutional court with the power to review regime-supported legislation. Instead of empowering judges to challenge regime policies or allowing citizens to advance claims of individual right, rapid institution building in the court system reveals the state's interest in a legalization project geared toward providing credible commitments to foreign investors and establishing an economic infrastructure for a largely market-based economy (Ginsburg & Moustafa, 2008; Moustafa, 2007, pp. 21–41; Y. Wang, 2015). The ecological approach to explaining a change in China's legal system employed in this book takes a more ambitious approach than other similar works by aiming to generate theories that examine the plausibility of causal relationships between macro- and micro-level institutional layers, actors, and events. While Liu is correct to suggest, for instance, that events shaping lawyer mobility might be "contingent on the particular social contexts in which lawyer migration, or other social processes of law, takes place" and are likely not statistically predictable, more modest causal claims might also be supported by an ecological framework, which could integrate the ecological study of courts in China and other authoritarian regimes with more positivistic social science research on the topic (Hurst, 2018; Y. Wang, 2015). Ultimately, research on seemingly disparate legal issue areas such as labor and employment law (M. E. Gallagher, 2017), environmental litigation (Stern, 2013), and intellectual property law (Dimitrov, 2009) could be better understood under a unified, ecology-based framework for researching the politics of courts and lawyers in China and other authoritarian regimes.

Lessons for Authoritarian Judiciaries

In earlier comparative law and politics research, scholars eschewed analysis of causal factors leading to changes in the judiciary, focusing instead on classifying various institutional legacies into civil, common, socialist, and religious law systems (Damaska, 1986; Hazard, 1969; Merryman, 1969; Quigley, 1989). In this endeavor, categorizing the socialist or Marxian legal tradition has proven slippery, with several communist states (e.g., Vietnam, Cuba, and the Eastern European bloc countries) reflecting the influence of civil law legal traditions inherited from Continental Europe. Even those scholars claiming that socialist legality is a unique legal type often drew ideological and economic distinctions rather than judicial, institutional, or legislative ones (Hazard, 1969, p. 521).

Although this book benefits from the legacy of these groundbreaking studies, it also engages much more directly with recent literature on comparative judicial politics, in which scholars have applied more positivistic social scientific approaches. Viewed in the context of previous studies on the categorization of legal systems, recent research represents a scholarly shift toward repackaging "legal system types" into discrete variables and factors that affect the rule of law and courts in specific polities. Scholars have turned their attention to the determinants of changes in judicial "empowerment" – which can refer to topics ranging from increased powers of judicial review and the authority of Constitutional Courts in authoritarian regimes (Ginsburg, 2003; Hilbink & Woods, 2009; Moustafa, 2007; Solomon, 2007a; Trochev, 2004, 2008). For example, in the Chilean case of judicial empowerment in democracy and dictatorship, institutions governing the promotion, appointment, and performance of judges continued to influence judicial practice despite changes to the broader political environment. Autonomous bureaucratic institutions in Chile that govern judicial salary, tenure, discipline, and punishment led judges, over time, to seek the favor of their institutional superiors rather than liberal judicial activism (Hilbink, 2007, pp. 33–36).[15]

Likewise, Trochev's study of the Russian judiciary documents the importance of bureaucratic support in implementing judicial decisions (Trochev, 2008), and rising caseloads and increased deadline pressure raise the probability of judicial error when deciding complex civil and economic cases (see Hendley, 2013, p. 1). Similar to courts in Chile and

[15] On a related topic, other researchers document the importance, especially in illiberal states, of bureaucratic support when implementing judicial decisions (see, e.g., Trochev, 2008).

Russia, bureaucratic evaluations and discipline shape the incentives of PRC judges (as discussed in Chapter 3). But whereas other authoritarian courts value secrecy regarding judicial evaluation (Hilbink, 2007, pp. 224–234), the hallmark of the Chinese bureaucratic evaluation of judges is widespread visibility of bureaucratic scores among peers, which serves as the tool that drives some judges to higher productivity levels and the next chance at promotion. Here, my findings are consistent with those of Hilbink and others that bureaucratic conditions can potentially be seen as factors that can influence outcomes related to judicial behavior. To paraphrase Shapiro, when the people's courts that helped legitimize the revolution become part of a larger modernizing and bureaucratization effort, the Party often discovers that more empowered courts are no threat to a workers' state so long as judges remain subject to the career discipline of the judicial bureaucracy (Hazard, 1969; Shapiro, 1981, pp. 61, 62).

This recent literature has done well to examine the mechanisms by which some of the relatively mundane dynamics of everyday justice can lead to change in the legal system. Although approaches that seemingly de-emphasize direct conflict and power struggles might not seem readily applicable to the oppressive contexts of authoritarian states, commonplace changes can and do occur continuously and alongside the systemic changes demanded by activists, mobilized groups, and others in the face of repression. This finding resonates with other studies of authoritarian legal systems that find plural power dynamics operating within individual authoritarian states. Take, for instance, Meierhenrich's analysis of the apartheid state in South Africa, regarding which he finds that the "prerogative state," which operated forcefully as an instrument of oppression, was nonetheless compelled to exercise power legally. This double-bind, a seeming reflection of the authoritarian judicial dilemma discussed in Chapter 2, can render authoritarian rulers vulnerable to contestation under certain conditions (Meierhenrich, 2008, pp. 129–130), and it is also based on a Weberian sense of forms and substance of law. Borrowing from Ernst Fraenkel's original conception and application to conflicting legal imperatives of Hitler's Nazi regime (Fraenkel, 1941; Meierhenrich, 2008, pp. 42–43), overtones of the "dual" state can be discerned in accounts of post-Mao China that find multiplicities of legal power employed in different conditions and contexts with differing degrees of tolerance and policymaking space for commercial versus criminal law, politically sensitive versus ordinary law, among others, which can lead to "rule by law," "partial rule of law," or thin versus thick rule of law (Hurst, 2018; S. Liu & Halliday, 2016; Mertha, 2009; Peerenboom, 2002; Stern, 2013; Y. Wang, 2015;

Y. Wang & Minzner, 2015). The key moving forward is enhanced precision when identifying the spatial-temporal parameters and boundaries of the multiplicity of these "states," "legal regimes," or "linked ecologies" operating within China's overarching state and society, which result in the heterogeneity of social forms in multiple dimensions of power (see S. Liu, 2008). Extensions of these concepts to socio-legal understandings of human ecology and the emerging research on the "legal complex" might be a path forward in examining the more mundane construction of China's commercial law within a "tolerance interval" acceptable to the state versus mobilized legal contestation outside this tolerance interval (Cain, 1974; Foucault, 1977; S. Liu & Au, 2020; S. Liu & Emirbayer, 2016; S. Liu & Halliday, 2016, 2019; Weber, 1978). Such approaches have potential to distinguish between conflict-based and noncontested legal system change, both with respect to China and to post-2016 law-related international and domestic change.

The findings of this study also have the potential to advance the understanding of the role of law as an instrument of power, as well as inequality and development in China and beyond, despite this book's focus on the formal aspects of legal change. In emphasizing the formal aspects of law, this book has mostly endeavored to articulate "the social structures and processes that constitute its spatial and temporal dimensions," mostly setting aside a precise analysis of how these legal shapes produce power asymmetries and allow them to operate (S. Liu, 2015, pp. 2–3). At the same time, an emphasis on legal forms and an analysis of power and inequality are "complementary for achieving a comprehensive and integrated sociological understanding of the legal system," and follow-up studies might examine more directly the substantive aspect of law more often associated with a power/inequality socio-legal approach, "…that is, the prevailing notions of justice and equality in society as well as the patterns of domination and resistance associated with them" (S. Liu, 2015). Recent studies whose findings could possibly be extended in this direction include those that have highlighted that the professional mobilization of lawyers "has a spatial logic" whereby "an ecology of activism can emerge initially from a state of isolation," and as "the social distances between actors are reduced, the meanings of mobilization are crystallized through boundary work between actors over positions, and this in turn leads to the emergence of a consolidated social space for activism" (S. Liu & Halliday, 2019, p. 453).

As it relates to social inequality and development, an implication of this book is that the development of the PRC judicial system is poised to provide more impartial judicial services to areas where courts commonly hear corporate litigation, whereas reforms aimed at professionalizing the judiciary in less developed urban localities and "battleground" legal markets appear to stall more easily. Much of China has not developed to the point that corporate litigation is often heard in courts, and other research on Chinese courts suggests that citizens in rural areas do not have access to fair, well-trained judges. Hence, this book could also serve as a stepping stone for understanding how to incorporate the study of access to justice across China into understandings of social inequality; in so doing, it also urges scholars studying the sources of judicial autonomy, especially in authoritarian regimes, to view the judiciary as part of a larger class of legal professionals whose specialized portfolio of skills, annual income, workload, and social status are all in flux when a regime seeks to empower law as part of a broader effort at enhancing regime legitimacy. Further studies on the legal complex might uncover whether greater judicial professionalism affects the judicial response to lawyer-led mobilization, thereby shaping patterns of power distribution (Cain, 1974; Foucault, 1977; Halliday et al., 2007; S. Liu & Halliday, 2016, 2019; Weber, 1978).

Whereas extant scholarship on judicial politics in new democracies or transitional political systems sees judicial autonomy as affected mainly by competition between multiple parties, the one-party dominance of the CCP precludes a finding that party competition produces the changes in judicial promotion described previously. Nonetheless, in some localities in China, court leaders appear to be willing to offer their judges better conditions, including professionalized selection and promotion mechanisms, as an unintended consequence of the interaction between central government standards for case quality and local demand for qualified legal talent (i.e., professional, capable lawyers, and judges).

Conclusion

Despite its shortcomings, this study is distinctive for challenging conventional approaches in judicial politics that largely cast in opposition civil society actors and the state officials who command the repressive apparatus, with judges as gatekeepers. An examination of constitutional rights activism in China illustrates this point: Whereas the regime has appeared to reverse itself since 2000 regarding judicial professionalization – an apparent recognition that the judiciary is, in the words of former SPC President Xiao Yang, a "special" profession (Michelson, 2003, p. 17) – it has strengthened its authoritarian grip on activist lawyers and rights claimants. Perhaps, no story captures this dramatic shift in state–society relations more than that of Xu Zhiyong, whose political advocacy played a major role in perhaps the most significant act of Chinese Party–State concession to liberal activists – the 2003 abolition of "custody and repatriation of vagrants and beggars in cities" (*shourongqiansong*). However, since 2003, the Party-State has leaned heavily on activist lawyers; for example, Xu's legal aid center was closed in 2009, resulting in Xu's temporary detention, and on August 22, 2013, Xu was arrested for "gathering a crowd to disrupt order in a public place" (Branigan, 2009)[16]; in January 2014, Xu was convicted and sentenced to four years in prison.[17] Since the 2003 abolishment of "custody and repatriation," constitutional petitions for greater rights protections were ignored and outright repressed by the Beijing leadership (Pils & Rosenzweig, 2014), building up into a wave of arrests of activist lawyers in July 2015 that essentially extinguished the rights-based activism that looked so promising just a decade earlier (Fu & Zhu, 2018; Michelson, 2020).

As this chapter and developments since the turn of the century demonstrate, legal politics in the PRC has at least these two sides: the increasingly harsh approach to the mobilizing tactics of activist lawyers on one hand, and the interest in modernizing attempts to professionalize the judiciary on the other. In focusing heavily on the latter phenomenon, this book acknowledges that in many legal systems, but especially in authoritarian states, contentious advocacy for political change can easily be severely circumscribed, but the lines between professional classes and state organs are often blurred, allowing symbiotic interaction between judges, lawyers, and state officials to bring about change in the operation of courts and the larger legal system (Halliday, Karpik, & Feeley, 2007; S. Liu, 2011a). This book's focus on local-level reforms occurring primarily in high-end cities reveals that this process of change can draw the attention of national-level policymakers, even in an authoritarian state like China: Central leaders and the SPC had the opportunity to advance wide-ranging reforms to judicial promotion and remuneration in the early 2000s, but instead moved forward at that time with a much more limited set of reforms under SPC President Xiao Yang, and even those were countered by Wang Shengjun's populist turn

[16] Full text of the verdict in the Xu Zhiyong case is available at http://chinalawtranslate.com/en/xu-zhiyong-opinion/, accessed February 24, 2015.

[17] The information in this paragraph is taken primarily from the Xu Zhiyong verdict.

in 2008, despite some limited professionalizing reforms (C. Minzner, 2011a; T. Zhang, 2012). I agree with scholars who find that the 2014–2016 reforms were particularly significant for distinguishing judges from other Party cadres, giving judges better status and pay, reconstituting basic internal structures of the courts, and abolishing counterproductive performance indicators. Based on the continued changes to China's legal system, it is clear that an understanding of the recent past is necessary to move forward.

APPENDIX

Summary of Interviews Regarding Local Lawyer Salaries (2014)

Informant identification number		Time of personal communication	Reported partner income (RMB)	Reported experienced associate (nonpartner) income (RMB)	Reported entry-level associate (nonpartner) income (RMB)
Shanghai	L7S	October 2014	N/A	300,000	100,000
	L1S	October 2014	2,000,000	N/A	92,000
	L4S	October 2014	840,000	720,000	150,000
	L9S	October 2014	2,000,000	400,000	140,000
Shenzhen	L7Z	October 2014	450,000	195,000	65,000
	L2Z	October 2014	300,000	300,000	N/A
	L1Z	October 2014	5,000,000	N/A	N/A
Chengdu	L4C	October 2014	2,000,000	150,000	45,000
	L2C	November 2014	750,000	150,000	N/A

REFERENCES

Abbott, A. (1988). *The system of professions: An essay on the division of expert labor.* University of Chicago Press.

Abbott, A. (2005). Linked ecologies. *Sociological Theory, 23*(3), 245–274. https://doi.org/10.1111%2Fj.0735-2751.2005.00253.x

Ahl, B. (2014). Retaining judicial professionalism: The new guiding cases mechanism of the supreme people's court. *The China Quarterly, 217*, 1–19. https://doi.org/10.1017/S0305741013001471

Alford, W. P. (1995). Tasselled loafers for barefoot lawyers: Transformation and tension in the world of Chinese legal workers. *The China Quarterly, 141*, 22–38. https://doi.org/10.1017/S0305741000032896

Alford, W. P. (2010). "Second lawyers, first principles": Lawyers, rice-roots legal workers, and the battle over legal professionalism in China. In W. P. Alford, W. Kirby, & K. Winston (Eds.), *Prospects for the professions in China* (pp. 48–77). Routledge. https://doi.org/10.4324/9780203843024

Amnesty International. (2018). Death sentences. In *Death sentences and executions 2017.* www.amnesty.org.au/wp-content/uploads/2018/04/amnesty-report-death-penalty-2018.pdf

Baker, G. P., Jensen, M. C., & Murphy, K. J. (1988). Compensation and incentives: Practice vs. theory. *The Journal of Finance, 43*(3), 593–616. https://doi/10.1111/j.1540-6261.1988.tb04593.x/full

Balme, S. (2009). Ordinary justice and popular constitutionalism in China. In S. Balme & M. W. Dowdle (Eds.), *Building constitutionalism in China* (pp. 179–198). Palgrave MacMillan.

Barnett, A. D., & Vogel, E. F. (1967). *Cadres, bureaucracy, and political power in communist China.* Columbia University Press.

Baum, L. (2006). *Judges and their audiences: A perspective on judicial behavior.* Princeton University Press.

BBC News. (2014, January 26). China court sentences Xu Zhiyong to four years in jail. www.bbc.com/news/world-asia-china-25900272

BBC News. (2019, December 13). Hong Kong–China extradition plans explained. www.bbc.com/news/world-asia-china-47810723

BBC News. (2020a, January 16). A quick guide to the US–China trade war. www.bbc.com/news/business-45899310

BBC News. (2020b, May 28). Hong Kong security legislation backed by China's parliament. www.bbc.com/news/world-asia-china-52829176

Bennett, A., & Elman, C. (2006). Qualitative research: Recent developments in case-study methods. *Annual Review of Political Science*, *9*(1), 455–476. https://doi.org/10.1146/annurev.polisci.8.082103.104918

Black, D. (n.d.). *The behavior of law* (2nd ed.). Emerald Group Publishing Limited.

Black, M., Moffitt, R., & Warner, J. (1990). The dynamics of job separation: The case of federal employees. *Journal of Applied Economics*, *245*(5), 245–262.

Blecher, M. (2003). *China against the tides* (2nd ed.). Continuum.

Bodde, D., & Morris, C. (1967). *Law in imperial China*. Harvard University Press.

Borjas, G. J. (1982). Labor turnover in the U.S. federal bureaucracy. *Journal of Public Economics*, *19*, 187–202. https://doi.org/10.1016/0047-2727(82)90042-1

Bourdieu, P. (1987). The force of law: Toward a sociology of the juridical field. *Hastings Law Journal*, *38*, 805–853.

Bourdieu, P., & Wacquant, L. J. D. (1992). *An invitation to reflexive sociology*. University of Chicago Press.

Boylan, R. (2004). Salaries, turnover, and performance in the federal criminal justice system. *Law and Economics*, *47*(1), 75–92.

Branigan, T. (2009, July 30). Chinese police detain human rights lawyer. *The Guardian*. www.theguardian.com/world/2009/jul/30/china-human-rights-lawyer

Brødsgaard, K. E. (2002). Institutional reform and the *bianzhi* system in China. *The China Quarterly*, *170*(June), 361–386. https://doi.org/10.1017/S0009443902000232

Brødsgaard, K. E. (2012). Cadre and personnel management in the CPC. *China: An International Journal*, *10*(2), 69–83.

Brinks, D. M. (2008). *The judicial response to police killings in Latin America*. Cambridge University Press.

Brinks, D. M., & Blass, A. (2018). *The DNA of constitutional justice in Latin America*. Cambridge University Press.

Buckley, C., & Bradsher, K. (2018, February 25). China moves to let Xi stay in power by abolishing term limit. *The New York Times*.

Burns, J. P., & Wang, X. (2010). Civil service reform in China: Impacts on civil servants' behavior. *The China Quarterly*, *201*, 58–78. https://doi.org/10.1017/S030574100999107X

Cai, Y., & Yang, S. (2005). State power and unbalanced legal development in China. *Journal of Contemporary China*, *14*(42), 117–134. https://doi.org/10.1080/1067056042000300817

Cain, M. (1974). The main themes of Marx and Engels' sociology of law. *British Journal of Law and Society*, *1*, 136–148. https://doi.org/10.2307/1409865

CASS: Chinese Academy of Social Sciences Legal Studies Department Rule of Law National Status Research Group. (2012). Problems and strategies for making written judicial opinions public on the internet (in Chinese; internal document). *Leadership Reference Material (Lingdao Canyue)*, 2.

Chan, H. (2019, March 31). In pictures: 12,000 Hongkongers march in protest against 'evil' China extradition law, organisers say. *Hong Kong Free Press*.

Chavez, R. B. (2004). The evolution of judicial autonomy in Argentina: Establishing the rule of law in an ultrapresidential system. *Journal of Latin American Studies*, *36*(3), 451–478. https://doi.org/10.1017/S0022216X04007758

Chen, J. (2008). *Chinese law: Context and transformation*. Brill.

Chengdu Bureau of Statistics. (2011). *Chengdu statistical yearbook 2011 (Chengdu tongji nianjian 2011)*. China Statistics Publishing House (Zhongguo tongji chubanshe). www.cdstats.chengdu.gov.cn/list.asp?ClassID=020703

Chengdu Intermediate People's Court. (1997). *Chengdu court gazette (Chengdu fayuanzhi)*. Sichuan People's Publishing House (Sichuan renmin chubanshe).

Cheung, G., & Ng, T. (2020, July 15). National security law: Beijing vows to retaliate after Donald Trump ends special treatment for Hong Kong and targets officials with sanctions. *South China Morning Post*. www.scmp.com/news/hong-kong/politics/article/3093344/national-security-law-beijing-vows-retaliate-after-trump

Chin, J. (2014, October 21). China tries to hold on to judges by offering freer hand: With judges quitting in droves, party plenum to focus on tweaking legal system. *Wall Street Journal*. http://online.wsj.com/articles/china-tries-to-hold-on-to-judges-by-offering-freer-hand-1413822462

China Daily Staff. (2017, March 14). Workload for judges addressed. *China Daily*. www.chinadaily.com.cn/m/chinalic/2017-03/14/content_28555039.htm

China Law Yearbook Editing Committee. (Various years). China Law Yearbook (*Zhongguo falü nianjian*). Beijing: China Law Yearbook Publishing House.

China Lawyers Yearbook Editing Committee. (2005). *China lawyers yearbook 2004 (Zhongguo lüshi nianjian 2004)*. Legal System Publishing House (Zhongguo fazhi chubanshe).

China Lawyers Yearbook Editing Committee. (2009). *China lawyers yearbook 2006–2008 (Zhongguo lüshi nianjian 2006–2008)*. People's Court Publishing House.

China Lawyers Yearbook Editing Committee. (2011). *China yearbook of lawyers 2009 (Zhongguo lüshi nianjian 2009)*. People's Court Publishing House.

Chinese Lawyers Yearbook Editing Committee. (2005). *Chinese yearbook of lawyers, 2001–2003 (Zhongguo lüshi nianjian, 2001–2003)*. Renmin fayuan chubanshe.

Clarke, D. C. (2003). Empirical research in Chinese law. In E. Jensen & T. Heller (Eds.), *Beyond common knowledge: Empirical approaches to the rule of law* (pp. 164–192). Stanford University Press.

Cohen, J. (1979). Due process (in China)? In *The China difference: A portrait of life today inside the country of one billion* (pp. 237–259). Harper and Row.

Cohen, J. (2016, February). A looming crisis for China's legal system. *Foreign Policy.* https://foreignpolicy.com/2016/02/22/a-looming-crisis-for-chinas-legal-system/

Cohen, J. A. (1980). China's new lawyers' law. *American Bar Association Journal, 66*(12), 1533–1535.

Council, H. K. L. (2019). Legal service division report on fugitive offenders and mutual legal assistance in criminal matters legislation (Amendment) bill 2019.

Dahl, R. (1957). Decision-making in a democracy: The supreme court as a national policy-maker. *Journal of Public Law, VI*(2), 279.

Damaska, M. (1986). *The faces of justice and state authority: A comparative approach to the legal process.* Yale University Press.

Davis, B. (2020, January 16). U.S.-China deal could upend the way nations settle disputes. *Wall Street Journal.*

Deng, J. (Ed.). (2001). *A record of the Shenzhen intermediate people's court Chuji level cadre leaders competitive promotion system (Shenzhenshi Zhongji Renmin Fayuan Chuji Lingdao Ganbu Jingzheng Shanggang Jishi).* China Legal System Publishing House (Zhongguo fazhi chubanshe).

DiFederico, G., & Guarnieri, C. (1988). The courts in Italy. In J. L. Waltman & K. M. Holland (Eds.), *The political role of law courts in modern democracies* (pp. 153–180). MacMillan.

Dimitrov, M. (2009). *Piracy and the state: The politics of intellectual property rights in China.* Cambridge University Press.

Donnan, S., Wingrove, J., & Mohsin, S. (2020, January 15). U.S. and China sign phase one of trade deal. *Bloomberg.*

Economy, E. (2019, October). China's neo-Maoist Moment. *Foreign Affairs.* www.foreignaffairs.com/articles/china/2019-10-01/chinas-neo-maoist-moment

Edin, M. (2003). State capacity and local agent control in China: CCP cadre management from a township perspective. *The China Quarterly, 173,* 35–52.

Epp, C. (1998). *The rights revolution: Lawyers, activists, and supreme courts in comparative perspective.* University of Chicago Press.

Epstein, L., Knight, J., & Shvetsova, O. (2001). The role of constitutional courts in the establishment and maintenance of democratic systems of government. *Law & Society Review, 35,* 117–164.

Finder, S. (2016). What China's judicial reform white paper says about its vision for its judiciary. *Supreme People's Court Monitor.*

Finder, S. (2020, May 4). Supreme people's court's new vision for the Chinese courts. *Supreme People's Court Monitor.* https://supremepeoplescourtmonitor.com/2020/05/04/supreme-peoples-courts-new-vision-for-the-chinese-courts/

Fioretos, O., Falleti, T., & Sheingate, A. (2016). *The Oxford handbook of historical institutionalism.* Oxford University Press.

Foucault, M. (1977). *Discipline and punish: The birth of the prison* (trans. A. Sheridan). Vintage Books.

Foucault, M. (2008). *The birth of biopolitics: Lectures at the College de France, 1978–1979* (M. Senellart [Ed.]). Palgrave MacMillan.

Fraenkel, E. (1941). *The dual state: A contribution to the theory of dictatorship.* Oxford University Press.

Fu, H. (2003). Putting China's judiciary into perspective: Is it independent, competent, and fair? In E. G. Jensen & T. C. Heller, (Eds.), *Beyond common knowledge: Empirical approaches to the rule of law* (pp. 193–219). Stanford University Press.

Fu, H., & Zhu, H. (2018). After the July 9 (709) crackdown: The future of human rights lawyering. *Fordham International Law Journal, 41*(5), 1135–1164.

Galanter, M. (1974). Why the "haves" come out ahead: Speculations on the limits of legal change. *Law & Society Review, 9*, 95–160.

Gallagher, M. (2005). *Contagious capitalism: Globalization and the politics of labor in China.* Princeton University Press.

Gallagher, M. E. (2017). *Authoritarian legality in China: Law, workers, and the state.* Cambridge University Press.

Gauri, V., & Brinks, D. M. (2008). Introduction: The elements of legalization and the triangular shape of social and economic rights. In V. Gauri & D. M. Brinks (Eds.), *Courting social justice: Judicial enforcement of social and economic rights in the developing world* (pp. 1–37). Cambridge University Press.

Geddes, B. (1990). How the cases you choose affect the answers you get: Selection bias in comparative politics. *Political Analysis, 2*(1), 131–150.

Gerring, J. (2007). Is there a (viable) crucial-case method? *Comparative Political Studies, 30*(3), 231–253.

Givens, J. (2014). Sleeping with dragons? Politically embedded lawyers suing the Chinese state. *Wisconsin International Law Journal, 31*(3), 101–140.

Ginsburg, T. (2003). *Judicial review in new democracies: Constitutional courts in Asian cases.* Cambridge University Press.

Ginsburg, T., & Moustafa, T. (Eds.). (2008). *Rule by law: The politics of courts in authoritarian regimes.* Cambridge University Press.

Guo, N. (2013, April 20). Shanghai courts' judicial fairness index and transparency level are highest in the country (in Chinese). *Liberation Daily (Jie'fang Ribao).* www.chinacourt.org/article/detail/2013/04/id/939740.shtml

Hall, P., & Taylor, R. (1996). Political science and the three new institutionalisms. *Political Studies, 44*, 936–957.

Halliday, T., & Karpik, L. (Eds.). (1997). *Lawyers and the rise of western political liberalism: Europe and north America from the eighteenth to twentieth centuries.* Oxford University Press on Demand.

Halliday, T., Karpik, L., & Feeley, M. (Eds.). (2007). *Fighting for political freedom: Comparative studies of the legal complex and political liberalism.* Hart.

Hand, K. J. (2007). Using the law for a righteous purpose: The Sun Zhigang incident and evolving forms of citizen action in the People's Republic of China. *Columbia Journal of Transnational Law, 45*(1), 1114–1195.

Hannan, M. T., & Freeman, J. (1977). The population ecology of organizations. *American Journal of Sociology, 82*(5), 929–964.

Hannan, M. T., & Freeman, J. (1989). *Organizational ecology*. Harvard University Press.

Harding, H. (1981). *Organizing China: The problem of bureaucracy, 1949–1976*. Stanford University Press.

Hazard, J. N. (1969). *Communists and their law: A search for the common core of legal system of the Marxian socialist states*. University of Chicago Press.

He, X. (2009). Administrative law as political control mechanism. In S. Balme & M. Dowdle (Eds.), *Building constitutionalism in China* (pp. 143–162). Palgrave MacMillan.

Hendley, K. (2012). The puzzling non-consequences of societal distrust of courts: Explaining the use of Russian courts. *Cornell International Law Journal, 45*(3), 517–567.

Hendley, K. (2013). Too much of a good thing? Assessing access to civil justice in Russia. *Slavic Review, 72*(4), 802–827.

Hernandez, J. C. (2018, September 28). For Xi Jinping, Being a man of the people means looking the part. *The New York Times*.

Hernandez, J. C., & Carlsen, A. (2017, November 9). Why Xi's (Airbrushed) face is plastered all over China. *The New York Times*. www.nytimes.com/interactive/2017/11/09/world/asia/xi-propaganda.html

Hilbink, L. (2007). *Judges beyond politics in democracy and dictatorship: Lessons from Chile*. Cambridge University Press.

Hilbink, L., & Woods, P. J. (2009). Comparative sources of judicial empowerment: Ideas and interests. *Political Research Quarterly, 62*(4), 745–752.

Ho, D. Y. (1976). On the concept of face. *American Journal of Sociology, 81*(4), 867–884.

Howson, N. C. (2010). Corporate law in the Shanghai People's Courts, 1992–2008: Judicial autonomy in a contemporary authoritarian state. *East Asia Law Review*, 5, 303–442.

Hsueh, R. (2011). *China's regulatory state: A new strategy for globalization*. Cornell University Press.

Hu, C. (2015). China judges professional satisfaction analysis: Detailed analysis of a survey of 2660 respondents (Zhongguo Faguan Zhiye Manyidu Kaocha: Yi 2660 Fen Wenjuan wei Yangben de Fenxi). *China Law Review (Zhongguo Falv Pinglun)*, 4. www.lawpress.com.cn/zgflplzazhi.html

Hui, M. (2020, April 1). *Hong Kong police are using coronavirus restrictions to clamp down on protesters*. Quartz.

Hurst, W. (2009). *The Chinese worker after socialism*. Cambridge University Press.

Hurst, W. (2011). Politics, society, and the legal system in contemporary China. In J. Garrick (Ed.), *Law, wealth, and power in China: Commercial law reforms in context* (pp. 72–88). Routledge.

Hurst, W. (2018). *Ruling before the law: The politics of legal regimes in China and Indonesia*. Cambridge University Press.

Jiang, Y. (2013). Some thoughts on China's system of judicial remuneration security (Qian tan woguo faguan de daiyu baozhang zhidu). *Guangming Online (Guangmingwang)*. http://court.gmw.cn/html/article/201301/30/118223.shtml

Johnson, I. (2016, January 2). China grants courts greater autonomy on limited matters. *The New York Times*. www.nytimes.com/2016/01/03/world/asia/china-grants-courts-greater-autonomy-on-limited-matters.html

Kapiszewski, D. (2012). *High courts and economic governance in Argentina and Brazil*. Cambridge University Press.

Karpik, L., & Halliday, T. C. (2011). The legal complex. *Annual Review of Law and Social Science, 7*, 217–236.

Katznelson, I., & Weingast, B. R. (2005). Intersections between historical and rational choice institutionalism. In *Preferences and situations: Points of intersection between historical and rational choice institutionalism* (pp. 1–24). Russel Sage Foundation.

King, G., Keohane, R. O., & Verba, S. (1994). *Designing social inquiry: Scientific inference in qualitative research*. Princeton University Press.

Kinkel, J. (2015). High-end demand: Markets for legal services and pressure for judicial autonomy in urban China. *Law & Social Inquiry, 40*(4), 969–1000.

Kinkel, J., & Hurst, W. (2011). Review essay – Access to justice in post-Mao China: Assessing the politics of criminal and administrative law. *Journal of East Asian Studies, 11*(3), 467–499. https://doi.org/10.1017/S1598240800007414

Kinkel, J., & Hurst, W. (2015). The judicial cadre evaluation system in China: Foundational institutional incentives and "intra-state legibility." *The China Quarterly, 224*, 933–954.

Kisilowski, M. (2014). The middlemen: The legal profession, the rule of law, and authoritarian regimes. *Law & Social Inquiry, 40*(3), 700–722.

Lague, D., Pomfret, J., & Torode, G. (2019, December 20). How murder, kidnappings and miscalculation set off Hong Kong's revolt. *Reuters*.

Landes, W., & Posner, R. (1975). The independent judiciary in an interest group perspective. *Journal of Law, Economics & Organization, 18*(3), 875.

Landry, P. F. (2008). *Decentralized authoritarianism in China: The communist party's control of local elites in the post-Mao era*. Cambridge University Press.

Leung, K., Xinqi, S., & Lok-kei, S. (2019, June 15). Hong Kong protest organisers vow to press ahead with Sunday march despite government backing down on extradition bill – but Monday's strike is off. *South China Morning Post*.

Li, Lin, & Tian, H. (2013). *Blue book of the rule of law: China rule of law development report, No. 11 (Fazhi lanpishu: Zhongguo fazhi fazhan baogao)*. Social Sciences Academic Press (Shehui kexue chubanshe).

Li, Ling. (2012). The "production" of corruption in China's courts: Judicial politics and decision making in a one-party state. *Law & Social Inquiry, 37*(4), 848–877.

Li, V. (1978). *Law without lawyers*. Stanford Alumni Association.

Li, X., & Cheng, J. (2013). Structural constraints on legal change: Chinese lawyers in the interaction between the state, the market, and society. *Social Sciences in China, 34*(1), 58–77.

Lieberthal, K. (2004). *Governing China: From revolution through reform*. W. W. Norton & Company.

Lieberthal, K., & Oksenberg, M. (1988). *Policy making in China: Leaders, structures, and processes*. Princeton University Press.

Liebman, B. L., Roberts, M. E., Stern, R. E., & Wang, A. Z. (2020). Mass digitization of Chinese court decisions: How to use text as data in the field of Chinese law. *Journal of Law and Courts*, *8*(2). https://doi.org/10.1086/709916

Lijphart, A. (1977). *Democracy in plural societies: A comparative exploration*. Yale University Press.

Liu, S. (2008). Globalization as boundary-blurring: International and local law firms in China's corporate law market. *Law & Society Review*, *42*(4), 771–804.

Liu, S. (2011a). Lawyers, state officials and significant others: Symbiotic exchange in the Chinese legal services market. *The China Quarterly*, *206*, 276–293.

Liu, S. (2011b). *The logic of fragmentation: An ecological analysis of the Chinese legal services market (in Chinese)*. Shanghai Sanlian Bookstore (China).

Liu, S. (2014). The shape of Chinese law. *Peking University Law Journal*, *1*(2), 415–444. https://doi.org/10.1080/20517483.2014.11424478

Liu, S. (2015). Law's social forms: A powerless approach to the sociology of law. *Law and Social Inquiry*, *40*(1), 1–28. https://doi.org/10.1111/lsi.12105

Liu, S., & Au, A. (2020). The gateway to global China: Hong Kong and the future of Chinese law firms. *Wisconsin International Law Journal*, *37*, 308–349.

Liu, S., & Emirbayer, M. (2016). Field and ecology. *Sociological Theory*, *34*(1), 62–79. https://doi.org/10.1177/0735275116632556

Liu, S., & Halliday, T. C. (2016). *Criminal defense in China: The politics of lawyers at work*. Cambridge University Press.

Liu, S., & Halliday, T. C. (2019). The ecology of activism: Professional mobilization as a spatial process. *Canadian Review of Sociology*, *56*(4), 452–471. https://doi.org/10.1111/cars.12258

Liu, S., Liang, L., & Michelson, E. (2014). Migration and social structure: The spatial mobility of Chinese lawyers. *Law & Policy*, *36*(2), 165–194. https://doi.org/10.1111/lapo.12016

Liu, S., & Wu, H. (2016). The ecology of organizational growth: Chinese law firms in the age of globalization. *American Journal of Sociology*, *122*(3), 798–837.

Liu, X. (2014, March 12). Shanghai courts lost 74 judges last year; representative suggests construction of a salary system for specialized professionals (Shanghai fayuan qunian liushi faguan 74 ren; Daibiao jianyi: shili yu zhuanye zhiwu xiangshiying de gongzi zhidu). *Youth Daily (Qingnian Bao)*. http://youthdaily.why.com.cn/epublish/node37623/node38420/userobject7ai392817.html

Liu, Z. (2009). Regarding the system of managing separate divisions within China's courts (Lun zhongguo fayuan de fenting guanli zhidu). *Legal System and Social Development (Fazhi Yu Shehui Fazhan)*, *89*(5), 124–135.

Liu, Z. (2012). The emergence of court presidents as structured by vertical and horizontal relations of authority (Tiao tiao yu kuai kuai guanxixia de fayuan yuanzhang chansheng). *Global Legal Forum (Quanqiu Falü Pinglun)*, *1*, 107–125.

Liu, Z. (2014). Specification, position, rank and the competition for office (Ge, zhi, ji yu jingzheng shanggang). *Tsinghua University Law Journal*, *8*(2), 146–163.

Lü, S., & Wang, X. (2014, April 10). Shenzhen explores judicial professionalization reforms; judicial wages might exceed that of court president (Shenzhen tansuo faguan zhiyehua gaige; faguan gongzi huo chao fayuan yuanzhang). *People's Daily (Renmin Ribao)*.

Lubman, S. (1999). *Bird in a cage: Legal reform in China after Mao*. Stanford University Press.

Ma, S. (2011). Shanghai court departmental vice leaders' selection through competitive promotion smoothly completed (Shanghai fayuan bumen fuzhi lingdao jingzheng shanggang gongzuo shunli wancheng). *China Court Web (Zhongguo Fayuanwang)*. http://old.chinacourt.org/html/article/201201/11/473401.shtml

Manion, M. (1985). The cadre management system, post-Mao: The appointment, promotion, transfer and removal of party and state leaders. *The China Quarterly*, *102*(June), 203–233. https://doi.org/10.1017/S030574100002991X

McCubbins, M. D., & Schwartz, T. (1984). Congressional oversight overlooked: Police patrols versus fire alarms. *American Journal of Political Science*, *28*(1), 165–179.

Meierhenrich, J. (2008). *The legacies of law: Long-run consequences of legal development in South Africa, 1652–2000*. Cambridge University Press.

Merry, S. E. (2011). Measuring the world: Indicators, human rights, and global governance: With CA comment by John M. Conley. *Current Anthropology*, *52*(S3), S83–S95.

Merryman, J. H. (1969). *The civil law tradition: An introduction to the legal systems of Europe and Latin America*. Stanford University Press.

Mertha, A. (2006). Policy enforcement markets: How bureaucratic redundancy contributes to effective intellectual property enforcement in China. *Comparative Politics*, *38*(3), 295–316.

Mertha, A. (2009). "Fragmented authoritarianism 2.0": Political pluralization in the Chinese policy process. *The China Quarterly*, *200*, 995–1012. https://doi.org/10.1017/S0305741009990592

Merton, R. K., Fiske, M., & Kendall, P. L. (1990). *The focused interview: A manual of problems and procedures* (2nd ed.). Free Press.

Miceli, T. J., & Cosgel, M. M. (1994). Reputation and judicial decision-making. *Journal of Economic Behavior and Organization*, *23*(1), 31–51.

Michelson, E. (2003). *Unhooking from the state: Chinese lawyers in transition*. University of Chicago Press.

Michelson, E. (2007). Lawyers, political embeddedness, and institutional continuity in China's transition from socialism. *American Journal of Sociology*, *113*(2), 352–414.

Michelson, E. (2020). In search of activist lawyers in China: A time machine back to the heyday of political activism in the Chinese legal profession. *Wisconsin International Law Journal*, *37*(2), 350–414.

Michelson, E., & Read, B. (2011). Public attitudes toward official justice in Beijing and rural China. In M. Y. K. Woo & M. Gallagher (Eds.), *Chinese justice: Civil dispute resolution in contemporary China* (pp. 169–204). Cambridge University Press.

Michener, G. (2015). Policy evaluation via composite indexes: Qualitative lessons from international transparency policy indexes. *World Development*, *74*, 184–196.

Min, J. (2006, January 18). Sichuan legislative meetings: Basic court judges leave courts in great numbers, making it difficult to resolve cases (Sichuan lianghui: Jiceng faguan daliang liushi nanyi duiying ban'an). *China Youth Daily (Zhongguo Qingnian Bao)*. http://news.163.com/06/0119/06/27QERUVU0001124T.html

Minzner, C. (2011a). China's turn against law. *American Journal of Comparative Law*, *59*, 935–984.

Minzner, C. (2011b). Judicial disciplinary systems for incorrectly decided cases: The imperial Chinese heritage lives on. In M. Woo & M. Gallagher (Eds.), *Chinese justice: Civil dispute resolution in contemporary China* (pp. 58–90). Cambridge University Press.

Minzner, C. F. (2009). Riots and cover-ups: Counterproductive control of local agents in China. *University of Pennsylvania Journal of International Law*, *31*(1), 53–123.

Minzner, C. F. (2013). The rise and fall of Chinese legal education. *Fordham International Law Journal*, *36*(2), 335–396.

Moustafa, T. (2007). *The struggle for constitutional power: Law, politics, and economic development in Egypt*. Cambridge University Press.

National Bureau of Statistics of the PRC. (2011). Communiqué of the National Bureau of Statistics of People's Republic of China on major figures of the 2010 population census[1] (No. 2). www.stats.gov.cn/english/NewsEvents/201104/t20110429_26450.html

Ng, K. H., & He, X. (2017). *Embedded courts: Judicial decision making in China*. Cambridge University Press.

North, D. (1990). *Institutions, institutional change, and economic performance*. Cambridge University Press.

North, D., & Weingast, B. R. (1989). Constitutions and commitment: The evolution of institutions governing public choice in seventeenth-century England. *Journal of Economic History*, *49*(4), 803–832.

O'Brien, K. J., & Li, L. (1999). Selective policy implementation in rural China. *Comparative Politics*, *31*(2), 167–186.

Paletta, D., Lee, C. E., & Browne, A. (2016, December 2). Trump spoke with Taiwan president in break with decades of U.S. policy. *Wall Street Journal*.

Pan, Y. (2003). The inflow of foreign direct investment to China: The impact of country-specific factors. *Journal of Business Research*, *56*(10), 829–833. https://doi.org/10.1016/S0148-2963(02)00470-8

Park, R. E., & Burgess, E. W. (1969). *Introduction to the science of sociology* (2nd ed.). University of Chicago Press.

Peerenboom, R. (2002). *China's long march to the rule of law*. Cambridge University Press.

Peerenboom, R. (Ed.). (2003). Varieties of the rule of law: An introduction and provisional conclusion. In *Asian discourses of rule of law: Theories and implementation of rule of law in twelve Asian countries, France, and the U.S.* (pp. 1–53). Routledge Curzon.

Peerenboom, R. (2006). Judicial independence and judicial accountability: An empirical study of individual case supervision. *The China Journal*, *55*, 67–92.

Peerenboom, R. (2009). Middle income blues: The east Asian model and implications for constitutional development in China. In S. Balme & M. Dowdle (Eds.), *Building constitutionalism in China* (pp. 77–96). Palgrave MacMillan.

Peerenboom, R. (2010). Judicial independence in China: Common myths and unfounded assumptions. In R. Peerenboom (Ed.), *Judicial independence in China: Lessons for global rule of law promotion* (pp. 69–94). Cambridge University Press.

Peerenboom, R. (2011). Economic development and the development of the legal profession in China. In M. Woo & M. E. Gallagher (Eds.), *Chinese justice: Civil dispute resolution in contemporary China* (pp. 114–138). Cambridge University Press.

Pieke, F. N. (2009). *The good communist: Elite training and state building in today's China*. Cambridge University Press.

Pils, E. (2007). Asking the tiger for his skin: Rights activism in China. *Fordham International Law Journal*, *30*, 1209–1287.

Pils, E., & Rosenzweig, J. (2014, January 26). Beijing confronts a new kind of dissident the new citizen movement can continue even as Xu Zhiyong sits in jail. *Wall Street Journal*. www.wsj.com/articles/SB10001424052702303553204579344160684807586

Press, H. K. F. (2020, June 30). Beijing unanimously passes national security law for Hong Kong as Chief Exec. Carrie Lam evades questions. *Hong Kong Free Press*.

Quigley, J. (1989). Socialist law and the civil law tradition. *The American Journal of Comparative Law*, *37*(4), 781–808.

Reuters Staff. (2020, August 3). France says it will not ratify extradition treaty with Hong Kong. *Reuters*.

Rigobon, R., & Rodrik, D. (2005). Rule of law, democracy, openness, and income: Estimating the interrelationships. *Economics of Transition*, *13*(3), 533–564.

Santos, B. de S. (1987). Law: A map of misreading. Toward a postmodern conception of law. *Journal of Law and Society*, *14*(3), 279–302.

Sapio, F. (2010). *Sovereign power and the law in China*. Brill.

Schlesinger, J. M., & Ailworth, E. (2018, January 22). U.S. imposes new tariffs, ramping up 'America First' trade policy. *Wall Street Journal*.

Schurmann, F. (1971). *Ideology and organization in communist China* (2nd ed.). University of California Press.

Scoggins, S. E., & O'Brien, K. J. (2016). China's unhappy police. *Asian Survey*, *56*(2), 225–242.

Scott, J. C. (1999). *Seeing like a state: How certain schemes to improve the human condition have failed*. Yale University Press.

Segal, J. A., & Spaeth, H. J. (2002). *The supreme court and the attitudinal model revisited*. Cambridge University Press.

Shanghai Bureau of Statistics. (2011). *Shanghai statistical yearbook 2011 (Shanghai tongji nianjian 2011)*. China Statistics Publishing House (Zhongguo tongji chubanshe). www.stats-sh.gov.cn/data/toTjnj.xhtml?y=2011

Shanghai High People's Court. (2011). Shanghai court IP adjudication mechanism research report (Shanghai fayuan zhishichanquan shenpan jizhi yanjiu, yanjiu baogao). www.hshfy.sh.cn/shzcw/gweb/xxnr_view.jsp?pa=aaWQ9MTY4MzIwJnhoPTEmdHlwZT0xz&jdfwkey=0jvgt

Shanghai Judicial Gazette Editing Committee. (2003). *Shanghai judicial gazette (Shanghai shenpanzhi)*. Shanghai Social Science Publishing House (Shanghai shehui kexue chubanshe).

Shapiro, M. (1981). *Courts: A comparative and political analysis*. University of Chicago Press.

Shapiro, M., & Stone Sweet, A. (2002). *On law, politics & judicialization*. Oxford University Press.

Shen, G. (Ed.). (1998). *Judges' handbook (Faguan Shouce), part I*. China Personnel Publishing Company (Zhongguo renshi chubanshe).

Shenzhen Bureau of Statistics. (2011). *Shenzhen statistical yearbook 2011, Vol. 21 (Shenzhen tongji nianjian 2011 zong di 21 qi)*. China Statistics Publishing House (Zhongguo tongji chubanshe). www.sztj.gov.cn/xxgk/tjsj/tjnj/201202/t20120221_1806408.htm

Shenzhen City Local Gazette Editing Committee. (2006). *Shenzhen city gazette, volume on legal system and politics (Shenzhen shi zhi, fazhi zhengwu juan)*. Local Gazette Publishing House (Fangzhi chubanshe).

Shenzhen Intermediate People's Court. (2010, January). Shenzhen court IP judicial protection situation white paper for 2006–2010 (Shenzhen fayuan zhishichanquan sifa baohu zhuangkuang).

Shenzhen Intermediate People's Court. (2011). Shenzhen intermediate people's court labor dispute litigation white paper. www.szcourt.gov.cn/shenwu/view.aspx?id=4208

Simard, S. (2021). *Finding the mother tree: Discovering the wisdom of the forest*. Knopf.

Solinger, D. J. (2006). Interviewing Chinese people: From high-level officials to the unemployed. In M. Heimer & S. Thogersen (Eds.), *Doing fieldwork in China* (pp. 153–168). NIAS Press.

Solomon, P. H. (2007a). Courts and judges in authoritarian regimes. *World Politics*, *60*(1), 122–145.

Solomon, P. H. (2007b). Review article: Courts and judges in authoritarian regimes. *World Politics, 60*(1), 122–145.

Stern, R. E. (2010). On the frontlines: Making decisions in Chinese civil environmental lawsuits. *Law & Policy, 32*(1), 79–103.

Stern, R. E. (2013). *Environmental litigation in China: A study in political ambivalence*. Cambridge University Press.

Stern, R. E., & Li, S. (2016). The outpost office: How international law firms approach the China market. *Law and Social Inquiry, 41*(1), 184–211. https://doi.org/10.1111/lsi.12138

Su, F., Tao, R., Xi, L., & Li, M. (2012). Local officials' incentives and China's economic growth: Tournament thesis reexamined and alternative explanatory framework. *China & World Economy, 20*(4), 1–18. https://doi.org/10.1111/j.1749-124X.2012.01292.x

Sun, Y. (2010, September 17). Shenzhen established specialized court divisions, pushes forward with 3 in 1 IP courts (Shenzhen she zhuanmen shenpanting tuixing zhishichanquan san shen he yi). *Southern Daily (Nanfang Ribao)*. www.sipo.gov.cn/mtjj/2010/201009/t20100917_537441.html

Tate, N. C., & Vallinder, T. (Eds.). (1995). *The global expansion of judicial power.* New York University Press.

The Economist. (2014). Realigning justice: Judges are often impotent in China's courtrooms. That might be changing. *The Economist.* www.economist.com/news/china/21612161-judges-are-often-impotent-chinas-courtrooms-might-be-changing-realigning-justice

Thelen, K. (1999). Historical institutionalism in comparative politics. *Annual Review of Political Science, 2,* 369–404. https://doi.org/10.1146/annurev.polisci.2.1.369

Tian, H. (2012). Gaijin Zhengfu Xinxi Gongkai Gongzuo, Tigao Yifa Xingzheng Shuiping (Improve government information transparency, improve the level of administration according to law). *Lingdao Canyue (Leadership Reference Reading), 16,* 3–9.

Tiffert, G. D. (2011). The Chinese judge: From literatus to cadre (1907–1949). 1–43. http://papers.ssrn.com/sol3/papers.cfm?abstract_id=1948259

Tiffert, G. D. (2015). *Judging revolution: Beijing and the birth of the PRC judicial system (1906–1958).* University of California.

Toharia, J. J. (1975). Judicial independence in an authoritarian regime: The case of contemporary Spain. *Law & Society Review, 9*(3), 475–496.

Trevaskes, S. (2011). Political ideology, the party, and politicking: Justice system reform in China. *Modern China, 37,* 315–344.

Trochev, A. (2004). Less democracy, more courts: A puzzle of judicial review in Russia. *Law & Society Review, 38*(3), 513–548.

Trochev, A. (2008). *Judging Russia: The constitutional court in Russian politics, 1990–2006.* Cambridge University Press.

Trubek, D., & Galanter, M. (1974). Scholars in self-estrangement: Some reflections on the crisis in law and development studies. *Wisconsin Law Review*, 1062–1101.

Tsai, K. (2007). *Capitalism without democracy: The private sector in contemporary China*. Cornell University Press.

Tsai, K. (2016). Adaptive informal institutions. In O. Fioretos, T. G. Falleti, & A. Sheingate (Eds.), *The Oxford handbook of historical institutionalism*. Oxford University Press.

Ulc, O. (1972). *The judge in a communist state*. Ohio University Press.

Valverde, M. (2009). Jurisdiction and scale: Legal "technicalities" as resources for theory. *Social and Legal Studies, 18*(2), 139–157. https://doi.org/10.1177/0964663909103622

Valverde, M. (2015). *Chronotopes of law: Jurisdiction, scale, and governance*. Routledge.

Van Evera, S. (1997). *Guide to methods for students of political science*. Cornell University Press.

Wang, A. L. (2013). The search for sustainable legitimacy: Environmental law and bureaucracy in China. *Harvard Environmental Law Review, 37*, 365–440.

Wang, J., & Liang, W. (2019). Political resources and divergent court empowerment in China: A subnational comparison. *Modern China, 45*(6), 629–665.

Wang, Y. (2015). *Tying the autocrat's hands: The rise of the rule of law in China*. Cambridge University Press.

Wang, Y., & Minzner, C. (2015). The rise of the Chinese security state. *The China Quarterly, 222*, 339–359.

Wang, Y., & Shen, M. (2009). Litigating economic disputes in rural China. *The China Review, 9*(1), 97–121.

Weber, M. (1946). *From Max Weber: Essays in sociology* (H. H. Gerth & C. W. Mills [Eds.]). Oxford University Press.

Weber, M. (1978). *Economy and society* (G. Roth & C. Wittch [Eds.]). University of California Press.

Wei, J. (2010, December 2). Shanghai courts fully carry out the work mechanism of competitive cadre promotion (Shanghai fayuan quanmian tuixing jingzhengxing xuanba ganbu gongzuo jizhi). *People's Court News (Renmin Fayuan Bao)*.

Whiting, S. H. (2000). *Power and wealth in rural China*. Cambridge University Press. https://doi.org/10.1017/CBO9780511571596

Whiting, S. H. (2004). The cadre evaluation system at the grass roots: The paradox of party rule. In B. J. Naughton & D. L. Yang (Eds.), *Holding China together: Diversity and national integration in the post-Deng era* (pp. 101–119). Cambridge University Press.

Wong, J., & Lo, C. (2021, December 16). Hong Kong's pro-democracy activists are running out of options. *Bloomberg*. www.bloomberg.com/news/features/2021-12-16/china-s-communist-party-crackdowns-leave-hong-kong-protesters-with-few-tactics

Xinhua News Agency. (2013). The salaries of civil servants in all 31 of China's Provinces revealed. (Quanguo 31 ge diqu gongwuyuan gongzi baoguang). http://news.xinhuanet.com/photo/2013-10/11/c_125512066.htm

Xinhua News Agency. (2017). China has 300,000 lawyers. (January 9). www.xinhuanet.com//english/2017-01/09/c_135967814.htm (last visited January 5, 2022).

Yan, F. (2007, March 7). Beijing adds three new IP tribunals (Beijing zhishichanquan fating xin zeng 3 ge). *Beijing Morning Post (Beijing Chenbao).* http://news.sina.com.cn/c/2007-03-07/012511352574s.shtml

Ying, Y. (2011). Comply with judicial regulations, improve the assessment system, diligently lead and implement the SPC's new case quality assessment system (Zunxun Sifa Guilü, Youhua Pinggu Tixi, Renzhen Linghui He Shishi Zuigao Fayuan Xin Anjian Zhiliang Pinggu Tixi). *Shanghai Shenpan Shijian (Shanghai Adjudication in Practice), 228*(12), 3–4.

Yung, L. H. (1991). *From revolutionary cadres to party technocrats in socialist China.* University of California Press.

Zhang, J. (2011). "Bawo pinggu tixi jingshen, tisheng anjian zhixiao shuiping" ("Grasp the assessment system spirit, raise the level of case quality and efficiency") (internal document). *Shanghai Shenpan Shijian (Shanghai Adjudication in Practice), 228*(12), 12–13.

Zhang, M., & Zhang, B. (2012). Specialized environmental courts in China: Status quo, challenges, and responses. *Journal of Energy and Natural Resources Law, 30*(3), 1–25.

Zhang, Q. (2003). The people's court in transition: The prospects of the Chinese judicial reform. *Journal of Contemporary China, 12*(34), 69–101.

Zhang, T. (2012). The pragmatic court: Reinterpreting the supreme people's court of China. *Columbia Journal of Asian Law, 25*(1), 1–61.

Zhang, X. (2014, August 26). The National People's Congress considers establishing IP courts in Shanghai, Beijing, and Guangzhou (Quanguo renda changweihui shenyi "bei shang guang" sheli zhishichanquan fayuan). *People's Court News (Renmin Fayuan Bao).* www.chinacourt.org/article/detail/2014/08/id/1426955.shtml

Zhejiang High Court. (2013). Circular of the Zhejiang High Court issuing "the guiding opinion regarding strengthening the operation of adjudication analysis work" (Zhejiangsheng Gaoji Renmin Fayuan Yinfa "Guanyu Jiaqiang Shenpan Yunxing Taishi Fenxi Gongzuo de Zhidao Yijian' de Tongzhi") (Doc. No. 58 [2013]).

Zhou, L. (2011). Toushi zhibiao shuju, cujin shenpan xiaoneng (Thoroughly Look at Index Statistics, Promote Adjudication Efficacy). *Shanghai Shenpan Shijian (Shanghai Adjudication in Practice), 12.*

Zhu, S. (2010). The party and the courts. In R. Peerenboom (Ed.), *Judicial independence in China: Lessons for global rule of law promotion* (pp. 52–68). Cambridge University Press.

Zhuang, G. (2010). *Theory and practice of the evaluation system for leading cadres (Lingdao ganbu zhengji pingjia de lilun yu shijian).* China Economics Publishing House (Zhongguo jingji chubanshe).

INDEX

www.ingramcontent.com/pod-product-compliance
Ingram Content Group UK Ltd.
Pitfield, Milton Keynes, MK11 3LW, UK
UKHW020111040726
472853UK00010B/495
* 9 7 8 1 0 0 9 0 7 8 1 8 4 *